Art and Architecture

Art and Architecture

Exploring Cultural Heritage Worldwide

Rafeal Mechlore

WSM Publisher

CONTENTS

INDEX 1

INTRODUCTION 3

Chapter 1 21

Chapter 2 37

Chapter 3 53

Chapter 4 69

Chapter 5 84

Chapter 6 97

Chapter 7 113

Chapter 8 128

Chapter 9 147

Chapter 10 162

Chapter 11 178

CONTENTS

Chapter 12 195

INDEX

Introduction

1. Definition of Cultural Heritage
2. The Significance of Art and Architecture
3. Purpose and Scope of the Book
4. Overview of Chapters

Chapter 1: Foundations of Cultural Heritage
1.1 Understanding Cultural Heritage
1.2 The Role of Art and Architecture in Cultural Heritage
1.3 Preservation and Conservation

Chapter 2: Prehistoric and Ancient Art and Architecture
2.1 Cave Art and Megalithic Structures
2.2 Ancient Egyptian Architecture
2.3 Greek and Roman Art and Architecture

Chapter 3: Art and Architecture in the Middle Ages
3.1 Gothic Cathedrals
3.2 Islamic Architecture
3.3 Byzantine Art and Architecture

Chapter 4: Renaissance and Baroque Periods
4.1 Italian Renaissance Art and Architecture
4.2 Baroque Splendor in Europe
4.3 Mesoamerican Art and Architecture

Chapter 5: The Age of Enlightenment and Neoclassicism
5.1 Enlightenment Ideals in Architecture
5.2 Neoclassical Revival

5.3 Colonial Architecture

Chapter 6: The 19th Century and Industrialization
6.1 Victorian Architecture
6.2 Art Nouveau and the Belle Époque
6.3 Impact of Industrialization on Cities

Chapter 7: Modernism and the Avant-Garde
7.1 The Bauhaus Movement
7.2 Frank Lloyd Wright and Organic Architecture
7.3 Post-World War II Architectural Innovations

Chapter 8: Contemporary Trends in Art and Architecture
8.1 Sustainable and Green Architecture
8.2 Postmodernism and Deconstructivism
8.3 Public Art and Urban Interventions

Chapter 9: Art and Architecture in Non-Western Cultures
9.1 Chinese Art and Architecture
9.2 Japanese Traditional and Contemporary Design
9.3 African and Indigenous Architectural Styles

Chapter 10: Preservation and Challenges in the Digital Age
10.1 Digital Documentation and Restoration
10.2 Cultural Heritage Preservation and Politics
10.3 The Threat of Climate Change

Chapter 11: Art and Architecture Tourism
11.1 The Role of Tourism in Cultural Heritage
11.2 Iconic Landmarks and World Heritage Sites
11.3 Responsible Tourism and Preservation

Chapter 12: Future Trends in Art and Architecture
12.1 Technological Advancements in Design and Construction
12.2 Cultural Exchange and Fusion
12.3 The Role of Art and Architecture in Shaping the Future

INTRODUCTION

Art and architecture are two of the few threads in the vast tapestry that makes up human civilization that are as lively, lasting, and important as they are. Paintings, sculptures, and colossal constructions that were created in the past are now considered to be pillars of our cultural history because they have withstood the test of time and geography to become works of art that are considered to be masterpieces. An ambitious excursion into this world of human ingenuity, "Art and Architecture: Exploring Cultural Heritage Worldwide" is a journey across history, across continents, and into the heart of communities that have left indelible impressions on the global stage.

Art and architecture are not merely aesthetic manifestations; rather, they are reflections of our views, goals, values, and identities. Art and architecture are much more than just aesthetic manifestations. They recount tales of success and failure, of breaking new ground and honoring the past, of diversity and of oneness. Through the study of art and architecture, we are able to get a glimpse into the very essence of mankind and gain an understanding of the goals and inspirations of people who came before us. We like the splendor that comes from the diversity of cultural traditions and the omnipresence of artistic expression. In this book, we set out on a voyage to discover, admire, and commemorate the diverse world of art and architecture. This is a trip that transcends time and location to provide a panoramic view of the cultural heritage that we share as a human race all over the world.

The Importance of Preserving Our Cultural Heritage

Before we set out on this adventure, it is essential that we have a fundamental comprehension of the value of our cultural legacy and the reasons why art and architecture play such essential roles in the maintenance and transmission of our common human history. Monuments, buildings, artifacts, traditions, languages, and ideals are all examples of tangible components of our history that are included in cultural heritage. Cultural heritage also includes intangible aspects of our past. It is the sum total of all that we inherit from our predecessors, including the tangible traces of their creativity as well as the collective wisdom that is embedded in the traditions that they have handed down to us.

Not only is our cultural history of interest from a historical perspective, but it also serves as the foundation of our modern identity and directs us in the direction we should go in the years to come. It is both a source of inspiration and a repository of knowledge, and it serves as a demonstration of our capacity for originality and inventiveness.

When we visit a gothic cathedral, take in the beauty of a picture from the Renaissance period, or examine the intricacy of the design on a Persian carpet, we are, in effect, dealing with the ideas, aspirations, and abilities of individuals who lived a very long time ago. We are trying to connect with the people who lived centuries ago by their experiences, beliefs, and the beautiful things they made.

In addition, the preservation of cultural heritage is an extremely significant tool for promoting international conversation and understanding. It instills in us a sense of empathy and respect for diversity, as well as an appreciation for the value of preserving the riches that give our world its distinctive character. When we investigate our cultural legacy, we move beyond the confines of space and time, entering a domain where individuals from all backgrounds can find common ground in their admiration for the accomplishments of the human race.

The Aims and Boundaries of the Present Work

The book "Art and Architecture: Exploring Cultural Heritage Worldwide" is an exhaustive effort to shed light on the myriad elements of cultural heritage and the ways in which art and architecture have played vital roles in defining it. The book is a part of a larger project titled "Art and Architecture: Exploring Cultural Heritage Worldwide." This book aims to be a resource that is interesting, educational, and visually compelling for those who are interested in the diversity of human expression, including enthusiasts, scholars, students, and anybody else who is intrigued about the range of human expression.

This book covers a wide variety of subjects, time eras, and geographical places, indicating that its breadth is quite comprehensive. It begins with the first examples of human inventiveness in prehistoric times and continues into the marvels of modern architecture that we find in the digital age. The geographical scope is similarly expansive, taking in both the Western and non-Western nations and illuminating the interdependence of artistic and architectural traditions on a worldwide scale.

In the following pages, we will embark on a journey through time, beginning with the mysterious cave paintings of our ancient ancestors, exploring the awe-inspiring wonders of the ancient Egyptians, and tracing the evolution of architectural design and artistic expression throughout the eras of the Middle Ages, the Renaissance, the Baroque period, the Enlightenment period, and the 19th century.

In this course, we will delve into the revolutionary ideas behind the Modernist and Avant-Garde movements, cover the present trends of green building, and investigate the thriving non-Western civilizations that have enriched our global heritage.

In addition to this, we will discuss the difficulties that have been brought on by the digital era as well as the significance of preservation in light of the climate change. In the final chapter of this book, we will take a look ahead at the developments that are likely to occur in the fields of art and architecture, focusing on the ways in which these fields will continue to have an impact on our world.

An Outline of the Chapters

In the course of our investigation of "Art and Architecture: Exploring Cultural Heritage Worldwide," we will move through a total of twelve chapters that have been painstakingly curated. Each of these chapters will concentrate on a different topic, period, or facet of the enthralling journey that is cultural heritage as it is expressed through art and architecture.

The Building Blocks of Our Cultural Heritage

We will start out by delving into the fundamental ideas behind cultural heritage, gaining a knowledge of its value as well as the part that art and architecture play in the process of conserving and passing on this legacy.

Architecture and artwork from prehistoric and ancient times

The trip will begin with an in-depth exploration of the ancient and prehistoric world, during which time the traveler will investigate mysterious cave art, enormous megalithic structures, and the splendor of ancient Egyptian temples and pyramids.

The Middle Ages were a golden age for art and architecture.

After that, we will take a trip back in time to the awe-inspiring Middle Ages, when the towering Gothic cathedrals of Europe, the intricate Islamic architectural marvels, and the Byzantine mosaics will capture our mind.

Periods of the Renaissance and the Baroque

As we proceed, we will enter the Renaissance and the Baroque periods, during which we will celebrate the inventiveness of Italian artists, the opulence of Baroque Europe, and the mysticism of Mesoamerican constructions.

The period that encompasses both the Enlightenment and Neoclassicism

Following that, we will investigate the Age of Enlightenment and the Neoclassical resurgence, focusing on the architectural manifestations of Enlightenment principles as well as the distinctive architectural forms that evolved from colonial architecture all over the world.

The nineteenth century and the beginning of industrialization

The 19th century was a time of tremendous upheaval and advancement in many fields. We are going to look into the architectural marvels of the Victorian era, the movement of Art Nouveau, as well as the effect that industrialization had on the urban landscape.

The movements known as modernism and the avant-garde

The 20th century was a time period that saw significant shifts in both art and architecture. The pioneering ethos of the Modernist and Avant-Garde movements, with a particular emphasis on the Bauhaus School and Frank Lloyd Wright, will be investigated in this class.

Recent Developments in the Fields of Art and Architecture

As we progress into the modern era, we will investigate the most recent movements in art and architecture, such as postmodernism, sustainable and green design, and public art.

The Non-Western World's Contribution to Art and Architecture

Our investigation extends to non-Western cultures, and we highlight the splendor and singularity of the architectural and creative traditions of China, Japan, Africa, and indigenous peoples.

Concerns Regarding Preservation in the Age of Digital Technology

The importance of preservation cannot be overstated in terms of cultural heritage. In this session, we will talk about the benefits and difficulties presented by the digital era, as well as the politics surrounding the preservation of cultural material.

The Worlds of Art and Architecture Visitor Industry

This chapter investigates the interaction of art, architecture, and tourism by focusing on famous landmarks, world heritage sites, and the roles that tourists play in the preservation of cultural artifacts.

Upcoming Developments in the Fields of Art and Architecture

Our excursion comes to a close with an optimistic outlook on the upcoming developments in the fields of art and architecture. In this session, we will talk about the influence that technology and intercultural dialogue have on the future of the globe, as well as the role that these fields play in that process.

A profound respect for the dynamic relationship between culture, creativity, and legacy will serve as our compass throughout each chapter as we proceed. We are going to investigate how these factors have had an impact in the past, how they continue to have an impact in the present, and how they provide us priceless insights into the future.

As we move forward with our investigation of "Art and Architecture: Exploring Cultural Heritage Worldwide," we are delving into the very core of human creativity and the very essence of the past that we all have in common. The subsequent chapters will shed light on the splendor of a variety of creative and architectural traditions, ranging from the majestic cathedrals of Europe to the tranquility of Japanese gardens, from the audacity of contemporary designs to the ageless elegance of ancient civilizations.

This book seeks to be an open door to the wonders of cultural heritage. It is a voyage that inspires you to ponder the creative genius of humanity, to appreciate the cultural tapestry of our planet, and to examine the need of preserving these irreplaceable legacy for future generations. The book's goal is to accomplish these goals. As we delve deeper into the complexities of art and architecture, we want you to not only admire the aesthetics but also gain an understanding of the tales, dreams, and enduring human spirit that are represented by these works of art and architecture.

Therefore, we invite you to accompany us on this journey as we investigate the overarching story of cultural heritage, one work of art and one architectural wonder at a time. Together, we will dig up the relics that connect us to our ancestors and provide us with the motivation to build the future while maintaining a healthy respect for the past.

1. **Definition of Cultural Heritage**

   The cultural heritage of a community or society is the community's or society's shared history, traditions, beliefs, and values. It is a rich tapestry of tangible and intangible aspects that encapsulates the shared history, traditions, beliefs, and values of that community or civilization. It works as a storehouse of collective memory, covering the material objects, customs, languages, and rituals that have been handed down from one generation to the next as well as the information that has been accumulated throughout time. Not only does a people's cultural history reflect their creative expressions, but it also displays their resiliency, their goals, and the intricate web of relationships that characterize their existence. The concept of cultural heritage may be broken down into its component parts, each of which contributes to a more complete comprehension of the identity of a society and its position within the larger story of human civilization. At its core, the definition of cultural heritage is multidimensional. Each of these components, whether tangible or intangible, plays an important part in determining the cultural heritage that a society leaves behind. These dimensions can be generically categorized as tangible or intangible aspects.

   Heritage of the Culture That Can Be Touched

   The physical representations of human creation are known as tangible cultural heritage. This type of heritage includes a wide variety of artifacts, architecture, and landscapes that attest to the inventiveness, craftsmanship, and aesthetic sensitivities of bygone civilizations. These physical vestiges offer a window into the material culture of a community, which enables us to comprehend the architectural prowess, artistic expressions, and scientific developments that distinguished distinct time periods in history.

   Ancient temples, medieval cathedrals, and enormous palaces are some examples of architectural marvels that stand as testaments to the architectural genius of their respective eras. These architectural wonders also represent the cultural, theological, and socio-political elements that influenced their development. Not only do these buildings act as landmarks, but they also symbolize the ideals, principles, and goals of the communities that were responsible for their construction. As such, they are enduring symbols of the cultural identity of those communities.

Artifacts, such as ceramics, sculptures, paintings, and textiles, provide insights into the artistic traditions and workmanship of different civilizations. These artifacts also demonstrate the development of artistic styles, techniques, and thematic preoccupations over the course of numerous eras. Every artifact has its own tale to tell, one that preserves the cultural nuances, historical events, and social norms that shaped the lives of the individuals who made them.

Archaeological ruins, ancient communities, and natural monuments are examples of historical sites and landscapes that provide insights into the ways in which human societies engaged with their environments, adapted to geographical challenges, and established environmentally responsible practices to assure their continued existence. These locations document the development of human settlements, the expansion of trade routes, and the intercultural exchanges that altered the course of human history and serve as living records.

Heritage of the Intangible Cultural Landscape

The concept of intangible cultural heritage, on the other hand, refers to those non-tangible facets of cultural expression that are passed down through the generations through verbal transmission, through the medium of performance, or through social practices, rituals, and ceremonial occasions. It embodies the knowledge, skills, and traditions that are handed down from one generation to the next, which helps to promote a sense of continuity as well as a sense of identity for the community as a whole. It is a symbol of the living heritage of a community.

Oral traditions, such as myths, folk stories, legends, and epics, are an essential component of the cultural heritage of a community. These traditions serve as a vehicle for the transmission of historical events, moral ideals, and societal standards from one generation to the next. Not only entertaining, but also educational, these oral narratives instill a sense of cultural pride and foster a communal memory that ties individuals to their common history.

The performing arts, which include things like music, dance, theater, and even ritualistic performances, are the creative manifestations of a community and reflect its emotional sensibility, spiritual beliefs, and social cohesion. Some examples of performing arts are music, dance, and theater. These kinds of artistic expression serve as vehicles for cultural expression, allowing communities to celebrate their heritage, express their joys and sorrows, and reinforce their common cultural identity through communal engagement in these forms of artistic expression.

Within a community, the customs, ceremonies, and celebrations that people participate in on a regular basis play a significant part in both the development of social relationships and the promotion of a sense of belonging. They are a reflection of the values, ethics, and belief systems that regulate the interactions that take place within society, which helps to build a sense of togetherness and mutual respect among the members of the community. These intangible traditions and rituals help to the maintenance of cultural diversity, the promotion of intercultural dialogue, and the development of a deeper comprehension of the common humanity that unites us all.

The Safekeeping and Passing Down of Cultural Heritage
When it comes to maintaining the integrity and vibrancy of a community's identity over time, the preservation and transmission of a community's cultural legacy are of the utmost importance. It entails making a determined effort to protect cultural assets, both real and intangible, by adopting a variety of tactics that place an emphasis on conservation, documentation, education, and community engagement.

The repair, preservation, and protection of historical sites, objects, and structures are all part of the conservation efforts for tangible cultural heritage. These activities have the goal of conserving the physical integrity of these cultural assets as well as its historical relevance for future generations. In order to be successful, these undertakings entail striking a careful balance between safeguarding the structural stability of the original items or structures while also keeping their authenticity and integrity.

The recording and dissemination of knowledge regarding historical sites, items, and practices of intangible cultural heritage is greatly aided by the utilization of documentation of cultural heritage as an essential tool. It entails the methodical gathering of information, images, and audio-visual assets, which are then curated and archived for the purposes of research, education, and marketing. Documentation not only helps in the process of generating exhaustive inventories of cultural heritage, but it also makes it easier to develop educational programs and promote cultural tourism.

Education and participation from the general public are two of the most important factors in cultivating a sense of cultural understanding, appreciation, and stewardship among members of a community. Individuals can be encouraged to take an active role in the preservation and promotion of their cultural inheritance through the use of educational programs that aim to increase knowledge about the relevance of cultural heritage. These programs can help develop a sense of pride and responsibility among individuals and are designed to do so. Communities are given the opportunity to share their history, gain new perspectives, and commemorate their distinct cultural identities through the participation in public engagement programs such as cultural festivals, exhibitions, and seminars.

In addition, the incorporation of cultural heritage preservation into programs for sustainable development is essential for assuring the continued existence of historical sites, cultural practices, and creative traditions in the long run.

Communities are able to strike a balance between economic progress and the preservation of their cultural identity by incorporating cultural heritage considerations into urban planning, infrastructure development, and tourism management. This helps to foster a sustainable and inclusive approach to the management of cultural heritage.

The Evolving Characteristics of Our Cultural Heritage

It is necessary to acknowledge that cultural heritage is not a fixed object but rather a living, ever-evolving phenomena that represents the shifting goals, values, and socioeconomic dynamics of a community. This is why it is so important to realize that cultural heritage is not a static entity. For the purpose of preserving and promoting cultural heritage, it is necessary to develop flexible solutions that can accommodate the varied requirements and goals of both the current generation and the generations to come. This is because societies will continue to change and adapt in order to meet the challenges posed by the modern world.

In a global world that is becoming more interconnected, it is necessary to recognize the interconnectivity of different cultural traditions and to encourage intercultural communication in order to build mutual respect, understanding, and harmony among varied populations. It is possible for societies to enhance their cultural fabric, foster social cohesion, and contribute to the common treasure of human heritage if they embrace cultural diversity as a source of strength and harmony.

2. The Significance of Art and Architecture

Art and architecture, in all their varied guises and manifestations, are of tremendous importance to the development of human civilization. These creative undertakings are not only aesthetic hobbies; rather, they are crucial to the way we see the world around us, engage with it, and shape it. The fabric of our civilizations is woven with art and architecture, and this fabric reflects our beliefs, our aspirations, and the dynamic interaction that exists between tradition and innovation. In the course of this investigation, we will dissect the varied significance that art and architecture have held throughout human history and in today's society. We will acknowledge the roles that art and architecture play as mirrors of culture, agents of change, and sources of inspiration.

The Role of Art and Architecture as Reflectors of Cultural Values

Art and architecture are like mirrors of culture because they reflect the norms, values, and beliefs of society at the time they were created. They act as narratives, both visually and spatially, that capture the spirit of a certain age and keep it alive for future generations. When we investigate the visual arts and built environments of a particular era or culture, we are able to gain understanding of the social, political, religious, and philosophical currents that were at work in that civilization at the time.

Art, whether in the form of painting, sculpture, or other visual forms, has the ability to express feelings, tell tales, and communicate concepts that are frequently too difficult to express using words alone. It functions as a language that is understood by all people regardless of their native tongue or culture, allowing for the expression of feelings and ideas that are shared by all people. Take, for instance, the evergreen appeal of Leonardo da Vinci's "Mona Lisa," a picture that has captivated people from all over the world for hundreds of years. The mysterious grin of the subject as well as the subtle nuances in the composition invite thought, conversation, and interpretation, and they symbolize the overarching human yearning for connection and comprehension.

Likewise, architecture is a concrete representation of a culture's identity. Not only do buildings and other structures provide functional space, but they also serve as symbols of the ideals held by a society. The soaring cathedrals of the Middle Ages, which conveyed the spiritual aspirations of their period, to the modern skyscrapers that reflect the ambition and invention of the 21st century, architecture encompasses the spirit of an age in a way that cannot be done by any other medium. The religious passion of the time and the aspiration to be closer to the holy are reflected in the complexity of a Gothic cathedral, which is characterized by its lofty spires and bright stained glass. On the other hand, the current ideals that characterize our society are reflected in the concepts of efficiency and sustainability that are reflected in the minimalist design of contemporary structures.

In addition, both art and architecture have the potential to act as vehicles for the preservation of cultural traditions. They offer a way to preserve cultural traditions while also celebrating them, as evidenced by the colorful tapestries, sculptures, and architectural forms that can be discovered in indigenous communities all over the world. In this sense, they not only stand for the continuation of culture but also serve as a means of fostering cultural resilience. This enables communities to fight against assimilation and keep their distinct identities, which is an important role that they play.

Art and Architecture as Forces of Social Transformation

Art and architecture are not immutable things; rather, they are active forces that have the capacity to mold and reshape communities. They have been driving forces behind transformation, whether it be in the field of politics, culture, or technology.

Art and architecture have frequently been utilized in the realm of politics as a means to both

disseminate ideals and consolidate power. Throughout history, kings, queens, and other people in positions of power have used monumental building projects to solidify their reign and leave a lasting mark on the world. One of the most famous examples of this kind of architectural power play is found in the Palace of Versailles, which was commissioned by King Louis XIV of France. The extravagance and magnificence of it were designed not only to display the wealth and power of the French monarchy but also to consolidate authority over the nobles, with the goal of lowering the likelihood of a rebellion occurring as a result of this.

On the other hand, art and architecture have also been used as weapons of political dissent and uprising throughout history. The Mexican muralist movement, which emerged in the 20th century and was led by painters such as Diego Rivera, utilized huge murals as a means of communicating revolutionary themes and advocating for social change. These artists used the visual power of art to inspire and mobilize the masses in their quest to bring about political change.

On a cultural level, art and architecture act as catalysts for innovation and the mixing of different cultural traditions. The resurgence of classical art and humanist ideals that occurred during the Renaissance period sparked a rush of creative energy and intellectual inquiry that irrevocably altered the path that Western civilization would take going forward. Not only did the architecture of the Renaissance period transform the urban landscapes of Europe, but it also offered a new way of thinking about aesthetics and human potential at the same time. The Renaissance architecture was distinguished by its harmonious proportions and rebirth of classical forms.

The evolution of technology has also been significantly aided by significant contributions from the arts and architecture. In the late 19th century, the construction of the Eiffel Tower demonstrated the possibilities of iron construction and architectural prowess. In the 21st century, the development of revolutionary materials and construction processes is revolutionizing the way that we design and create our cities.

Inspirational and creative antecedents and antecedents

Art and architecture are wellsprings of creativity; they revitalize the human spirit and ignite innovation across a wide range of disciplines. They not only inspire people to pursue artistic endeavors, but they also have an impact on other fields, such as science, literature, and music.

There are innumerable pieces of literature that have been influenced in some way by works of visual art as well as architectural achievements. For instance, Marcel Proust's magnum opus "In Search of Lost Time" was shaped by the author's consideration of the visual arts, specifically the works of Vermeer. The ability of Proust's writing to transmit complex emotional and sensory experiences through the strength of visual imagery is a tribute to the profound ties that exist between art and literature.

Even musical compositions frequently take cues from visual art and building

design. Composers such as Mussorgsky and Ravel were influenced by works of visual art when they were writing pieces such as "Pictures at an Exhibition" and "Boléro." The visual aspects of art are translated into the realm of sound in their compositions, which results in a rich tapestry of artistic
expressions that are interconnected with one another.

The advancement of science and technology is also intimately interwoven with artistic creation and architectural design. The elegant shapes of birds and the structural wonders of Gothic cathedrals have had an impact on the study of aerodynamics and engineering, respectively. In the rapidly developing discipline of science and design known as biomimicry, creative engineering and problem-solving are inspired by the natural world and the ingenious solutions that may be found there.

In addition to this, both art and architecture have the power to inspire individual creativity on a deeper level. People frequently have fleeting moments of inspiration and an increased capacity for imaginative thought when they encounter with works of art and architecture. Those who interact with works of art can have their imaginative capacities stoked as a result of the works' breathtaking aesthetics, intricate details, and profound meanings. An experience of standing in front of an entrancing painting or within the awe-inspiring walls of a church can serve as a refuge for contemplation and meditation, igniting a spark of creative thought or providing a starting point for new ideas.

Opportunities for Intercultural Communication and Completion

The creation of art and architecture is a powerful means of fostering cultural understanding and communication since it is able to traverse both physical and linguistic barriers, so facilitating the formation of linkages between various cultures. They have the ability to break down cultural barriers, increase empathy, and facilitate communication among individuals.

Museums and art galleries play an important role in the dissemination of culture by organizing exhibitions that bring together works of art and artifacts originating from many regions of the world. Not only do these places let people to learn about the art and traditions of cultures other than their own, but they also provide chances for interaction amongst people of different cultural backgrounds. People gain a deeper appreciation for the diversity of human creativity when they are exposed, for example, to the artistic traditions of different countries through the medium of international traveling exhibitions.

Public art, such as sculptures, murals, and installations, can act as a platform for fostering understanding and conversation amongst people of different cultural backgrounds. Public displays of art encourage participation from a large audience in a variety of artistic expressions, frequently leading to conversations and fostering an awareness for a variety of cultural perspectives. Public art has the potential to become a symbol of inclusiveness and cultural exchange, reflecting the diversity of a society comprised of people of many different backgrounds.

In addition, the many types and practices of architecture have the potential to operate as bridges to intercultural understanding. Buildings that include components from a variety of architectural forms are a great example of how the beauty of cultural diversity can be highlighted via the process of fusing architectural traditions from other civilizations. This practice also demonstrates the possibilities for collaborative design. The sharing of architectural concepts between different cultures frequently results in the creation of urban areas that are both forward-thinking and welcoming, able to cater to the many requirements and goals of a multiethnic community.

3. **Purpose and Scope of the Book**

The intention of the author, as well as the content of the book, can be inferred from elements such as the book's goal and its scope. These facets offer the reader a road map to comprehend what they may expect from the book and determine whether or not it corresponds with their interests and requirements. In this essay, we are going to look into the idea of a book's purpose, as well as its breadth, and investigate their significance, as well as the ways in which they influence the whole experience of reading.

Acquiring an Understanding of the Goal of the Book

The goal of a book is the fundamental reason that it was written in the first place. It lays the groundwork for the author's aims and what they hope to accomplish with their writing throughout the process. It is essential for authors as well as readers to have a solid understanding of the goal of the book they are reading, as this purpose directs the book's content and assists readers in determining whether or not the book is relevant to their interests.

1. **To both educate and inform.**

   A great number of novels are written with the reader's enlightenment and information as their primary focus. The objective of these books, which most of the time are classified as non-fiction, is to give readers with factual facts, insights, or knowledge about a specific topic. These books are often written in third person. Textbooks, scientific journals, and instruction manuals, for example, are all written with the intention of educating and informing readers about a certain subject.

   You can also discover works of history, biographies, and memoirs in this category. These types of writing are written with the intention of enlightening readers about previous occurrences, notable people, or personal experiences. These books are important because they help keep information alive while also making it accessible to a wider readership.

2. **Amuse and enthrall**

   Readers are meant to be entertained, amused, and enthralled by the content of books written specifically for the entertainment industry. This genre frequently include works of fiction such as novels, short tales, and other fictional works. The purpose of the authors of these works is to provide entertainment and an escape from the monotony of everyday life by transporting readers to exotic realms, creating engaging characters, and crafting exciting narratives.

   In addition, humor and comedy books are written with the intention of making the reader laugh and improving their disposition. These novels are meant to be enjoyable to read and to bring a sense of contentment to the reader.

3. **Convince and Fight for Your Cause**

   There are some books that are created with the specific intention of arguing for a particular ideology, way of thinking, or cause through the medium of the written word. These publications can include works from a variety of genres, such as political manifestos, books on self-help, and literature advocating for environmental causes.

   Authors employ various persuasive strategies and arguments in the hope of persuading readers to adopt a particular mindset, carry out specific actions, or alter their ideas.

   Not only are readers meant to be informed by works of this nature, but they are also meant to be motivated and inspired to adopt the author's point of view.

4. **Inspire others and get them motivated**

   Some authors write novels with the intention of encouraging and energizing readers. These works frequently explore topics such as personal growth, success tales, or ways to better oneself. The objective is to inspire readers to think critically about what they want out of life, work hard to get what they want out of life, and triumph over the things that stand in their way.

   This type of books may contain the autobiographies of successful people, such as business owners, athletes, or artists, who reflect on their individual paths through life and the lessons they've picked up along the way. The goal is to inspire and direct readers by offering real-life instances of people who have triumphed while facing challenging circumstances.

5. **Record and maintain cultural traditions**

The documentation and upkeep of culture, traditions, and heritage can all be accomplished through the use of books. The purpose of these works is to document historical occurrences, cultural practices, and the accumulated knowledge of a particular civilization or community. Many times, encyclopedias, cultural studies, and ethnographies are the kind of books that serve this function.

In addition, publications of this sort might take the form of cookbooks that record traditional recipes, collections of oral histories, and travelogues that investigate and record the distinctive characteristics of a variety of cultures and areas.

Acquiring an Understanding of the Book's Contents

The limitations of a book's content, the themes that it discusses, and the extent to which it digs into those issues are all determined by the book's scope. The scope gives the readers an idea of what they might anticipate finding within the pages of the book based on the information provided.

1. **Scope, both Wide and Specific**
   Books can be written with either a broad or a narrow scope, depending on the readers and purposes for which they were written. A book can be said to have broad breadth if it addresses a wide variety of subjects that are connected to its subject matter. An beginning textbook on biology, for instance, can provide a broad overview of the topic by covering a variety of subfields within biology, such as ecology and genetics, amongst others.
   On the other hand, a book with a narrow scope focuses on a particular feature or subtopic within a subject that is more generally covered. A book, for instance, that digs rather thoroughly into one particular branch of biology and focuses on the genetics of one particular species of butterfly, would have a very limited scope.

2. **The extent of the coverage**
   The breadth of topics covered in a book is a good indicator of how deeply it investigates its subject matter. While some books merely provide a high-level overview of the subject at hand, others go into considerable depth in both their analysis and their presentation of the material. The goal of the book as well as the readers it is intended for often influence the breadth of its coverage.
   A children's book on space travel, for instance, might provide a fundamental introduction to the solar system. This might include covering the names of planets as well as the features of each planet. On the other hand, an astrophysics textbook geared toward more advanced students would go significantly deeper into intricate mathematical and scientific concepts associated with the universe.

3. **The Intended Observers**
   The readers who are most likely to like a book are directly responsible for determining its scope. Books are often created with the intention of appealing to a certain audience, whether that audience is comprised of children, adolescents, adults, professionals, or academics. The scope ought to be tailored to the reading level, as well as the knowledge and interests of the audience for whom it is meant.
   For instance, a young adult fantasy novel will have a scope that caters to the interests and reading abilities of teens, but a scholarly research monograph on a

specific issue within the social sciences will be targeted to academic experts and researchers in that field. Both types of novels, however, will have a scope that serves to the general public.

4. **Principal and Primary Concerns**

   Different books may place more or less of their attention and emphasis on various facets of the subject they cover. It's possible that certain books put more of an emphasis on theoretical notions, while others put more of an emphasis on practical applications. For instance, a book on photography may have an emphasis on technical particulars and camera settings that are applicable to photographers, whereas a book on the history of photography may place more of an emphasis on the development of photographic art and its influence on culture.

   The emphasis that is placed throughout a book can have an effect on the kinds of facts that are discussed as well as the level to which various facets of the topic are investigated in depth.

5. **Interdisciplinarity or Specialization: Which Is Better?**

Books can be multidisciplinary, which means that they cover various fields of study, or they can be specialized, which means that they focus on a single subfield within a discipline. Books that use an interdisciplinary approach typically help bridge the gap between several fields of study and offer a more comprehensive viewpoint on a subject.

On the other hand, specialist publications focus on a certain sector of knowledge and delve deeply into its various aspects. For instance, a book on environmental ethics might draw from philosophy, biology, and sociology, which would make it an interdisciplinary work; on the other hand, a book on the protection of a particular endangered species would be very specialized.

The Importance of Determining a Book's Aims and Boundaries

1. **Clarity for the Audience of Readers**

   When trying to understand what a book has to offer, readers rely on the book's goal as well as its overall scope. The reader will be able to assess if the book meets their interests and needs if these components are defined in a clear and concise manner. This enables consumers to make educated decisions regarding whether or not to read the book, ensuring that their time and effort are spent effectively.

2. **Making Effective Use of Available Resources**

   It is crucial for authors and publishers alike to have a distinct understanding of the goal and scope of a book in order to effectively allocate resources. It guarantees that the content of the book, as well as the marketing efforts and distribution techniques, are suited to the audience that the book is meant for and the goals that it aims to achieve.

3. **Compatibility with the Aims of the Author**

   When authors have a purpose and scope that are clearly outlined, it is easier for them to maintain concentration on the objectives and targets they have set for themselves. It serves as a guide for the writing process, making it much simpler to select relevant content, organize the book, and keep the same tone and style throughout.

4. **Communication That Is Effective**

   The author and the reader are able to communicate with one another through the medium of a book through the book's goal and scope. They communicate the goals of the author as well as what the reader might anticipate gaining from reading the book. In this context, having effective communication helps develop trust with the audience, which in turn increases their level of involvement.

5. **Importance to One's Field of Study and Career**

   For purposes of determining a book's value and significance in academic and professional contexts, having a purpose and a scope that are crystal apparent is absolutely necessary. On the basis of these considerations, academics and industry professionals can evaluate the significance of a book's contribution to the field of study or practice to which it pertains.

6. **Aspects of Art and Literature to Take Into Account**

The intent and range of coverage of a book have a substantial impact on the author's choice of voice and tone, as well as the organization of the story. This is true in both the realm of literature and creative writing. For instance, a book written with the intention of amusing its readers might utilize vivid storytelling tactics, whereas a book written with the intention of educating its readers might adopt an approach that is more instructive and didactic.

D. Overview of Chapters

The first chapter is titled "Introduction to the Cosmos"

The reader is taken on an incredible journey into the wondrous universe of the cosmos in the very first chapter of the book. The relevance of space travel, the mysteries of the universe, and the fundamental questions that drive humanity's quest to understand the cosmos are all explained in this chapter, which serves to set the stage for the rest of the book.

The history of space exploration is covered in Chapter 2

This chapter examines the evolution of humankind's quest to discover what is beyond our planet's atmosphere. It all starts with early astronomers and the observations they made, which eventually led to the invention of rocketry in the middle of the 20th century. The Space Race, the first human landing on the moon, and other significant events in the history of space travel up to the present day will all be covered in this article.

The third chapter is titled "Our Solar System"

The third chapter is an in-depth exploration of the solar system that we inhabit. It offers in-depth knowledge concerning the sun, planets, moons, asteroids, and comets that are part of our cosmic neighborhood. Recent discoveries and continuing missions to investigate these heavenly bodies are being given a particular focus of attention here.

It is titled "The Search for Extraterrestrial Life"

This chapter delves into the fascinating subject of the hunt for life on other planets and in other solar systems. It digs into the conditions necessary for life and highlights missions and experiments dedicated to this search, such as the investigation of exoplanets, the exploration of Mars, and the search for microbial life beyond Earth.

Beyond the Boundaries of Our Solar System, which is Chapter 5

The reader is taken on an adventure that takes them beyond the confines of our solar system and into the depths of the Milky Way and the larger cosmos. This chapter explores topics such as galaxies, nebulae, black holes, and other astronomical phenomena in an effort to shed light on the unfathomable secrets of the cosmos.

Chapter 6 and Its title is "Cosmic Time and Origins"

The notion of cosmic time is dissected in Chapter 6, which covers topics ranging from the Big Bang to the birth of galaxies and stars. The origins of the universe, the fundamental forces of existence, and the cosmic microwave background radiation are all topics that are investigated in this book. The beginning and development of the cosmos are broken down in greater detail for the reader.

The seventh chapter is titled "Space Technology and Exploration"

This chapter takes a more in-depth look at the technology that underpins the field of space exploration. Spaceships, telescopes, rovers, and other tools that are used to investigate the cosmos will all be included in this book for readers to learn about. In addition to it, the chapter talks about the difficulties and advances that have been made in space technology.

Human Spaceflight and the Prospects for Future Space Travel

Human spaceflight is the topic of discussion in Chapter 8, which provides a historical overview of various space expeditions that involved astronauts. In addition to this, it discusses the trajectory of future space travel, including plans for trips to the moon and Mars as well as the possibility of commercial space tourism. The reader investigates the opportunities and threats that come with expanding human habitation into space.

It is titled "Cosmic Mysteries and Unsolved Questions"

The reader is given an introduction to some of the most perplexing riddles in the cosmos in this chapter. Topics covered include black holes, dark matter, and the nature of dark energy. This chapter focuses on contemporary scientific initiatives and speculations that are being undertaken in an effort to solve these mysteries.

"The Ethical and Philosophical Dimensions of Space Exploration"

The final chapter explores the moral and philosophical dilemmas that arise from conducting research in outer space. The author encourages readers to consider topics such as our role in the universe, the repercussions of our endeavors in space, and the obligations that come along with cosmic exploration.

The final thought

The final chapter of the book provides a brief summary of the most important points and

emphasizes the relevance of expanding our understanding of the cosmos through space travel. It invites readers to continue their discovery of the cosmos, whether through scientific research or simply by staring at the night sky in wonderment as they do so.

The conclusion

In the conclusion, we take a look into the foreseeable future of space exploration and discuss some of the exciting new developments and missions that are on the horizon. The content encourages readers to maintain their involvement in the rapidly advancing field of space research and technology.

This fictitious book is titled "Exploring the Universe: A Journey Through Space and Time," and it takes readers on an enthralling adventure through the cosmos. Topics covered in the book include the history of space travel, the mysteries of the universe, and the ethical issues that come into play when venturing beyond Earth. The author approaches the topic of space exploration from a variety of angles throughout each chapter, making this book an interesting and educational read for space fans of all experience levels.

Chapter 1

Foundations of Cultural Heritage

The collective legacy of a community is known as its cultural heritage, and it includes both the material and non-material manifestations of that group's identity and history. It is a rich fabric of artifacts, traditions, values, knowledge, and practices that bind individuals to their history and affect the present as well as the future of those individuals. The diversity and inventiveness of human communities are reflected in their cultural history, which can shed light on how these societies evolved, as well as their core values and highest goals.

The Importance of Preserving Our Cultural Heritage

1. **One's Sense of Self and Belonging**
   The preservation of cultural traditions is important because it provides a sense of identity and belonging. It fosters a sense of belonging to a particular cultural, regional, or national community by connecting individuals to their roots, so assisting individuals in better comprehending where they stand in the world and providing a sense of connection to that group. People are given the opportunity to learn more about the customs and beliefs of their ancestors, which helps them develop a stronger connection to their cultural identity.

2. **The Maintenance of Historical Accuracy**
   The preservation of a society's past through its cultural legacy. It does this by providing insights into the experiences, successes, and problems of previous generations through the use of artifacts, documents, and oral traditions. It offers a direct connection to history, making it possible for both current and future generations to gain insight from studying the past.

3. **The Diversity of Cultures**
   The preservation and celebration of cultural heritage are essential to maintaining cultural diversity. This emphasizes the singularity of each culture as well as the contributions that each has made to the cultural mosaic of the world. In a

world that is becoming more interconnected, respect for one another, tolerance, and understanding are fostered among different nations through the preservation of cultural legacy.

4. **The Value of Tourism and the Economy**
   The value of cultural heritage can sometimes be quantified monetarily. It frequently attracts tourists, which is beneficial to the local businesses and encourages cultural interaction. When it comes to increasing tourism and consequently a region's revenue, museums, historical sites, and cultural events are major drivers.

5. **Integration of society**
   The preservation of cultural traditions is important to the development of cohesive communities. It offers communities shared tales and symbols, which fosters a sense of connection and encourages collaboration among members of the community. This common legacy has the potential to assist different societies in overcoming their internal differences and conflicts.

6. **Sources of Inspiration for the Arts and the Creative Process**
   The preservation of cultural traditions can serve as a wellspring for artistic and creative endeavors. In order to create new works that both commemorate and reinterpret tradition, creatives such as writers, musicians, and artists seek inspiration from the intricate pattern of history. Heritage can serve as a source of inspiration for creative endeavors.

7. **Manifestations of the Cultural Heritage**

There are many different manifestations of cultural legacy, each of which contributes to a more comprehensive comprehension of the heritage of a society. Both tangible and intangible legacy are two main categories that can be used to classify these types.

Heritage of the Culture That Can Be Touched

1. **Architectural Landmarks and Historic Structures**
   Historic structures, which can range from ancient temples to contemporary skyscrapers, are concrete examples of a culture's architectural prowess and the progression of its historical development.

2. **Galleries, Museums, and Other Collections**
   The large collections of art, antiquities, and historical objects that are housed at museums provide a glimpse into the creative and historical development of a society.

3. **Locations of Archaeological Interest**
   Archaeological sites, which might include historical towns, burial grounds, and shipwrecks, offer vital insights into the lifestyles of bygone civilizations and the activities they participated in.

4. **Works of Art and Handicrafts**

   Expressions of one's ingenuity, cultural background, and appreciation for beauty can be found in works of art and handicrafts such as paintings, sculptures, fabrics, and pottery.

5. **Landscapes of Cultural Significance**

   Gardens, ancient city centers, and agricultural landscapes are examples of cultural landscapes that have been influenced by human activity over many generations. Cultural landscapes include natural and cultural aspects in their composition.

6. **Memorials and Archeological Sites**

The commemoration of historical occasions, persons, and sacrifices through monuments and memorials helps to keep the memory of significant turning points alive.

Heritage of the Intangible Cultural Landscape

1. **Traditions Passed Down Orally**

   The knowledge, history, and cultural values of a society can be preserved through oral traditions, which include tales, myths, legends, folktales, and the spoken word, among other forms of storytelling.

2. **Traditions, Celebrations, and Holidays**

   When it comes to expressing a community's ideas, values, and cultural identity, the importance of cultural and religious rites, festivals, and ceremonies cannot be overstated.

3. **Conventional Ways of Knowing and Doing Things**

   The accumulated wisdom of generations, as well as their adaptations to their circumstances, is represented by traditional knowledge, which might include farming skills, medicinal practices, and handicrafts.

4. **The Languages and Dialects of the World**

   Because they communicate a community's one-of-a-kind linguistic identity as well as its history, languages and dialects are an essential component of cultural heritage.

5. **Performers of Song and Dance**

   Expressions of culture such as music, songs, and dance are crucial components because they convey the sentiments, narratives, and rhythms of a people.

6. **Culinary Customs and the History of Food**

Traditions around food and cooking can shed light on a culture's gastronomic preferences, farming methods, and inventiveness in the kitchen.

The Safekeeping of Our Cultural Traditions

1. **Environmental Protection and Rehabilitation**
   The preservation of physical items and structures is the primary focus of conservation and restoration activities. Artworks, buildings, and relics can be repaired, restored, and preserved with the help of skilled conservators who apply scientific approaches.
2. **Documentation and Storage of Records**
   Even if the actual items of cultural heritage get damaged in some way, the significance of these artifacts can still be maintained by the meticulous documentation of their history, which can include images, written descriptions, and historical records.
3. **Administration of Museums and Exhibitions**
   Museums are extremely important institutions for the preservation and presentation of cultural heritage. Objects are curated, cataloged, and displayed by museum experts in order to make them available to the general public.
4. **Legislation and Administrative Requirements**
   A significant number of nations have put legal structures in place to safeguard their cultural heritage. The unearthing, exporting, and selling of cultural items, in addition to the preservation of historical monuments and buildings, are all regulated by these rules.
5. **Spreading Knowledge and Being Aware**
   Educational endeavors and public awareness campaigns have the dual purpose of informing the general public about the significance of cultural heritage and encouraging them to take an active role in the conservation of this legacy.
6. **Preserving the Digital Record**

In this day and age, there are attempts being made to digitally preserve cultural heritage. These efforts include 3D scans, virtual reality experiences, and online archives. This helps to ensure that legacy is available even if the actual pieces that make up the heritage are lost.

The Function of Historical and Cultural Relics in Modern Society

1. **Travel and the Promotion of Economic Growth**
   Many of the places and practices that make up a culture's legacy are also popular tourist destinations, which helps both the local and national economies. In many areas, tourism that focuses on local history and culture is a major contributor to economic growth.
2. **Instruction and Investigation**
   The study of history, society, and culture can all be enriched by tapping into the vast resources that are contained within cultural heritage. It is a very helpful resource for scholarly research and educational pursuits.

3. **An Exchange of Cultures**
   The preservation of cultural heritage encourages the sharing of other cultures and cooperation across international borders. The promotion of intercultural understanding and appreciation can be achieved through cultural diplomacy as well as through programs such as UNESCO's World Heritage Sites.
4. **Establishing a Sense of Belonging and Community**
   The preservation of a community's heritage can assist in the formation of its identity and the strengthening of social ties. It gives a sense of belonging as well as pride and a sense of history that is shared.
5. **Originality and Sources of Motivation**
   For creative people such as musicians, writers, and artists, a rich cultural legacy can be a rich source of ideas. It maintains its power to inspire creative and innovative practices in the modern era.
6. **Sustainable and Environmentally Friendly Business Practices**

The value of traditional knowledge in fields such as agriculture, conservation, and environmentally responsible activities is becoming increasingly acknowledged as a factor in the solution to environmental problems.

Obstacles to Be Confronted When Preserving Cultural Heritage

1. **Dangers Posed by Nature and the Environment**
   There is a high risk that tangible cultural heritage will be damaged or destroyed as a result of natural catastrophes, climate change, and other environmental problems such as pollution and erosion.
2. **The Role of Urbanization in the Development Process**
   Frequently, the change or elimination of historical sites and landscapes is an unavoidable consequence of urban expansion and development.
3. **Plundering and Engaging in Illicit Trade**
   Illegal digging up of archaeological sites and trafficking in cultural relics are continuous problems, and things are regularly taken from the locations where they were first discovered and sold on the black market.
4. **Armed Conflict and War**
   It is possible for cultural heritage places to be purposefully destroyed during times of armed conflict, as well as for priceless objects to be stolen.
5. **Neglect and the Accumulation of Decay**
   Structures and things that are part of a culture's legacy might deteriorate over time if they aren't properly maintained or if there aren't enough resources to do so.
6. **A lack of consciousness as well as education**

It's possible that a large number of people don't completely comprehend the worth of cultural heritage, which might lead to apathy or a lack of support for efforts to preserve it.

Efforts Being Made All Over the World to Preserve Our Cultural Heritage

In light of the widespread significance of the world's cultural heritage, a number of international organizations and treaties have been founded with the purpose of preserving and guarding it.

1. **UNESCO**
   The United Nations Educational, Scientific, and Cultural Organization, more often known as UNESCO, is an organization that plays a significant part in the process of safeguarding cultural assets. The United Nations Educational, Scientific, and Cultural Organization (UNESCO) maintains a number of treaties and maintains a list of sites that are of extraordinary cultural and natural significance on its World Heritage List.
2. **The Convention of The Hague**
   During times of armed conflict, the Hague Convention for the Protection of Cultural Property in the Event of Armed Conflict, which was signed in 1954, as well as its two Protocols, which were signed in 1954 and 1999, aim to preserve cultural property.
3. **The World Monuments Fund**
   This charitable organization's mission is to safeguard the cultural traditions of people all around the world. It provides financial assistance to conservation projects and educates people about the need of preserving cultural and natural heritage.
4. **ICOMOS**
   The International Council on Monuments and Sites (also known as ICOMOS) is an international non-governmental organization that works to encourage the preservation of cultural assets all around the world. It offers expertise as well as recommendations regarding the protection of history.
5. **Protective Blue Shield**

A network of organizations and individuals striving to conserve cultural heritage during times of armed war and other types of emergencies is known as the Blue Shield.

A community's identity, history, and traditions are all parts of its cultural legacy, and the term "cultural heritage" refers to all of these components, both the tangible and the ethereal ones. It is extremely important since it serves as a foundation for one's identity, a repository for historical knowledge, a platform for the appreciation of cultural variety, and a motivator for both economic and social solidarity. There are many different manifestations of cultural heritage, some of which are tangible, such as

ART AND ARCHITECTURE

artifacts, sites, and rituals, while others, such as practices, knowledge, and traditions, are intangible.

The conservation of cultural heritage, along with its documentation and legal safeguarding, is essential to its continued existence. It is of the utmost importance to make sure that future generations will still have access to the heritage that we have. The impact that tourism, education, cultural interchange, identity, creativity, and sustainability all have on cultural heritage is something that continues to be a critically important factor in modern society.

There are international efforts and treaties aimed at protecting cultural heritage, despite the fact that there are problems like as natural catastrophes, urbanization, looting, and neglect. The World Monuments Fund and the International Council on Monuments and Sites (ICOMOS) are only two of the organizations that are actively involved in heritage protection with UNESCO and the Hague Convention. The collective obligation to protect cultural heritage continues to be an international enterprise, one that acknowledges the inherent worth of maintaining the cultural legacy of the world for future generations.

1.1 Understanding Cultural Heritage

Without a doubt, I will be able to present to you an in-depth investigation of your quest to comprehend cultural heritage. Heritage is the legacy of a society's cultural history and tradition, and it includes both the tangible and intangible parts of a society's identity. Heritage is the legacy of a group's cultural history and tradition. For the purpose of gaining an understanding of cultural heritage, it is necessary to investigate the myriad of aspects that comprise this complex web, as well as to investigate the relevance of cultural heritage's many forms, how it should be preserved, and the role it plays in forming communities and identities.

Acquiring Knowledge of Our Cultural Heritage

The idea of cultural heritage is somewhat complex, as it attempts to capture the myriad ways in which human history, creativity, and morals have evolved over time. It is a complex network of rituals, rites, beliefs, artifacts, and practices that have been handed down from generation to generation. Recognizing the myriad components that make up a culture's heritage and respecting the fundamental role it plays in the formation of a society are necessary steps toward gaining an understanding of cultural heritage.

The Importance of Preserving Cultural Heritage

1. **One's Sense of Self and Belonging**
   Individuals and communities derive a sense of pride and cohesiveness from their cultural history because it gives them a sense of identity and a sense of belonging to the group. It fosters a common sense of history and tradition, which enhances social relationships, thereby connecting people to their ancestors and providing a link to their family trees.

2. **The conservation of historical sites**
   The cultural heritage of a society acts as a storehouse for the historical narrative of that society, maintaining the communal memory of events, accomplishments, and difficulties that occurred in the past. It works as a window into the cultural evolution of societies, enabling present and future generations to gain insight from the experiences of their predecessors and learn from the lessons their ancestors passed down to them.
3. **Diversity of cultures and an awareness of other countries**
   The celebration of the diversity of human expression that is a part of cultural heritage helps to cultivate mutual understanding and respect amongst different societies. It fosters conversation between other cultures and encourages an appreciation of the myriad of beliefs, practices, and traditions that exist in different parts of the world.
4. **Importance of Education**
   A large amount of educational value is provided by cultural heritage in the form of a vast repository of material suitable for study and investigation by academics, students, and members of the general public. It makes it possible to investigate various historical eras, artistic trends, and socioeconomic systems, which contributes to an overall comprehension of human civilization.
5. **Manifestations of the Cultural Heritage**

There are many different manifestations of cultural heritage, each of which exemplifies a different facet of the cultural legacy of a culture. Both tangible and intangible heritage are important aspects of a culture, and both contribute to an overall comprehension of the concept of cultural identity. These forms can be roughly classed as heritage.

Heritage of the Culture That Can Be Touched

1. **Historic Structures and Preserved Monuments**
   Castles, temples, and palaces are some examples of historic buildings that serve as visible memories of a society's achievements in architecture as well as its historical milestones.
2. **Artifacts and objects of artistic creation**
   The artistic and creative expressions of bygone civilizations are preserved in the form of artifacts and items of art, such as sculptures, paintings, and pottery. These artifacts and pieces of art reflect the cultural values and aesthetic sensitivities of the people who created them.
3. **Landscapes in Their Cultural Context**
   Ancient towns, gardens, and agricultural terraces are examples of cultural landscapes that demonstrate the seamless blending of human creativity with natural

ART AND ARCHITECTURE

settings. These examples of cultural landscapes exemplify the symbiotic link that exists between culture and nature.

4. **Locations of Archaeological Interest**

Archaeological sites, which might include historical ruins, burial grounds, and prehistoric villages, offer invaluable insights into the way of life and practices of ancient civilizations. These sites also throw light on the social, religious, and economic dynamics of these societies.

Heritage of the Intangible Cultural Landscape

1. **Expressions and Traditions Passed Down Verbally**
   Folk stories, legends, and proverbs are examples of oral traditions that are part of the oral history of communities. These traditions encapsulate the communities' collective knowledge, values, and beliefs.
2. **Traditional Practices and Performing Arts**
   The spiritual and cultural rituals that have always been an essential part of the social fabric of societies are embodied in the performing arts and rituals, which might include traditional dances, music, and ceremonial acts.
3. **Festivities and Occasions for Commemoration**
   Festivals and celebrations, which are denoted by particular cultural practices and customs, offer communities the opportunity to express their cultural identity, values, and social solidarity via the experiences that they share together.
4. **Craftsmanship and expertise rooted in the past**

Craftsmanship and skills that have been practiced for years, such as weaving, woodcarving, and pottery making, are examples of artisanal knowledge and practices that have been handed down from generation to generation, and they are a reflection of the cultural history of a community.

The Protection and Maintenance of Our Rich Cultural Heritage

1. **Environmental Protection and Rehabilitation**
   The physical preservation of cultural heritage is the primary focus of conservation and restoration activities. This involves the repair, maintenance, and protection of objects, buildings, and historical sites in order to stop the degradation and destruction from occurring.
2. **Documentation and Storage of Records**
   The systematic categorization and preservation of historical and cultural artifacts is enabled by thorough recording and archiving of cultural heritage objects. This documentation and archiving of cultural heritage items includes complete records, pictures, and digital databases.

3. **Legislation and policy pertaining to culture**
   Cultural policies and legislative frameworks set standards and laws for the conservation and administration of cultural heritage. This helps to ensure that cultural heritage is protected from unauthorized exploitation, destruction, and illegal commerce.
4. **Engagement with and participation in the community**
   The engagement and participation of local communities are essential components in the process of preserving cultural heritage. This is because these components cultivate a sense of communal duty and ownership within local communities, which in turn encourages residents to take an active role in the preservation of cultural heritage.
5. **Spreading Knowledge and Being Aware**

Educational programs and awareness campaigns play a significant role in improving public understanding and appreciation of cultural heritage. These programs and campaigns highlight the relevance of cultural heritage and the necessity of maintaining and protecting it.

The Importance of Historical and Cultural Artifacts in Today's World

1. **International Travel and the Sharing of Cultures**
   Heritage tourism efforts that highlight the one-of-a-kind cultural character and history of a region serve as a substantial driver of economic growth and serve to promote cultural exchange. Cultural heritage also serves as a significant draw for tourism, which in turn promotes cultural interaction.
2. **International Cultural Diplomacy and Comprehending Other Cultures**
   In the field of cultural diplomacy, the significance of cultural heritage in developing global cooperation and conversation, as well as fostering cross-cultural understanding, is of the utmost importance. This is accomplished through efforts that showcase the varied cultures' shared values and legacy.
3. **The promotion of sustainable development and the protection of the environment**
   By encouraging environmental preservation and sustainable practices that are founded in traditional knowledge and indigenous wisdom, cultural heritage makes a contribution to the cause of sustainable development. This helps to build a holistic approach to the process of community development.
4. **Identities and the Bonding of Societies**

By giving a feeling of continuity and shared history, cultural heritage helps to strengthen social

ART AND ARCHITECTURE

cohesion and identity. This, in turn, helps to foster a sense of belonging and solidarity among communities, which in turn helps to promote mutual respect and understanding.

To have a proper comprehension of cultural legacy, one must be aware of its profound significance, the variety of forms it can take, and the myriad functions it plays in modern society. Communities may assure the continuation of their rich cultural legacy for future generations by maintaining and protecting their cultural heritage. This can create a greater understanding and appreciation of their collective identity and history. The preservation of cultural legacy continues to be a communal obligation that exemplifies humanity's common cultural ideals and goals, despite the fact that cultural heritage is always changing and adapting to the difficulties presented by the modern world.

1.2 The Role of Art and Architecture in Cultural Heritage

The formation of cultural heritage and its continued existence are both substantially aided by the contributions of art and architecture. They are potent vehicles through which a culture's history, values, beliefs, and identity can be represented and passed down to succeeding generations of people. In this essay, we will investigate the crucial roles that art and architecture play in cultural heritage, ranging from the maintenance of historical narratives to the celebration of distinctive cultural identities. These functions include the preservation of historical narratives and the development of unique cultural identities.

1. **Keeping our past and our memories alive**

   Art and architecture are examples of historical artifacts that provide a culture with a tangible record of its previous existence. Documentation of a society's history and the significant events that have influenced its identity can be found in the form of paintings, sculptures, architecture, and monuments. These pieces of art have the ability to tell stories, memorialize historical events, and pay tribute to great personalities, all of which serve to keep the memory of these events alive for future generations. The biblical stories that are depicted in the paintings that cover the walls of the Sistine Chapel in Vatican City, for instance, have been maintained for millennia along with the chapel's religious and artistic heritage.

2. **Reflecting the cultural beliefs and values of the community**

   Art and architecture act as mirrors that reflect the cultural values, beliefs, and worldviews of the society they are a part of. The aesthetic preferences, styles, and symbols that are incorporated into works of art and architecture shed light on the prevalent worldviews of the time and location in which they were produced. For instance, the elaborate carvings on the temples of Angkor Wat in Cambodia represent the deep intertwining of Hindu and Buddhist practices in Khmer culture. These carvings may be found in Cambodia.

3. **Instilling a Strong Sense of Identity in Others**
   The production and maintenance of a cultural identity are inextricably linked to the fields of art and architecture. They highlight the specific qualities and distinctions that make a community unique and so exemplify the community's shared identity. Symbols of a country's or a region's identity can take the form of architectural styles, artistic traditions, or recognizable landmarks. The Taj Mahal in India, with its spectacular blend of Mughal and Persian architectural styles, stands as an enduring symbol of India's rich cultural legacy and artistic accomplishments. The Taj Mahal was built in the 16th century and was designed to be a mausoleum for the Emperor Shah Jahan.

4. **Educational Methods and the Transmission of Culture**
   The transmission of cultural information and values from one generation to the next can be facilitated by the use of educational resources such as art and architecture. These various modes of cultural expression are capable of communicating complicated ideas, myths, and historical accounts. People are taught about their ancestors' beliefs and practices, as well as their own heritage through these programs. For example, prehistoric cave paintings in places like Lascaux, France, provide as visual records of prehistoric life and offer insights into the cultural practices and beliefs of early human communities. These paintings were created thousands of years ago.

5. **Promoting Creative Thinking and Innovative Ideas**
   The creative process and innovative thinking are fostered by art and architecture. They motivate succeeding generations to expand upon the accomplishments of their ancestors and to push the envelope in terms of artistic expression and architectural design. The works of the past are a common source of creativity for current architects, artists, and designers, who frequently reimagine conventional shapes and patterns for use in modern settings. The Guggenheim Museum in Bilbao, Spain, which was created by Frank Gehry, serves as a prime example of how forward-thinking architectural design can revolutionize a community and inspire original thought.

6. **Encouragement of Intercultural Communication**
   Through providing insights into the aesthetics, histories, and values of many civilizations, art and architecture serve as a catalyst for the exchange of cultural ideas. The exchange of ideas between people of different cultures is facilitated and promoted by institutions such as museums, art shows, and architectural landmarks. The Louvre Museum in Paris and the British Museum in London are two examples of international organizations that house significant collections of artwork and artifacts from a variety of cultural traditions. These museums offer possibilities for cultural appreciation and exchange on a worldwide scale.

7. **Preserving and protecting for future generations**

The protection of cultural heritage frequently calls for preservation and conservation initiatives, particularly in the realm of art and architecture. These efforts also include the upkeep of historical structures, the safeguarding of artistic masterpieces, and the prevention of the deterioration of cultural assets. The techniques of conservation guarantee that these substantial contributions to cultural heritage will continue to be available to future generations so that they can be appreciated and learned from.

1.3 Preservation and Conservation

The preservation and conservation of our cultural and natural heritage are both essential practices that have the same overarching goal: to protect and assure the legacy's continued existence. These efforts are absolutely necessary in order to preserve the variety and richness of the planet, to protect historical narratives, and to guarantee that ecosystems will retain their integrity. In this essay, we are going to discuss the relevance of preservation and conservation, as well as their fundamental principles and the roles they play in resolving the challenges that endanger our history and the environment.

The Importance of Keeping Things in Their Original Form and Conserving Them

1. **The Maintenance of a Preserved Cultural Identity**

   Protecting historical items, structures, and practices through preservation and conservation efforts is an important step in preserving cultural identities. The ideals, beliefs, and history of a civilization are reflected in its cultural heritage, which includes things like art, architecture, and oral traditions. It is via the preservation of these components that cultures are able to transmit their distinct cultural identities to subsequent generations.

2. **Ensuring the Continuity of Historical Events**

   The preservation of historical tales guarantees their continued existence. It grants societies the ability to record their histories and draw lessons from both their successes and failures in the past. Maintaining a society's historical continuity is essential to the process of molding a society's identity and directing its path toward the future.

3. **Responsible Management of the Environment**

   The practice of conservation is an essential component of environmental stewardship. It is absolutely necessary for preserving the ecological balance and the health of ecosystems. The protection of habitats, biodiversity, and natural resources through conservation initiatives ensures that these features will continue to be accessible to subsequent generations.

4. **Methods That Are Ecologically Sound**

   Both in terms of cultural heritage and the environment, preservation and conservation are practices that contribute to the development of sustainable practices. Communities are able to establish environmentally friendly practices that are harmonious with their surroundingss if they take steps to preserve traditional knowledge such as agricultural practices that are sustainable.

5. **Education and Scientific Investigation**

These techniques are beneficial to the fields of education and research. Academic research is made significantly more fruitful by the protection of historical and cultural artifacts, as well as natural habitats and ecosystems; this, in turn, leads to a greater comprehension of the interactions between humans and their environments.

Principles Crucial to the Processes of Preserving and Conserving

1. **Health and Safety Measures**
   Taking preventative care entails acting in such a way as to reduce the likelihood of potential hazards and dangers to cultural assets and natural habitats. It encompasses procedures such as routine maintenance, the installation of protective enclosures, and the monitoring of the surrounding environment.

2. **Creating Documentation**
   Documentation in its fullest form is absolutely necessary for the conservation of both natural and cultural resources. The collecting of detailed records, images, and data helps in cataloging and comprehending the changes that have occurred in the environment and the legacy throughout time.

3. **Doing Research and Dissecting It**
   The preservation and conservation strategies that are used are informed by in-depth research and analysis. In order to make decisions based on accurate information, it is essential to have a solid understanding of the relevant materials, structures, or ecosystems.

4. **Intervention of the Barest Necessity**
   The "minimal intervention" approach states that any action done for preservation or conservation should strive to interfere with the original state of the thing being preserved or conserved as little as is humanly practicable. This method protects the authenticity of cultural items as well as the natural environments in which they are found.

5. **Measures That Can Be Undone**
   When it is practicable to do so, preservation and conservation efforts should make use of reversible measures. In the event that more up-to-date information or methods become available in the future, it will be possible to reverse these steps.

6. **Long-term viability**

The concept of long-term viability is central to the field of conservation. It is important that such efforts be coordinated with sustainable practices, since this will increase the likelihood that both natural and cultural settings may be preserved for the foreseeable future.

Attempts at Preserving and Conserving Face Difficulties

1. **The changing climate**
   The effects of climate change pose a substantial danger to the world's natural ecosystems. Temperature increases, altered patterns of precipitation, and the occurrence of extreme weather can all be detrimental to ecosystems and pose a threat to biodiversity.
2. **The problem of pollution**
   Both the natural world and the world's cultural traditions are at danger when pollution of any kind—whether it be in the air, the water, or the soil—is allowed to continue. For instance, pollution in the air can cause the facades of old buildings to deteriorate, whilst pollution in the water can destroy aquatic habitats.
3. **The Growth of Cities and Development**
   The elimination of natural habitats and the transformation of cultural landscapes are frequently the unintended consequences of urbanization and unbridled growth. The problem that preservation and conservation face is striking a balance between preserving heritage and allowing for growth.
4. **Plundering and Engaging in Illicit Trade**
   The destruction of cultural heritage and the illegal sale of priceless artifacts are two major
   problems that need to be addressed. This trading on the underground market deprives communities of their legacy and undermines attempts to preserve these cultural assets.
5. **An Insufficient Amount of Money and Resources**
   Efforts made toward preservation and conservation frequently face difficulties due to insufficient financing and resources. For these initiatives to succeed, financial backing is necessary for study, upkeep, and restoration.
6. **Awareness of the Public and Participation**

Awareness and participation on the part of the public are absolutely necessary for the successful preservation and protection of resources. The task is to educate the general people about the significance of these practices and to encourage their active participation.

The Importance of Preserving and Conserving Existing Resources in Responding to Challenges

1. **Measures to Reduce the Impact of Climate Change**
   The preservation of natural ecosystems is the primary goal of conservation activities; this, in turn, helps to mitigate the effects of climate change. Carbon dioxide

is captured by healthy ecosystems, which also help to preserve biodiversity and build resistance to the effects of extreme weather.

2. **Development that is Sustainable**
The preservation and conservation movement supports environmentally responsible economic growth. It is possible for communities to strike a harmonic balance between expansion and preservation if urban planning and development are carried out with environmental stewardship and the protection of cultural assets at the forefront.

3. **The protection of biological diversity**
The defense of biodiversity and the maintenance of threatened animal populations are the two primary focuses of conservation efforts. This is absolutely necessary in order to keep the ecological balance intact and stop the extinction of species that are important.

4. **The revitalization of culture and the strengthening of community**
The preservation of heritage can result in the revitalization of culture and the strengthening of communities. Communities can reclaim their feeling of identity and pride via the careful preservation and revitalization of ancient customs.

5. **The Encouragement of Responsible Vacationing**
Responsible tourism is supported by preservation and conservation efforts. To ensure that tourism is beneficial to the surrounding communities without having a negative impact on the environment, sustainable tourism practices place a priority on the preservation of natural and cultural resources.

6. **Promotion of Awareness and Advocacy**

Advocacy and awareness-raising are two of the most important roles that can be played by preservation and conservation activities. These activities raise awareness about how critical it is to preserve natural and cultural settings, thereby gaining support from the general public, governments, and other groups.

The safeguarding of both our cultural and natural heritage requires the unavoidable implementation of preservation and conservation techniques. They are vital to the maintenance of historical narratives, the defense of ecological systems, and the promotion of environmentally responsible practices. These efforts, in spite of the difficulties they encounter, are absolutely necessary for guaranteeing that our cultural and natural riches will be around for future generations to enjoy. By sticking to fundamental principles and advocating actions that are responsible, preservation and conservation contribute to the overall well-being of societies as well as the planet as a whole. This helps to develop a healthy coexistence between humanity and the natural world.

Chapter 2

Prehistoric and Ancient Art and Architecture

Creativity, innovation, and the progression of culture can be seen most clearly in the world's artistic and architectural creations. They shed light on the ideas, principles, and practices that guided ancient societies' technological development as well as their beliefs and values. The prehistoric and ancient eras are key landmarks in the history of art and architecture, exhibiting the development of human thought as well as advancements in aesthetics and technical expertise. This in-depth investigation of prehistoric and ancient art and architecture will take you on a journey through time, beginning in the Paleolithic period and ending with the collapse of the Roman Empire. Along the way, you will learn about the transforming power of human expression and invention.

1. **The Paleolithic Period, Also Known as the Beginning of Art**

The period of time known as the Paleolithic era extends from around 2.5 million years ago to approximately 10,000 years before the common era (BCE). The Old Stone Age is another name for this time period. During this time period, early humans were responsible for the creation of a few of the world's oldest and most mysterious kinds of art. Although they had a restricted selection of tools and materials to work with, they had an unbounded capacity for inventiveness.

1. **The Art of Caves**
   The caves of Lascaux and Chauvet
   The Lascaux and Chauvet caverns in France are considered to be two of the most famous examples of Paleolithic cave art. These websites have some very wonderful renderings of humans, animals, and non-representational symbols. These images were brought to life by the artists through the use of a variety of techniques, including natural paints, engravings, and sculptural relief. These works of art shed light on the ancient worldview, which may have been

connected to shamanic practices, hunting rites, or narrative storytelling.

The Cave of Altamira
Another well-known cave in Spain that contains art from the Paleolithic period is Altamira Cave. It is filled with intricate paintings of bison and other animals, all of which are produced with an impressive level of finesse. The early artists had a sharp eye for detail and a strong connection to the natural world, as evidenced by the animals' vivid colors and accurate anatomical depictions, which are both featured in the paintings.

2. **Art Work That Can Be Transported**
The Paleolithic period saw the creation of movable works of art in addition to the preexisting cave paintings. These featured miniature sculptures, such as the Venus figurines like the Venus of Willendorf, which lauded the beauty of the female form and may have honored fertility or the rites associated with reproduction.

3. **Technology and Materials**

Ochre and charcoal were two of the natural colors that Paleolithic artists used to produce their works of art throughout the Paleolithic period. In order to carve and sculpt, they created hand-made instruments out of bone, like as needles and chisels. These early innovations were a reflection of humanity's need to exert control over its natural surroundings and to articulate its place in the natural order of things.

II. The Neolithic Revolution, When Architecture First Begins to Take Form
During the Neolithic period, which roughly lasted from 10,000 BCE to 2,000 BCE, there was a significant cultural transition that affected human culture. The advent of agriculture made it possible for people to dwell in one place, which in turn led to the development of architecture that brought about major shifts in the way humans lived and organized their areas.

1. **The Built Environment**
The catalhoyuk
The site of Catalhoyuk, which may be found in what is now the country of Turkey, is considered to be one of the earliest examples of Neolithic building. This prehistoric community was characterized by dwellings built from mud bricks and arranged in close proximity to one another. The rooftops that were connected to one another served as walkways. The layout of the buildings gives the impression of community life and a well-organized civilization.

Stonehenge is referred to as
Stonehenge, located in England, is a Neolithic structure that is both mysterious and impressive. Ancient astronomy and technical knowledge can still be seen in the arrangement of large standing stones in such a way that they are aligned to the movements of celestial bodies. To this day, academics aren't entirely sure

what the function of Stonehenge was supposed to be—whether it was a place of worship, a burial ground, or an astronomical observatory.
2. **Art**

Art throughout the Neolithic period frequently took the shape of ceramics and earthenware that were embellished with complex patterns. These items displayed sophisticated artistic sensibility in addition to superior techniques for producing pottery. As societies got more stable and evolved, the level of complexity and symbolic import in their artwork increased.

III. The Ancient Middle East and the Origins of Civilization in the Near East

Some of the world's earliest civilizations, such as Sumer, Akkad, Babylon, and Assyria, originated in the region that is now known as the Ancient Near East. Around the years 3500 BCE and 500 BCE, the area now known as Mesopotamia witnessed the rise and flourishing of the cultures described below. Not only did their art and architecture represent the evolved social systems of their society, but also the political and theological ideas of the day.

1. **Ziggurats, to begin:**
   Ziggurats were massive stepping pyramids that were built as administrative and religious sites. For example, the Ziggurat of Ur, which was located in ancient Sumer, was a great architectural achievement that was supposed to promote communication between the mortal realm and the divine realm. Traditions of architecture have been profoundly impacted by the ziggurat, both in terms of its physical appearance and the meanings it conveys.
2. **Cuneiform Writing System**
   An important development that took place in the ancient Near East was the creation of cuneiform script, which consisted of markings that resembled wedges. The recording of laws, literary works, and religious texts was made possible as a result, ensuring that both knowledge and culture would be passed down to future generations. Clay tablets and monuments sometimes contain cuneiform inscriptions, which provide insights into the intellectual and bureaucratic lives of the communities in which they were located.
3. **Seals for the Cylinders**

Small and cylindrical in shape, cylinder seals were carved with complex motifs on their surfaces. These seals were utilized for a variety of tasks, including the identification of property, the verification of documents, and the invocation of guardian deities. It is possible to get insight into the religious practices and symbolism of ancient Mesopotamians through the examination of these objects, which are both works of art and useful instruments.

IV. Ancient Egypt's Everlasting Markers (Monuments to Eternity)

One of the most well-known and long-lasting civilizations in human history is ancient Egypt, which is famous for its artistic achievements as well as its pyramids and temples. It flourished for nearly 3,000 years, from around 3100 BCE to 30 CE, and it left behind a remarkable legacy of creative and architectural accomplishments.

1. **The Giza Pyramids**

   The pyramids of Giza, which were built during the time of the Old Kingdom in Egypt, continue to be among the most recognizable buildings in the entire world. These enormous tombs were constructed so that the pharaohs would have a place to stay in the afterlife. In particular, the Great Pyramid of Khufu serves as a testament to the excellent engineering talents that were prevalent during that time period.

2. **The Hieroglyphic Language**

   The ancient Egyptian writing system known as hieroglyphics incorporated aspects of alphabetic writing and logographic writing. These elaborate symbols were used as decoration on tombs, monuments, and temples. The ancient Egyptians used hieroglyphics not only as a tool of communication but also as a vehicle for conveying religious and historical ideas.

3. **The Art of the Funeral**

   The ancient Egyptian funerary art, which included paintings and sculptures found inside tombs, was an essential component in ensuring a peaceful transition into the next life. These pieces of art portrayed the deceased together with their ideal depictions of the hereafter, which frequently included agricultural prosperity, gatherings of surviving family members, and gifts from the living.

4. **Temples**

The architecture of Egyptian temples, which were built as shrines to both gods and pharaohs, paid careful attention to both proportion and symbolism. Intricate relief carvings and hieroglyphic inscriptions cover the walls of the temples of Karnak and Luxor, which are both excellent examples of monumental architecture.

V. The Birthplace of Classical Art and Architecture: Ancient Greece

The artistic and architectural traditions of the Western world can be traced back to ancient Greece, which flourished from about 800 BCE to 146 BCE. Their dedication to proportion, balance, and the idealized human form laid the groundwork for the classical aesthetics, which continue to have a significant impact on the visual arts and architecture to this day.

1. **The Acropolis of Athens**

   The Parthenon, which is a temple that was built to honor the goddess Athena, is considered to be an outstanding example of Doric architecture. It is renowned for the harmonious proportions and ornate decorative elements that it possesses. The frieze that wraps around the temple is an excellent example of the Greeks' ability to tell stories through the medium of art. It depicts various mythological events.

2. **Sculpture**
During the Classical period, Greek sculpture reached its highest point of development. Sculptors
such as Phidias and Praxiteles were responsible for creating statues that exemplified the perfect human form. The Doryphoros, also known as the Spear Bearer, was sculpted by Polykleitos and is an excellent example of the search of perfection in terms of both anatomical and artistic beauty.

3. **Pottery**

Greek pottery served a dual duty as both useful vessels and works of art. The pots were often decorated with recognizable motifs in red and black. These ceramics frequently depicted motifs from Greek mythology as well as scenes from everyday life, so shedding light on the culture and ideals of the historical period.

VI. The Engineering Wonders of Ancient Rome and the Imperial Art

During its existence from 27 BCE to 476 CE, the Roman Empire covered all of Europe, Africa, and Asia, and its art and architecture reflected the empire's enormous power and reach. The Romans were pioneers in the fields of engineering and urban design, and their contributions have left an indelible mark on the modern world.

1. **Roads and Waterway Structures**
   The Roman road network and aqueducts are both excellent examples of the engineering prowess of the Romans. The aqueducts ensured that cities had a consistent supply of water, while the road network made it easier for troops and traders to move about. The Romans' commitment to creating facilities that were both functional and aesthetically pleasing was on display in the building and upkeep of these infrastructures.

2. **The Colosseum**
   The Colosseum, located in Rome, was a large amphitheater that served as a testament to Roman entertainment as well as Roman engineering. It had the capacity to house up to 80,000 spectators and was used for various public events such as gladiatorial bouts and chariot racing. The ground-breaking architecture of it made it possible to effectively manage crowds and stage magnificent shows.

3. **Mosaics**
   Roman mosaics were used to decorate the floors and walls of public buildings, palaces, and temples throughout the Roman Empire. These elaborate graphics portrayed a wide variety of topics, ranging from legendary storylines to everyday settings and all in between. In the past, mosaics were a well-liked kind of decorative art because they successfully combined use and beauty.

4. Architecture with Arches and Vaults

The Romans were the first people to use arches and vaults in building construction, which led to the development of new architectural ideas such as aqueducts, triumphal arches, and the creation of huge interior spaces. These structural components ushered in a new era of innovation in building design and were essential contributors to the development of magnificent buildings like the Pantheon.

VII. The Ancient Chinese Practice of Striking a Balance

The aesthetics of ancient Chinese art and architecture place a strong emphasis on harmony, balance, and a profound connection to the natural world. This tradition dates back thousands of years. The fundamental tenet of Chinese aesthetics is the idea that works of art and architecture should be an embodiment of the guiding principles of harmony and proportion.

1. **The Great Wall of China**
   The Great Wall of China is a monumental work of architecture that was constructed over the course of several centuries. This massive fortification serves as a representation of China's resiliency and its commitment to safeguard the frontiers of its territory. The construction of it demonstrates the inventiveness of Chinese engineering in a multitude of ways, including the use of a wide range of materials and methods.

2. **The location of the Forbidden City**
   The architectural legacy of the Chinese imperial dynasties can be seen on display in Beijing's Forbidden City. From the beginning of the Ming Dynasty in 1368 to the end of the Qing Dynasty in 1912, it served as the imperial palace of China.
   Because of the layout's adherence to the concepts of feng shui and cosmic harmony, it is an excellent example of how Chinese architectural ideals should be represented.

3. **A Painting Done in China**

The Daoist and Confucian ideologies are frequently expressed through the medium of Chinese painting, which is typically carried out using ink and a brush on silk or paper. Landscapes and other aspects of nature are frequent subjects in Chinese art, which demonstrates the culture's profound respect for the natural world and its search of harmony.

VIII. Mesoamerica: An Overview of the Oldest Civilizations in the Americas

The pre-Columbian civilizations of Mesoamerica, such as the Maya, Aztec, and Inca, produced intricate artistic practices and architectural marvels that competed with those of the older civilizations of the Old World. These societies have left behind works of art and architecture of tremendous proportions.

1. **The Art and Architecture of the Maya**
   The Maya civilization, which had its heart in what is now Mexico and Central America, is famous for its ornate buildings and complex stone sculptures. The Maya built towering structures, such as Temple IV in Tikal, as well as stelae that were decorated with hieroglyphic inscriptions that recounted their history as well as their religious beliefs.
2. **Art and Architecture of the Aztecs**
   The Aztec Empire, which was based in what is now Mexico, was known for its massive architecture. One example of this is the Templo Mayor, which was the principal temple in Tenochtitlan, the Aztec capital. The intricate religious and cosmological ideas of the Aztecs were reflected in their art through the use of a wide variety of different mediums, such as featherwork, codices, and sculptures.
3. **Architecture of the Inca Empire**

Machu Picchu, which was built during the time of the Inca Empire and can be seen in South America, is famed for the inventive stonework that it featured. Walls and buildings made of dry stone were created with great accuracy by the Inca, demonstrating their mastery of geometry and engineering. Their artistic expressions and architectural designs frequently incorporated elements of their religious observances and astronomical observations.

Art and architecture from prehistoric and ancient times are examples of human creativity, inventiveness, and the wide variety of cultures that have existed throughout history. The passage of millennia has not diminished the importance of these writings, which continue to shed light on the thoughts and experiences of our predecessors.

We appreciate the enduring power of art and architecture to communicate across time and space as we explore the Paleolithic caves, marvel at the Pyramids of Giza, and contemplate the grandeur of the Parthenon. The cultural legacies left behind by these long-vanished civilizations continue to motivate, test, and direct contemporary artistic and architectural practices.

2.1 Cave Art and Megalithic Structures

Cave art is recognized as one of the earliest forms of artistic expression by humans. It provides a mesmerizing look into the thoughts and lifestyles of our ancient ancestors. Contemporary audiences continue to be captivated and motivated by the mysterious and intricate artworks that have been around for thousands of years and can be discovered in many different regions of the world. Cave art research not only reveals new information about the artistic abilities of early humans but also offers important new perspectives on their beliefs, rituals, and relationships with the natural environment.

A General Introduction to Paleolithic Cave Art

The Paleolithic period, which was defined by early human communities that relied on hunting and gathering for their existence, is where the origins of cave art can be traced back to. Cave paintings date back to this time period. Caves in many parts of the world, including Europe, Africa, and some areas of Asia, include notable examples of art that dates back to the Paleolithic period. These ancient works of art, which were frequently made with natural pigments and simple tools, represent a wide variety of subjects, including animals, human figures, abstract symbols, and complicated geometric patterns. Some of these artworks date back as far as 30,000 years.

The Lascaux Cave Provides an Insight into Ancient Artwork

The Lascaux Cave, located in the southwest of France, is a wonderful example of the artistic skill possessed by early people. The cave complex was not discovered until 1940, but it already contained a sizable collection of vibrant and detailed paintings that dated back more than 17,000 years. The artworks that can be found within the Lascaux Cave primarily depict a wide range of animals, such as horses, bulls, deer, and a number of other species of flora and fauna. The early artists' keen observation and strong connection to the natural world around them is reflected in the employment of methods such as natural colors, engravings, and sculptural relief in their work.

The Altamira Cave showcases the sophisticated craftsmanship of prehistoric artists

The Altamira Cave, located in northern Spain, is another important site that is famous for the extraordinary Paleolithic cave art that it contains. Intricate and lifelike images of bison and other animals may be found in a cave that was discovered during the end of the 19th century. The level of complexity displayed in these depictions is amazing.

The early artists had a sophisticated understanding of the topics they portrayed, as seen by the vivid colors and minute anatomical features depicted in their works of art depicting animals. The artwork discovered in Altamira Cave provides invaluable insights into the cultural and symbolic significance of animals within the life of early human groups. The cave is located in Spain.

The Chauvet Cave: A Window Into Our Ancestors' Cleverness and Innovation

The Chauvet Cave, which is located in the southeast of France and was found in 1994, is yet another extraordinary site that reveals important information regarding the artistic ability of Paleolithic humans. The cave's walls are covered in elaborate murals that were done with a high level of competence. These paintings include pictures of prehistoric animals such as mammoths, rhinoceroses, and others. The painters who worked in Chauvet Cave displayed an advanced awareness of perspective and movement, which enabled them to create an immersive and lifelike portrayal of the natural world that surrounded them.

Cave art's symbolic meanings and modern interpretations

Despite the fact that scholars are still debating the precise meanings underlying Paleolithic cave art, there are several prevalent hypotheses that aim to shed light on the possible uses and significance of these ancient artworks. Cave paintings have been interpreted as having served a variety of purposes, including as a type of storytelling, as a means of chronicling successful hunting journeys, and as a sort of ritual and ceremonial expression. Some people think that these artworks may have had some sort of symbolic or spiritual importance within the belief systems of these ancient communities. These beliefs may have been connected to fertility rites, shamanistic practices, or early representations of myths.

Megalithic structures are enduring testimonies to the ingenuity of ancient engineers

Megalithic structures, which are characterized by the use of enormous stones to construct gigantic architectural feats, have captured the imaginations of historians and archaeologists for ages. Megalithic structures are characterized by the use of large stones to construct monumental architectural feats. These mysterious constructions, which can be found all over the world in a wide variety of locations, are a testament to the engineering prowess and cultural relevance of ancient civilizations. Megalithic buildings serve as enduring testaments to the intellectual and technological achievements of our predecessors. These structures range from towering stone circles to intricate dolmens and are found all over the world.

Unraveling the Mysteries of Ancient Astronomy at Stonehenge

Stonehenge, which can be found in Wiltshire, England, and is widely considered to be one of the most recognizable megalithic structures in the world, has for a very long time been the focus of both fascination and conjecture. Stonehenge is a prehistoric monument that is thought to have been built between the years 3000 and 2000 BCE.

It is made up of enormous standing stones that are arranged in a round configuration. Stonehenge continues to be a topic of discussion among academics, with several hypotheses positing that it served various functions throughout its history, including those of an astronomical observatory, a religious place, and a ceremonial burial ground. Many people believe that because of its accurate alignment with astronomical events such as the summer and winter solstices, it played a key part in the ancient astronomical procedures and religious rites of that time period.

Dolmens and menhirs are examples of ancient burial practices that have been preserved

Dolmens are recognizable by the huge, vertical stones that support a capstone that is laid flat on top of them. These structures were frequently utilized as communal burial grounds or as chambers for the interment of the deceased. The burial practices and religious beliefs of ancient cultures can be better understood with the help of these buildings, which can be discovered in a variety of locations across Europe, Asia, and Africa. In a similar vein, massive vertical stones known as menhirs, which were frequently set in alignments or stood alone, are thought to have held some sort of ceremonial or sacrificial significance in the societies of antiquity.

The earliest known megalithic site is Gobekli Tepe

Gobekli Tepe, which can be seen in what is now Turkey, is widely regarded as one of the world's earliest and most fascinating examples of megalithic architecture.

Gobekli Tepe is an ancient site in Turkey that dates back to around 9600 BCE and features a number of stone pillars that have been beautifully carved and set in circular shapes. The antiquity of the site is only one component of the site's significance; its implications for the study of early human societal development and the evolution of complex religious beliefs and community organizations also contribute significantly to the site's relevance.

The Carnac Stones: Ancient Alignments with Significant Implications

The Carnac Stones are located in Brittany, France, and are made up of hundreds of standing stones that have been arranged in intricate rows and alignments. These constructions, which date back to the Neolithic period and the Bronze Age, continue to serve as emblems of the cultural and spiritual traditions that were prevalent in ancient communities. The specific use of the Carnac Stones is still a topic of discussion among academics; some hypotheses propose that they were utilized in religious rites, while others propose that they were used for astronomical observations or seasonal rituals connected to agricultural operations.

Importance of Megalithic Structures from a Cultural and Spiritual Standpoint

In the societies who erected them, megalithic buildings frequently carry great cultural, spiritual, and ritualistic importance. These gigantic works of engineering not only serve as physical expressions of communal identity, religious beliefs, and societal organization, but they also serve as a demonstration of the technical capabilities of ancient civilizations.

This is because these structures were built thousands of years ago. These ancient societies appear to have had a comprehensive grasp of astronomical occurrences, as evidenced by the alignments and orientations of megalithic monuments with celestial events. This information was likely integrated into the cultural and spiritual fabric of these communities.

2.2 Ancient Egyptian Architecture

The architecture of ancient Egypt is widely regarded as one of the most recognizable and long-lasting relics that have survived from the ancient world. Ancient Egyptian architecture displays the sophistication, grandeur, and spiritual beliefs of this exceptional culture. Examples of ancient Egyptian architecture include enormous monuments, exquisite temples, and complicated funeral complexes. The architectural feats of ancient Egypt continue to captivate and inspire contemporary audiences, offering significant insights into the culture, religion, and engineering capabilities of this ancient society. From the magnificent pyramids of Giza to the enormous temples of Karnak and Luxor, the architectural achievements of ancient Egypt continue to captivate and inspire contemporary audiences.

The Pyramid Complexes: Examples of Outstanding Construction

The pyramids of Egypt, and in particular the ones that may be found in Giza, are among the most lasting and instantly identifiable examples of ancient Egyptian architecture. Ancient Egyptians possessed an engineering prowess that was unprecedented

ART AND ARCHITECTURE

in its scope, as seen by the monumental tombs that they constructed for their pharaohs. The Great Pyramid of Giza is the largest and most well-known of all the pyramids. It was built during the time of Pharaoh Khufu and stands as a tribute to the inventiveness and technical prowess of the ancient Egyptians. The superior knowledge of mathematics, engineering, and astronomy that enabled the construction of the pyramids is evident in their precise alignment, enormous stone blocks, and complicated internal passageways.

Architecture of Religious Buildings as a Portal to the Sacred

The grandiosity, intricacy, and profound religious importance of the architecture of ancient Egyptian temples are distinguishing characteristics of this style. Temples were essential focus of religious, social, and political life in ancient Egyptian culture. They served as sacred sanctuaries dedicated to the gods and were also used for other purposes. Both the Karnak and Luxor Temple Complexes are excellent examples of the massive scale and architectural intricacy of ancient Egyptian religious architecture. These enormous temple complexes were embellished with huge columns, ornate reliefs, and towering pylons, so creating awe-inspiring sanctuaries that fostered the connection between the mortal realm and the divine realm.

Structures Dedicated to the Afterlife, Such as Funerary Complexes and Tombs

The ancient Egyptians' conceptions of the afterlife were deeply entwined with the processes that guided their construction of buildings. Pharaohs, queens, and other members of the royal court had elaborate funeral complexes built for them in order to serve as their final resting places. Some examples of these complexes were the Valley of the Kings and the Valley of the Queens. These complexes contained massive tombs that were embellished with artistic murals, hieroglyphic inscriptions, and intricate burial chambers; all of these elements were supposed to assure a safe journey into the hereafter for the deceased. The significant significance of the afterlife in the religious beliefs and cultural practices of ancient Egypt is demonstrated by the ornate building and decoration of these tombs, which are intricately detailed.

Obelisks and Temples: Symbolic Representations of Authority and Worship

Obelisks, which are tall, slender, tapering monuments, were major characteristics of ancient Egyptian architecture. They served as emblems of divine might and devotion to the gods, and they were a prominent part of ancient Egyptian architecture. These enormous buildings were frequently carved from a single block of granite and decorated with hieroglyphic writings. These inscriptions depicted the accomplishments and religious dedication of the ruling pharaohs. The obelisks that can be found in the Temple of Karnak and the Temple of Luxor, amongst other temples, served as symbols of the pharaoh's divine authority. Additionally, these obelisks were essential parts of the temple complexes, contributing to the overall splendor and spiritual importance of the temples.

Components of Architecture and Methods of Building Construction

Ancient Egyptian architecture made use of a wide variety of architectural components and construction techniques, all of which contributed to the impressiveness and longevity of the structures that were built in that culture. The construction of huge temples, tombs, and statues was made significantly easier by the utilization of massive stone blocks, such as limestone and granite. In order to move and position these enormous stones, the ancient Egyptians resorted to sophisticated methods, such as the utilization of ramps, levers, and pulleys, demonstrating the depth of their expertise in the fields of engineering and construction. The ancient Egyptians had a comprehensive understanding of astronomy, as evidenced by the precise alignment and orientation of structures with celestial events and cardinal directions. They also integrated cosmological principles into their architectural designs, which shows that their designs were influenced by this knowledge.

Inscriptions in Hieroglyphic and Other Decorative Arts

The ancient Egyptian architecture was adorned with decorative arts and hieroglyphic inscriptions, both of which played an important part in the transmission of religious, historical, and cultural tales. Walls of temples and tombs were often ornamented with intricate relief carvings that depicted religious rituals, historical victories, and other divine rites. These carvings were often made of stone.

These elaborate reliefs served as visual tales that conveyed the divine ancestry of the pharaoh, the achievements of the Egyptian state, and the significance of religious rites and beliefs to the Egyptian people. The walls of temples and tombs were covered in hieroglyphic writings, which included a script that was both complicated and symbolic. These inscriptions acted as conduits for religious incantations, historical chronicles, and offerings to the gods. This helped to ensure the longevity of the pharaoh's rule and the continuation of the afterlife.

2.3 Greek and Roman Art and Architecture

Ancient Greece and Rome are known for producing works of art and architecture that have had an everlasting impact on the development of human culture. These two major civilizations, which existed at different times and in different parts of the world, are responsible for producing some of the most recognizable and enduring examples of Western art and architecture. Greek art and architecture laid the groundwork for what we now refer to as classical aesthetics thanks to the emphasis placed on proportion, equilibrium, and an idealized human form in Greek art and architecture. On the other hand, Roman art and architecture expanded upon and modified the legacy left by the Greeks, integrating architectural marvels and a huge imperial reach. This in-depth investigation of Greek and Roman art and architecture will dive into the origins, evolution, and ongoing significance of these two exceptional cultural legacies. The focus of this investigation will be on Greek and Roman art and architecture.

1. **The Origin of Classical Aesthetics in Greek Art and Architecture**
   The Beginnings of Greek Art Can Be Traced Back to Archaic Greece

ART AND ARCHITECTURE

The Archaic period, which occurred around 800-480 BCE, is considered to be the beginning of Greek art. During this time period, some artistic traditions that were uniquely Greek came into existence; these conventions would go on to form the basis for later advancements in classical art. In particular, Archaic sculptures typically exhibited a rigid, frontal posture with exaggerated smiles, which came to be known as the "Archaic smile." Another important medium for creative expression was pottery, which included both black-figure and red-figure vases.

During the Archaic period, notable examples include the sculptures known as kouros and kore. These sculptures depicted idealized, youthful male and female forms and were frequently offered up as sacrifices in sanctuaries. One such sculpture is known as the "Kritios Boy," and it is famous for the novel contrapposto position that it strikes. This pose signaled the beginning of a movement to a more naturalistic depiction of the human figure.

The Age of Classical Perfection in Terms of Aesthetics

The peak of artistic creativity in ancient Greece occurred during the Classical period of Greek art, which lasted from about 480 to 323 BCE. During this time period, artists were interested in portraying the idealized human form, placing a strong emphasis on balance, harmony, and authenticity in their work. The transition from the Archaic to the Classical style can be seen in the Temple of Athena Parthenon, which is located on the Acropolis in Athens.

The Parthenon, which was built in honor of the Greek goddess Athena, is often regarded as the finest example of Doric architecture. The ideals of classical aesthetics are reflected in the building's precise architecture and proportions that are harmonious with one another. Sculptors such as Phidias were commissioned to create works of art for the pediments and frieze of the Parthenon. These works of art praised the valiant actions of the gods as well as mythical tales. These sculptural reliefs were a good example of how architectural and artistic elements may be successfully combined.

The Doryphoros, often known as the "Spear Bearer," was created by Polykleitos and is a well-known example of Classical sculpture. It is a model that adheres to accurate anatomical proportions and exemplifies the image of the human body that is idealized. This statue, which displays the essential principles of Greek sculpture during the Classical period, is distinguished by its use of a contrapposto posture and its concentration on harmonic proportion.

Realistic Expressionism Defined as Hellenistic Art

During the Hellenistic period (323–31 BCE), there was a shift in artistic goals away from the idealized perfection of the Classical period and toward a greater emphasis on emotional and expressive realism. This occurred as a direct result of the Hellenistic culture's influence on Greek art. The sculpture known as "Laocoon and His Sons" is an excellent illustration of this shift in aesthetic. This sculpture signified a change from the tranquil and balanced forms that were typical of older Greek art because of its depiction of pain, agony, and dynamic movement.

The "Winged Victory of Samothrace" is an additional well-known Hellenistic artwork. A sense of motion and victory is communicated through the dynamic, wind-swept draperies and the implied movement of the figure in the piece. During the Hellenistic period, there was an increase in the research of a wide variety of subject matter, including genre scenes, portraits, and foreign topics.

The Contribution of Greek Columns to the Development of Architecture

The unusual column designs used in Greek architecture have made it famous around the world. Doric, Ionic, and Corinthian columns are the three most common varieties of ancient Greek column styles. The proportions and decoration of each style are unique to the type.

Doric columns are the most straightforward and durable of the column types; they have a plain shaft, a capital with flutes, and no base. Doric columns, which are well-known for their proportion and understated elegance, can be found in the Parthenon.

Ionic columns are more delicate and decorative than Doric columns; the capitals of these columns have volutes, which are spiral scrolls. The Erechtheion, another building located on the Acropolis of Athens, is characterized by the presence of Ionic columns.

Acanthus leaf ornamentation is seen on the capital of the most decorative type of column, which is called a Corinthian column. They are frequently connected with buildings from the Hellenistic and Roman periods.

2. **Extending and Adapting the Greek Legacy in Roman Art and Architecture**
   Art from the Roman Republic and the Early Empire
   Greek art and architecture served as the basis upon which Roman art and architecture were built. Greek Hellenistic art was influential on Roman art during the Republican era (509–27 BCE), which lasted from 509 to 27 BCE. Realistic depictions of political personalities, like as the bust of Scipio Africanus, revealed a preoccupation with individual likeness as well as a fixation on realism.

   In addition, throughout the time of the Roman Republic, temples and public structures were constructed that were modeled after the architectural styles of ancient Greece. For example, the layout of the Temple of Portunus in Rome is typical for Roman temples, but it also has columns of the Ionic style, which derives from ancient Greece.

   Imperial Rome: Architecture and Ornaments of Grandeur
   The rise of the Roman Empire (27 BCE - 476 CE) coincided with a proliferation of artistic and architectural accomplishments. This was made possible by the broad imperial reach of the empire as well as the technological breakthroughs of the time. The Romans were masters of engineering, which allowed them to

ART AND ARCHITECTURE

build some of the world's most impressive monuments, including aqueducts, roads, bridges, and arenas.

The Colosseum, also known as the Flavian Amphitheatre, is among the most well-known buildings to have been constructed in ancient Rome.

This vast amphitheater had the capacity to house up to 80,000 spectators and was used for a variety of public events, including gladiatorial bouts and chariot races. The ground-breaking architecture of it made it possible to effectively manage crowds and stage magnificent shows.

Aqueducts were gigantic buildings that brought water to Roman cities and were examples of which may be found in France at the Pont du Gard. These feats of engineering were stone arches and perfect gradients that brought fresh water to metropolitan areas. They were engineering marvels.

Roman Architecture, Particularly the Temples and Arches
Roman temples, which were frequently erected in honor of deities or emperors, were characterized by a particular architectural style. In contrast to the usage of freestanding columns in Greek temples, engaged columns, which were partially linked to the building's facade, were frequently used in Roman temple architecture. The Maison Carrée in Nimes, France, is a prime illustration of a Roman temple that has been kept exceptionally well.

Roman arches are yet another significant architectural feature that saw extensive use in a variety of structures, such as bridges, gateways, and aqueducts, during Roman times. The portrayal of triumphal scenes on the magnificent Arch of Titus in Rome is a prominent example of the Roman practice of honoring military victories.

A Commemoration of the Uniqueness of Each Person Through Portraits and Mosaics
Roman portraiture had a significant emphasis on individual likeness and authentic representation of the subject being portrayed. The passage of time was depicted in the portraits of famous individuals, as well as emperors and senators, and their distinctive face features and personality traits were highlighted. The bust of Emperor Augustus, the first Roman emperor, is a prime example of the idealized yet individualized portrait style that was prevalent during that time period.

Roman mosaics were elaborate works of art that were crafted from little colored stones known as tesserae. These mosaics were used to decorate the floors and walls of public buildings, private villas, and religious temples. These intricate drawings frequently showed a diverse selection of topics, ranging from legendary themes to scenes from everyday life. The "Alexander Mosaic" from Pompeii is a well-known example of Roman mosaic art that captures the great drama and intricate details of the medium. The mosaic depicts the Battle of Issus.

Construction Using Arches and Vaults

The Romans were the first to use arches and vaults in building design, which fundamentally altered the way buildings were constructed. Arches and vaults were effective at distributing weight, which made it possible to build monumental constructions with expansive interiors. The Roman baths, the Basilica of Maxentius, and the Pantheon are just a few examples of buildings that made considerable use of this architectural innovation.

3. **The Inheritance of Art and Architecture from Ancient Greece and Rome**

The impact of Greek and Roman art and architecture is incalculable; it has persisted over the course of several centuries and had a significant impact on the aesthetics, engineering, and cultural identity of Western societies.

The revival of the Renaissance

The 14th century is considered to be the beginning of the Renaissance period, which is characterized by a renewed interest in the art and architecture of ancient Greece and Rome. Classical architecture served as a source of creativity for many architects, like Andrea Palladio and Leon Battista Alberti, who used it as a foundation for the design of palaces, churches, and other public structures. Michelangelo, Raphael, and Leonardo da Vinci were just a few of the Renaissance painters who found inspiration in classical sculptures and themes to incorporate into their works of art. Other artists that did the same include Leonardo da Vinci.

A Return to the Neoclassical Tradition

Neoclassicism, a movement that aimed to imitate the classical aesthetics of Greece and Rome, experienced a resurgence in popularity throughout the 18th and 19th centuries. The design of governmental structures, museums, and other public monuments was influenced by the neoclassical architectural style, which is typified by the use of columns, pediments, and classical orders. The United States Capitol Building in Washington, DC, and the British Museum Building in London, both in the United Kingdom, are prime examples of this Neoclassical pattern.

Influence of the Present Day

Art and architecture from ancient Greece and Rome continue to have an influence on current art and design. Numerous artistic fields, such as architecture, sculpture, painting, and design, continue to be influenced by the classical ideas of proportion, balance, and the idealized human form.

Chapter 3

Art and Architecture in the Middle Ages

A crucial period in European history that may be roughly dated from the 5th to the 15th century, the Middle Ages were distinguished by social, political, and religious shifts that occurred throughout this time period. During this time period, art and architecture served as important manifestations of faith, power, and cultural identity. These expressions reflected the complicated interplay that existed between religious devotion, feudal hierarchy, and the growing influence of rising city-states. The art and architecture of the Middle Ages provide testament to the enduring legacy of creativity and spirituality that distinguished this unique age in the annals of human history. This legacy can be seen in everything from the towering Gothic cathedrals to the exquisite illuminated manuscripts.

1. **Art and Architecture of the Early Middle Ages: Belief in the Midst of Unrest**
   The Pictorial Expressions of Cultural Identity in the Art of the Migration Period
   The period known as the Migration Period, which roughly spans the 5th to the 8th century, was marked by the movement of a number of Germanic tribes all throughout Europe. The art of this time period, which is exemplified by complex metalwork, extravagant jewelry, and other beautiful artifacts, is an excellent example of the integration of a wide variety of cultural influences and artistic styles. The Sutton Hoo burial site in England offers a fascinating look into the visual culture of early medieval Europe thanks to its extensive collection of items. These artifacts include the famous Sutton Hoo helmet as well as elaborate shoulder clasps.
   Art of the Carolingians: The Renaissance of the Empire
   In the eighth and ninth centuries, Charlemagne was the driving force behind what is known as the Carolingian Renaissance, which was characterized by a

renaissance of study, culture, and artistic patronage inside the Frankish Empire. The illuminated manuscripts had excellent calligraphy, complex ornamentation, and vivid narrative settings. Some examples of these illuminated manuscripts were the Coronation Gospels and the Utrecht Psalter. The intimate connection that existed in early medieval Europe between art, spirituality, and the dissemination of information is reflected in the close link that these manuscripts served as vital religious and educational aids.

The Sacred Majesty and Legitimacy of the Imperial State in Ottonian Art
Throughout the Ottonian period, which occurred throughout the 10th century, a distinctive artistic style came into being. This style was distinguished by the fact that it blended classical inspirations with Christian imagery. The majesty of the church and the divine power of the ruling class were highlighted through the monumental buildings, metalwork, and illuminated manuscripts that were produced during the Ottonian period of art. The Bernward Doors and the Gero Cross are two examples of outstanding works of Ottonian craftsmanship that are also prime examples of the delicate combination of imperial sponsorship with spiritual symbolism.

2. **Art and Architecture of the Romanesque Period: Belief in Stone**
The Healing Potential of Romanesque Architecture and the Pilgrimage
Romanesque architecture, which was popular from the 10th to the 12th century, may be identified by its sturdy construction using masonry, its use of rounded arches, and its thick walls. The establishment of pilgrimage routes, such as the Camino de Santiago in Spain and the Via Francigena in Italy, resulted in the construction of a great number of religious buildings, including monasteries and cathedrals, along the routes. Both the Abbey of Cluny in France and the Cathedral of Santiago de Compostela in Spain are well-known examples of Romanesque religious architecture. These buildings are symbolic of the spiritual ambitions of medieval civilization as well as the material resources that it possessed.

Romanesque sculpture is characterized by its emphasis on narrative and devotion in stone
Romanesque sculpture functioned as a visual narrative of biblical stories and religious teachings. It was commonly integrated into the entrances and façade of churches and cathedrals during this time period. The tympanum sculptures at the Autun Cathedral in France and the Gislebertus' Last Judgment are two examples of Romanesque sculptures that exemplify the spiritual passion and didactic intent of Romanesque sculpture. Both of these works vividly illustrate biblical scenes and moral allegories.

Murals and manuscripts are examples of Romanesque painting
Romanesque painting, which was primarily portrayed through mural art and illuminated manuscripts, was characterized by its vivid colors, stylized shapes,

and biblical subject matter. Religious histories and allegorical depictions of the divine were communicated through the use of mural paintings in churches. Examples of such paintings may be seen at the San Baudelio de Berlanga in Spain and the Saint-Savin-sur-Gartempe in France. Both the Lectionary of Henry II and the Winchester Bible are excellent examples of the meticulous craftsmanship and spiritual dedication that are inherent in Romanesque manuscript illumination.

3. **The Art and Architecture of Gothic: The Ascent Toward Heaven**

   The Aspirational Strive for Perfection in Gothic Architecture

   The focus placed on verticality, light, and innovative structural design throughout the Gothic period, which began in the 12th century and lasted until the 16th century, was crucial in the revolutionization of architectural design. The pointed arches, ribbed vaults, and flying buttresses that are characteristic of Gothic cathedrals were designed with the intention of producing a sensation of ethereal transcendence and spiritual elevation. The Notre-Dame Cathedral in Paris, the Chartres Cathedral in France, and the Cologne Cathedral in Germany are three instances of Gothic ecclesiastical architecture that are quintessential examples of the massive scale and celestial aspirations of Gothic design.

   The Sacred and the Beautiful Carved into Stone Gothic Sculpture

   The ever-evolving aesthetic sensibilities and increasing spiritual zeal of the time period were mirrored in the sculpture that was integrated into the entrances, façade, and inner spaces of Gothic cathedrals. The celebration of biblical stories and the devotion of saints and martyrs was highlighted by the sculptural programs at both the Reims Cathedral and the Amiens Cathedral in France. These cathedrals are located in France. Their sculptural programs featured intricate details, expressive forms, and dramatic narratives. A change toward a more humanistic and empathic approach to religious art can be traced back to the development of naturalism and expressive expression in Gothic sculpture.

   The Shining of Devotion as Depicted in Gothic Painting

   The goal of Gothic painting was to produce a sense of divine brilliance and spiritual transcendence. This was commonly accomplished by incorporating the style into stained glass windows and altarpieces. The Sainte-Chapelle in Paris is an excellent example of the complex interplay of light, color, and religious symbolism that is characteristic of Gothic painting. It is famous for the brilliant stained glass windows that depict biblical narratives. Both the Ghent Altarpiece by Jan van Eyck and the Maestà by Duccio di Buoninsegna are excellent examples of the combination of the naturalistic tendencies of the late medieval period with the Gothic aesthetics that were prevalent at the time.

4. **Art and Architecture in the Middle Ages Outside of Europe**

Art of the Byzantine Empire: Glamour and Sacredness

Byzantine art, which flourished in the Eastern Roman Empire from the 4th to the 15th century,
was characterized by its incorporation of a diverse range of artistic inspirations from both the East and the West. The spiritual majesty and divine splendor of the Christian religion were highlighted via the use of religious iconography and beautiful mosaics in Byzantine architecture. This style of architecture is known for its dome-shaped buildings. Both the Hagia Sophia in Istanbul and the San Vitale in Ravenna, Italy, are well-known examples of the architectural and artistic achievements of the Byzantine civilization.

The Harmony and Sacred Geometry of Islamic Art

The period beginning in the seventh century and continuing onwards saw the development of a wide variety of artistic styles known as Islamic art. These styles included calligraphy, geometric patterns, and arabesque designs. The beautiful domes, delicate tile work, and geometric motifs that were common in Islamic architecture revealed a profound synthesis of mathematical precision with spiritual symbolism. Both the Alhambra in Granada, Spain, and the Great Mosque of Cordoba are excellent examples of the perfect marriage of the aesthetics of Islamic architecture with a profound appreciation for the spiritual harmony and cultural identity of the people who built them.

3.1 Gothic Cathedrals

Not only do Gothic cathedrals stand as the iconic architectural achievements of the Middle Ages, but they also symbolize the pinnacle of architectural innovation and the highest form of artistic expression. This is because Gothic cathedrals were built during the height of Christian devotion. The age of Gothic architecture, which lasted from the 12th to the 16th century and left an unmistakable mark on Europe with its towering spires, elaborate brickwork, and dazzling stained glass windows, lasted from the 12th to the 16th century. These colossal buildings, which include well-known cathedrals such as Chartres, Notre Dame, and Reims, are enduring testaments to the religious fervor, artistic prowess, and technological prowess of medieval society. This investigation into Gothic cathedrals will dive into their history, architecture, and cultural significance, shedding light on the enduring legacy of these awe-inspiring edifices as they continue to stand the test of time.

1. **The Initial Development of the Gothic Style in Historical Context**
   Romanesque architecture is representative of the pre-Gothic period
   From the 10th to the 12th century, Romanesque architecture was the predominant style in Europe. This was the time period just prior to the development of the Gothic style. Romanesque cathedrals were distinguished by the robust construction of their buildings, which included strong walls, rounded arches, and sturdy construction. The volatile conditions of the century were reflected in the design of these churches, which sought to achieve stability and protection

through their architecture.
The Beginning of Gothic Design and Style
The move from Romanesque architecture to Gothic architecture was defined by a desire to construct rooms that were larger, brighter, and more ethereal in order to accommodate rising Christian congregations. This ambition is what led to the development of Gothic architecture. It is commonly believed that Abbot Suger, who oversaw the construction of the Abbey Church of Saint-Denis near Paris in the 12th century, is responsible for the creation of the Gothic style of architecture. The name "Gothic" was initially used in a derogatory manner to describe this new architectural style, suggesting a lack of delicacy or elegance. However, since that time, the term has come to represent the grandeur and creativity of the time period it was coined during.

2. **Specific Aspects of Gothic Cathedral Design and Construction**
The Struggle for Verticality: A Search for the Divine
It is characteristic of Gothic architecture to place a strong focus on verticality, with the goal of bringing the human spirit closer to the divine. The use of flying buttresses, pointed arches, and ribbed vaults made it possible to create constructions that were both taller and more graceful. The goal of the architects who worked in the Gothic style was to design structures that reached upwards into the heavens to represent the journey of the soul to God.

Structural Marvels Presented by the Ribbed Vaulting
Ribbed vaulting was a structural innovation that was utilized in Gothic cathedrals. This allowed for a more effective distribution of the building's overall weight. This architectural element not only contributed to the structure's overall stability but also produced fascinating patterns on the ceilings of the interior spaces. The utilization of ribbed vaulting enabled the building of rooms that were not only larger but also more open, which in turn made it possible to install broad stained glass windows.

Arches with Pointed Tops Offer Both Elegance and Height
The pointed arch is one of the most recognizable characteristics of Gothic architecture. This is in contrast to the rounder arches that are characteristic of the Romanesque style. The interiors were given a sense of height and openness by the use of pointed arches, which also added to the feeling of elegance and grace that was present in the spaces. Because of this design option, there was more leeway in terms of how architectural elements were combined.

Grace and Support Provided by Flying Buttresses
Gothic cathedrals are easily identifiable by the presence of flying buttresses. The lateral force that was produced by the weight of the stone and the height of the walls was counterbalanced by these external supports that were arched in shape. They did not only contribute to the structural soundness of the cathedral's exterior, but they also contributed to the aesthetics of the outside, giving it a

sense of elegance and lightness.

Divine Illumination Through the Use of Stained Glass Windows

Gothic cathedrals were distinguished by their extensive use of stained glass windows, which served as a medium for communicating religious narratives, a source of illumination within the cathedral, and a sign of the presence of God. The purpose of the vibrant colors and intricate designs of the windows was to create an atmosphere that was comparable to that of heaven for those who were within. Craftsmen skilled in the craft of stained glass, also referred to as glass painters, produced detailed scenes from the Bible and the lives of saints to turn the cathedral into a visual catechism for those who were illiterate at the time.

Rose Windows: A Shining Example of Symbolism

The facades of many Gothic cathedrals were embellished with rose windows, which were characterized by their exquisite tracery and dazzling stained glass. Not only did these circular or semicircular windows function as architectural focus points, but they also imparted spiritual symbolism through their shape. The purpose of the complicated geometry of rose windows was to represent both the oneness of God and the depth of the divine intelligence.

Lessons Learned from Stone: A Portal Sculpture

The gateways and façade of Gothic cathedrals were typically decorated with vast amounts of sculptural detail. For the faithful who were illiterate, the sculpted images, which frequently represented biblical narratives, saints, and virtues, functioned as visual instruction. These sculptures, which occasionally incorporated features that were both whimsical and grotesque, transmitted theological lessons, moral teachings, and stories from religious traditions.

3. **Remarkable Examples of Gothic Architecture**

The Royal Road to Heaven Leads Through Chartres Cathedral

The Cathedral of Chartres, which can be seen in Chartres, France, is widely regarded as one of the finest specimens of Gothic architecture. The building of this historic cathedral began in the 12th century, and it is home to the Chartres Labyrinth. Pilgrims used the labyrinth as a means of meditation, and it represented their spiritual journey as they made their way closer to the divine. The breathtaking stained glass windows of the cathedral, in particular the North Rose Window, continue to be one of its most notable characteristics. These windows capture the spirit of medieval devotion as well as the artistic brilliance of the time period.

The Notre-Dame Cathedral: A Crowning Achievement for Paris

With its twin towers, rose windows, and stunning interior, the Notre-Dame Cathedral in Paris is another outstanding masterpiece of Gothic architecture. The cathedral is located in the city of Paris. Construction on the cathedral began in the 12th century, and it was featured prominently in Victor Hugo's novel "The Hunchback of Notre-Dame." It is a monument to the harmony that exists

ART AND ARCHITECTURE

between art and religion and represents the spiritual center of the French city.

Cathedral of Reims, often known as the Cathedral of the Coronation

It is well known that the French monarchs had their coronations performed at the Reims Cathedral, which is a church that is devoted to the Virgin Mary. The artistic prowess of the time period is attested to by the breathtaking sculptures and spectacular rose windows that can be found in the cathedral. The majestic cathedral of Reims is a potent representation of the royal legacy and religious devotion of France.

The Amiens Cathedral, Also Known as the Heavenly Heights

The astounding height of Amiens Cathedral as well as its complex architectural details have

earned it widespread acclaim and make it the tallest Gothic cathedral in France. The outside of the cathedral is covered in a profusion of sculptural motifs that depict religious iconography and biblical narratives. The magnificence and originality of Gothic architecture may be seen at Amiens Cathedral, which stands as a witness to these qualities.

The Magnificence of the English: Canterbury Cathedral

The Canterbury Cathedral is often regarded as the finest example of English Gothic architecture and may be seen in Canterbury, England. It is noted for its elaborate ribbed vaulting as well as its large stained glass windows, some of which are known as the Miracle Windows. Pilgrims continue to visit the cathedral because it is an important emblem of the ecclesiastical power of the English church.

4. **Importance to the Culture and History of the Area**

Symbolism with Theological Undertones

Not only were Gothic cathedrals works of architecture of the highest caliber, but they also made profound spiritual and theological statements. The intention was to portray the majesty of heaven and generate a sense of heavenly transcendence by placing an emphasis on the building's height, light, and exquisite design. It was common practice to organize the interior of cathedrals in the form of a cross to represent both the crucifixion of Christ and the paramount importance of Christianity in medieval society.

Both a Pilgrimage and an Act of Devotion

The construction of numerous Gothic cathedrals along pilgrimage routes resulted in the arrival of countless pilgrims at the cathedrals' doors. Pilgrimages were an essential part of the spiritual life of Christians during the middle ages, and cathedrals were an essential part of the infrastructure that made these excursions possible. Pilgrims would travel enormous distances to visit these cathedrals in the hopes of receiving heavenly grace, spiritual enlightenment, or physical healing.

Importance From Both a Political and Cultural Perspective

Not only were they used as places of worship, but gothic cathedrals also served as emblems of governmental and cultural authority. Not only did numerous monarchs and aristocratic families make contributions to the building of these massive monuments, but they did so not just as manifestations of their religious beliefs but also as affirmations of their political power. Cathedrals evolved into pivotal locations for civic activity, cultural expression, and the development of a sense of community identity.

Protection as well as Reconstruction

There has been a continuous effort made toward maintaining these architectural masterpieces for future generations, and one of those endeavors is the preservation and restoration of Gothic churches. Even though many cathedrals have sustained damage over the course of the ages, including damage caused by wars and natural disasters, efforts have been made to ensure that they will continue to survive and maintain their cultural significance. The unwavering dedication to the conservation of historic structures is exemplified by the fact that cathedrals such as Chartres and Notre-Dame have been rebuilt following devastating fires and other types of devastation.

5. **Influence and a Lasting Legacy**

Renaissance and Its Aftermath

In the 14th century, when the Renaissance was beginning to take shape, there was a shift away from the verticality and symbolism of Gothic design and toward the architectural principles of the classical era. The Gothic style of architecture, on the other hand, placed a strong focus on light, proportion, and structural innovation, all of which continued to impact architectural advancements during the Renaissance and other centuries.

Revivals and imagination both play a role

The upsurge of interest in Gothic architecture that occurred in the 19th century ultimately resulted in the movement known as the Gothic Revival.

Vital contributions were made by architects such as Augustus Pugin and Eugene Viollet-le-Duc toward the revitalization and restoration of Gothic cathedrals. These efforts, which aimed to recreate the magnificence and spirituality of the Gothic period, resulted in the construction of new buildings designed in the Gothic style and the restoration of cathedrals that were already in existence.

Inspiration from the Present Day

Cathedrals built in the Gothic style continue to serve as a source of motivation for architects, painters, and cultural manifestations of the modern era. These cathedrals, with their soaring spaces, elaborate designs, and bright stained glass, continue to be sources of surprise and inspiration even after centuries have passed. They are a powerful reminder of the ability of architecture to communicate profound cultural and spiritual ideas in a way that is independent of both time and location.

3.2 Islamic Architecture

Over the course of more than a millennium, Islamic architecture has played a significant role in determining the physical appearance of the built environment throughout the Islamic world. Islamic architecture developed from its beginnings on the Arabian Peninsula and has since extended across the entirety of the Middle East, as well as North Africa, South Asia, and even further afield. This architectural style is a reflection of the great influence that Islam has had on the material, spiritual, and cultural components of the communities that it has affected. This examination of Islamic architecture will delve into the historical evolution, key aspects, and cultural relevance of Islamic architecture, showing the continuing legacy of this unique heritage. From the awe-inspiring domes of mosques to the exquisite geometry of Islamic tile work, this exploration of Islamic architecture will cover a wide range of topics.

1. **The Evolution of Islamic Architecture Throughout History**
   Architecture in the Early Stages of Islam: During the Formative Period
   The establishment of Islam on the Arabian Peninsula in the seventh century coincided with the beginning of the development of Islamic architecture. The first examples of Islamic architecture were uncomplicated and concentrated primarily on serving functional and practical purposes. Both the Prophet's Mosque and the Quba Mosque, both located in Medina, are considered to be among the earliest examples of Islamic architecture. Both mosques are recognized for their simple, unadorned designs.
   The Umayyad Dynasty Is Responsible For The Construction Of The First Major Islamic Buildings
   During the reign of the Umayyad Caliphate, which stretched from the seventh to the eighth century, significant advances were made in the field of architecture. One of the most important examples of early Islamic architecture is located in Damascus and is known as the Umayyad Mosque. It was constructed by Caliph Al-Walid I. It is characterized by a remarkable architectural element in the form of a horseshoe-shaped arch, which was later adopted in Islamic architecture in Spain. Additionally, it contains a beautiful prayer hall that is mosaicked.
   Golden Age of the Abbasid Empire: The House of Wisdom and More
   The Abbasid Caliphate, which lasted from the eighth to the thirteenth century, is considered to be the golden age of Islamic culture. Along with this, the continued development of Islamic architecture also occurred during this time. The Round City of Baghdad, which Caliph Al-Mansur was responsible for designing, is an excellent illustration of effective urban planning due to its round layout and systematic design. The House of Wisdom in Baghdad developed into a hub for learning, since it became a repository for a large number of texts and represented the body of Islamic knowledge.
   The Islamic Kingdom of Spain and the Al-Andalus Legacy

A flowering of Islamic architecture took place during the period of Islamic sovereignty in Spain (Al-Andalus), which lasted from the 8th to the 15th century. The Great Mosque of Cordoba is a well-known example of Islamic architecture in Spain. It is distinguished by its intricate system of horseshoe arches, its alternating red and white voussoirs, and its exquisitely crafted mihrab. The Alhambra, located in Granada, is a prime example of the superb Islamic palatial architecture that can be seen across the Islamic world. This building is characterized by its detailed plasterwork, lush gardens, and intricate courtyards.

The Flourishing of the Mosque in the Architecture of the Seljuks and the Ottomans

The Seljuk Empire, which existed from the 11th to the 13th century, and the Ottoman Empire,

which existed from the 13th to the 20th century, were both extremely influential in the development of Islamic architecture. The Seljuks were responsible for the construction of great mosques, such as the Great Mosque of Isfahan in Iran, which is known for its famous blue-tiled mosaics and soaring domes. Other mosques that the Seljuks built include the Blue Mosque in Konya, Turkey. The Ottoman Empire left behind an enduring heritage of mosque design, one of the most famous examples of which is the Blue Mosque in Istanbul. This mosque is renowned for its towering minarets, imposing domes, and ornate tile work.

2. **Principal Characteristics of Islamic Architecture**

   The mosque is the most important building in Islamic architecture

   The mosque is the most important building in Islamic culture and serves as the spiritual and social focal point of the community. It is the most iconic example of Islamic architecture. The qibla wall, which points in the direction of Mecca, the mihrab, which is a niche in the qibla wall for the imam, and the minbar, which is a pulpit where sermons are delivered, are the primary architectural elements of a mosque. The prayer hall is often distinguished by a big central dome, which is supported by arches and columns, and is surrounded by smaller domes on either side. The layout and ornamentation of mosques are highly variable and often reflect the architectural traditions of their respective countries or regions.

   The Symbolic Significance and Peaceful Atmosphere of Gardens and Courtyards

   Islamic architecture typically includes both enclosed and open-air spaces, such as courtyards and gardens. They are helpful in both an operational and a symbolic sense. Gardens promote a sense of peace and provide an area for spiritual meditation, while courtyards serve as a meeting place for the community. In Islamic gardens, the concept of the chahar bagh, which literally translates to "four gardens," is a reoccurring motif. These gardens strive to achieve harmony via the use of water, plants, and geometric forms.

ART AND ARCHITECTURE

The Dome and the Minaret: Two Iconic Components of Architecture

The minaret and the dome are two of the most recognizable features of Islamic architecture. In many mosques, the dome, which represents the heavens, is the most prominent architectural element. It is a representation of the order of the cosmos as well as the link between the earthly realm and the heavenly realm. The minaret is a tall, slender structure that acts as both a functional and beautiful element. It is from this tower that the call to prayer is made. The structure and decoration of minarets can look very different from one another, which contributes to the aesthetic variety of Islamic architecture.

The Artistry of Design Embedded in Calligraphy and Decoration

Intricate calligraphy and intricate decorative patterns are frequently included into Islamic architecture. The walls and domes of mosques and other buildings are often decorated with Arabic calligraphy. This calligraphy may feature verses from the Quran or other religious literature. Commonly used decorative motifs include geometric patterns such as stars, polygons, and designs that interlace with one another. These patterns are not only decorative; rather, in addition to their aesthetic value, they communicate both symbolic and mathematical meaning.

3. **Variations in Islamic Architectural Styles Across the World**

The Moorish Architectural Tradition and Its Impact on North Africa and the Maghreb

The Maghreb region, which encompasses all of North Africa, is famous for its extensive architectural history, which is frequently exemplified by the legacy of Moorish architecture. One of the most significant examples of Islamic architecture in all of North Africa is the Grand Mosque of Kairouan, which can be found in Tunisia and dates all the way back to the seventh century. It is a tribute to the influence of North African architectural forms on the Iberian Peninsula that the Alhambra, which is located in Granada, Spain, still stands today.

The Craft of Ceramic Tiling in the Architecture of Persia and Central Asia

The elaborate tile work, lush gardens, and grand mosques that can be found in Persian and Central Asian architecture have made these regions famous. The intricate geometric designs and calligraphy found in the tile work of the Imam Mosque in Isfahan, Iran, are exemplary of the artistic prowess of Islamic tile work. The Registan in Samarkand, Uzbekistan is another example of the Islamic architecture that can be seen across Central Asia. It is known for its magnificent tile work and towering arches.

The Indian Subcontinent as a Melding Pot for Many Cultures

The Islamic architecture of the Indian subcontinent exhibits a combination of both indigenous traditions and Islamic influences on design and construction. The Badshahi Mosque in Lahore, Pakistan and the Taj Mahal in Agra, India are two examples of spectacular buildings that were created by fusing Islamic architectural elements with Indian craftsmanship. Both of these structures are located in Pakistan and India, respectively. In particular, the Taj Mahal is renowned for its construction out of pure white marble, its intricate inlay work, and its expansive gardens.

The Maritime Trade and the Architecture of Mosques in Southeast Asia

The marine trade routes and indigenous construction materials in Southeast Asia all had an
impact on the Islamic architecture that was built there. The Sultan Omar Ali Saifuddin Mosque in Bandar Seri Begawan, Brunei, is an excellent example of how Islamic aesthetics may be combined with the architectural styles of the surrounding region. The utilization of native materials and skilled craftsmanship may be seen in the construction of wooden mosques in Indonesia, such as the Masjid Agung Demak and the Menara Kudus Mosque, amongst others.

4. **Meaning and Importance to Cultures and Spirituality**

The importance of Symbolism and Spirituality

The spiritual and cosmological ideas of Islam are reflected in Islamic architecture, which is filled to the brim with many symbols. The design of mosques often incorporates geometric patterns, calligraphy, and domes—all of which have significant symbolic significance. The mihrab, which indicates the direction in which one should pray, is particularly represented by the mosque, which is a symbol of both the cohesiveness of the Muslim community and the preeminence of faith.

Protection as well as Reconstruction

Efforts to safeguard these architectural gems are always being made, and two of those efforts are the preservation and restoration of traditional Islamic architecture. There are institutions and organizations all around the world that are committed to preserving the Islamic cultural heritage. For example, the Aga Khan Trust for Culture is instrumental in the revitalization and protection of historical structures and landscapes across the Islamic world.

5. **The Influence of Modern Times and the Obstacles They Present**

Interpretations in the Modern Era

Modern designers and architects continue to draw inspiration from Islamic architecture, resulting in contemporary reinterpretations that make use of classic themes and materials. This synthesis of traditional practices and cutting-edge innovations makes it possible to maintain cultural distinctiveness while yet catering to the requirements of modern living.

Urbanization as well as Environmental Preservation

The maintenance of traditional Islamic architecture is becoming increasingly difficult as a result of rapid urbanization and the spread of modern development. It is a challenge for many cities in the Islamic world to find a middle ground between the pressures of rapid urbanization and the imperative to preserve cultural traditions. Architects and urban planners are working together to discover solutions that can satisfy both of these goals.

Heritage and identity rooted in culture

In many nations with predominantly Muslim populations, Islamic architecture is still an essential
component of the cultural heritage and national identity. It is a source of pride and serves as a reminder of the historical and spiritual roots upon which Islamic civilization was built.

3.3 Byzantine Art and Architecture

A legacy that was born out of the Eastern Roman Empire, also known as the Byzantine Empire, which lasted for more than a thousand years, art and architecture from the Byzantine period represent a magnificent chapter in the history of art. Byzantine culture was distinguished by a novel fusion of Roman, Christian, and Eastern elements, which resulted in the development of a distinctive artistic and architectural style. This culture sprang from the ruins of the Roman Empire. This investigation of Byzantine art and architecture will dig into its historical evolution, significant aspects, and cultural relevance, illuminating the extraordinary heritage that will continue to be passed down from generation to generation as a result of this remarkable tradition.

1. **The Beginnings of Byzantine Art in Their Historical Context**
The transition from Rome to Byzantium

Art and architecture that came to be known as Byzantine can be traced back to the Eastern Roman Empire, which is now more commonly known as the Byzantine Empire. When Emperor Constantine moved the Roman capital east in the year AD 330, he established the Byzantine Empire and renamed the city of Constantinople, which is now known as Istanbul. The capital of this empire was Byzantium, which is now known as Istanbul. The Byzantine Empire persisted until 1453, when Constantinople was finally overthrown, and over this millennium, its art and architecture saw significant development.

The Influence of Christianity

The influence of Christianity was significant in the growth of art during the Byzantine period. A pivotal moment in the evolution of the Roman Empire occurred in the early fourth century, when Emperor Constantine became one of the first Christians. This event is referred to as the "Conversion of Constantine." Christianity was adopted as the official religion of the state, and as a result, artwork and buildings dedicated to worship played an important part in Byzantine culture.

2. **The Principal Characteristics of Byzantine Art and Architecture**
The Spiritual Magnificence of Mosaic Art

One of the most defining characteristics of Byzantine culture is its mosaic art.

Intricate works of art known as mosaics are produced by assembling tiny pieces of colored glass or stone, known as tesserae, in order to create various designs and patterns. Mosaics were used to decorate the interiors of Byzantine churches, most notably the apse, the nave, and the dome of the structure. The mosaic program in the dome of the Hagia Sophia in Constantinople is considered a masterpiece of Byzantine art.

It has a massive picture of Christ Pantocrator, also known as the Almighty. Mosaics were used as a form of visual theology, in that they taught religious narratives and placed an emphasis on the presence of God within the church.

Iconography: the Art of Creating Sacred Images

The construction of religious icons and their subsequent veneration had a pivotal role in the practice of faith in Byzantine culture. Iconography. Icons are usually depictions of Christ, the Virgin Mary, other saints, or scenes from the Bible that have been painted on a surface. The veneration of icons, a tradition that is still observed by adherents of Eastern Orthodox Christianity in modern times, places an emphasis on the notion that the sacred can be found even in the most mundane of places. Icon painters, who are often referred to as iconographers, adhered to stringent norms when creating their works in the hopes of communicating spiritual truths and leading viewers into a state of contemplative devotion.

Elements of Architecture: The Basilica of Saint Mary in Byzantium

Churches in Byzantium were primarily constructed in the basilica form, which consists of a central nave, side aisles, and an apse at the east end of the building that is used for the primary altar. The Hagia Sophia is the most well-known and well-preserved example of Byzantine basilica architecture. Its enormous central dome is a structural miracle that is held up by pendentives, which made it possible to create an enormous, open interior space that was filled with light. The narthex, also known as the entrance hall, was a place that served as a transitional zone between the secular and the sacred. It was decorated with exquisite mosaics, and its construction was lavish.

Wall art is also known as fresco painting.

In addition to icons and mosaics, fresco painting was an important part of the artistic tradition of the Byzantine era. Frescoes are a type of mural painting that are produced by applying pigments to a plaster surface while it is still wet. They were used as decoration on the walls of monasteries, palaces, and cathedrals. The Chora Church in Istanbul is well-known for the exquisite frescoes that adorn its interior. These frescoes show episodes from the lives of Christ, the Virgin Mary, and many saints. Frescoes typically performed a teaching function, enlightening devout Christians on the doctrines and stories that are central to the Christian religion.

3. **Regional Differences in the Art and Architecture of the Byzantine Empire**
   Ravenna and the Basilica as Examples of Early Byzantine Art
   Figural depiction and religious iconography were at the forefront of artistic endeavors throughout the early Byzantine period.
   This was before the iconoclastic debates that followed. Ravenna, which is located in what is now the Italian region of Veneto, is renowned for being an important hub of early Byzantine art and architecture. The beautiful mosaics that cover the Basilica of San Vitale in Ravenna are a prime example of the incorporation of Christian imagery in the aesthetics of early Byzantine art. The significance of the Eucharist is emphasized by the structure's octagonal plan, central dome, and elaborate mosaics.
   Iconoclasm: A Controversy Regarding Aesthetics and Religion
   During the 8th and 9th centuries, there was a religious disagreement on the practice of veneration of sacred images that led to the destruction and removal of many religious images, including icons and mosaics. This was known as the time of iconoclasm. This period had a significant influence on Byzantine art and architecture, which resulted in a reduction in the complexity of religious iconography and an increase in the priority placed on abstract adornment. Iconoclasm came to an end with the ultimate success of iconophiles, who pushed for the adoration of icons. This brought an end to the practice of iconoclasm.
   The artistic renaissance known as the Palaiologan Renaissance
   A revitalization of artistic production can be traced back to the Palaiologan Renaissance, which took place during the late Byzantine Empire (the 13th to 15th century). The combination of Hellenistic aesthetics with the artistic tradition of the Byzantine empire produced a flowering of Byzantine and Hellenistic art and culture. It is well known that churches built during this time period, such as the Chora Church in Istanbul, are renowned for the beautiful mosaics and paintings that decorate their interiors.

4. **Meaning and Importance to Cultures and Spirituality**
   Relationship with the Divine
   The art and architecture of the Byzantine period had a significant impact on the development of a sense of spiritual connection. The faithful were educated about the life of Christ, the Virgin Mary, and the saints through the employment of mosaics, icons, and paintings in sacred places, which served as visual catechisms. The architectural features, such as the dome that is located in the center of Hagia Sophia, were designed with the intention of evoking the holy and spiritual realms.
   Preserving and protecting for future generations
   In order to preserve and conserve Byzantine art and architecture, there are continuing preservation and conservation efforts. In order to preserve the creative riches housed within them, some Byzantine churches have been transformed

into museums.

There are a number of institutions, such as the Hellenic Ministry of Culture and Sports and the Greek Orthodox Church, that are committed to the preservation and refurbishment of Byzantine cultural artifacts.

5. The Influence of Modern Times and the Obstacles They Present

Influence from the Arts

Art and architecture from the Byzantine Empire continue to be influential on contemporary artists, particularly those whose work is influenced by Eastern Orthodox Christianity. In the works of contemporary iconographers and painters, who strive to capture the spiritual and visual essence of Byzantine art, the legacy of iconography, mosaic art, and architectural architecture is still present.

Problems Associated with Preservation

Especially in countries where these historical assets are endangered by conflict, urbanization, and environmental concerns, preserving Byzantine art and architecture is a constant problem. This is especially true in the case of historical buildings. Efforts are being made by a variety of entities, including museums, organizations, and government programs, to secure the preservation of these priceless artifacts.

Chapter 4

Renaissance and Baroque Periods

In Western art, culture, and history, the Renaissance and Baroque periods were two different epochs that were yet interwoven with one another. These epochs, each with their own distinctive qualities and contributions, were crucial in determining the path that European culture would take over the course of its history. In this essay, we will conduct a deep dive into a detailed analysis of the Renaissance and Baroque periods, examining their beginnings, important characteristics, creative developments, and their lasting impact on various elements of society.

Before we begin:

The term "renaissance" comes from the French word meaning "rebirth," and it refers to a significant cultural and artistic transformation that occurred in Europe. It is believed to have originated in Italy during the 14th century and then expanded throughout Europe in the centuries that followed. The subsequent time period is known as the Baroque period, which began in the 17th century and lasted into the 18th century. These two eras, when considered together, mark a time in the annals of Western civilization that was one of profound change.

The Renaissance (Language)

The Beginnings and the Context:

The intellectual and artistic foundations of the Renaissance can be traced back to the rediscovery of classical Greek and Roman literature, philosophy, and art. Although the Renaissance began in Italy in the late 14th century, its intellectual and artistic origins can be traced back far further. This renaissance of classical study was further fueled by the fall of Constantinople in 1453, which sent Greek professors and literature to Italy. It was a desire to embrace the ideals of antiquity as well as a reaction against the dogmas that were prevalent during the Middle Ages.

Humanism consists of:

One of the most important intellectual currents to emerge throughout the Renaissance was humanism. It stressed the significance of human potential and the uniqueness of each person. Humanists were interested in reviving ancient ideals by placing an emphasis on human accomplishments, rationality, and the quest of knowledge. Petrarch, Erasmus, and Pico della Mirandola are examples of notable personalities associated with the humanist movement.

The Arts and the Built Environment:

The artistic movement known as the Renaissance is distinguished by its return to naturalism as well as its heavy focus on perspective, proportion, and light. Famous artists such as Leonardo da Vinci, Michelangelo, and Raphael produced works of art that have stood the test of time due to the technical prowess and emotional intensity of their creations. During this time period, buildings saw significant transformations as a result of advancements in architecture. These advancements included the usage of classical components such as columns, domes, and arches.

The written word:

The written word thrived during the Renaissance period, which contributed to the development of Renaissance literature. The "Divine Comedy" written by Dante Alighieri is considered to be an early example of Italian Renaissance literature. William Shakespeare, who lived during a later period of the Renaissance in England, is responsible for producing some of the most enduring works written in the English language. The development of the printing press by Johannes Gutenberg in the 15th century was a crucial factor in the widespread diffusion of information and the rise in popularity of written works.

The pursuit of knowledge and adventure:

The Renaissance was not just a time for progress in the arts and humanities; it was also a time for progress in the sciences and intellectual pursuits. Copernicus, Galileo, and Kepler were among the early innovators who made significant contributions to our understanding of the cosmos. Explorers like as Christopher Columbus and Ferdinand Magellan set sail at the same time to discover new regions, broadening the scope of European knowledge and influence.

Both Political Science and Philosophy:

The resurgence of interest in classical ideas throughout the Renaissance period had an impact on the political philosophy of the time. The political works of historical authors like Machiavelli, who is best known for penning "The Prince," place an emphasis on the practical application of power. Additionally, during this time period, the concepts of the Enlightenment began to form, which would eventually go on to impact the contemporary world. Thinkers such as Thomas More advocated for utopian societies throughout this time period.

Patrimony inherited from the Renaissance:

The Renaissance had a significant influence that persisted throughout the development of Western civilization. It laid the groundwork for the Age of Enlightenment, which in turn paved the path for the development of modern democratic countries.

The Renaissance's contributions to the worlds of art, literature, and science are still held in high esteem and extensively researched in modern times.

The Era Known as the Baroque

The Beginnings and the Context:

The Renaissance was followed by the Baroque period, which began in the latter half of the 16th century and lasted into the early 18th century. The word "baroque" originates from the Portuguese word "barroco," which literally translates to "irregular" or "imperfect" pearl. The Renaissance was marked by a return to harmony and balance, while the Baroque era saw a shift toward drama, emotion, and decoration as its defining characteristics.

The Arts and the Built Environment:

The extravagance, grandeur, and dynamic compositions of baroque art and architecture are some of the characteristics that have made them famous. In order to create works that were dramatic and emotionally charged, artists like Caravaggio, Peter Paul Rubens, and Artemisia Gentileschi adopted the use of chiaroscuro, which is a stark contrast between light and shade. Baroque architecture was characterized by the use of extravagant facades, sumptuous interiors, and illusionistic techniques such as trompe-l'oeil in order to produce a sense of awe in the viewer.

Tuning in:

The visual arts of the time were accompanied by a lively and emotive kind of music known as baroque music. It was during this time that opera, sonatas, and concertos came into being. The world of classical music will forever be shaped by the contributions of composers such as Johann Sebastian Bach, George Frideric Handel, and Antonio Vivaldi. The fact that the orchestra became such a famous musical unit during this time period is evidence of the musical innovation that occurred during that era.

The written word:

In the same way that its visual and musical counterparts are defined by intricacy and emotional intensity, so too is the literature of the Baroque period. Both "Paradise Lost" by John Milton and "Don Quixote" by Miguel de Cervantes are excellent examples of the preoccupation with the human condition, suffering, and the search for meaning that characterizes the Baroque period.

Philosophy and scientific inquiry:

The Baroque period was characterized by the continuation of scientific advancement, with pioneers such as Isaac Newton making crucial contributions to the fields of physics and mathematics throughout this time. In the field of philosophy, the writings of René Descartes and Blaise Pascal were essential in reshaping the intellectual landscape because they questioned conventional concepts of knowing and reason.

Politics and Religious Beliefs:

The Counter-Reformation, which was the Catholic Church's response to the Protestant Reformation, took place at the same time as the Baroque period. This resulted in the construction of magnificent buildings and the production of art for religious purposes as a way to reaffirm Catholic beliefs. The period was also marked by political upheavals and conflicts, the most notable of which were the English Civil War and the Thirty Years' War, both of which had a considerable impact on the art and literature of the time period.

The Baroque Period Left Behind:

The Baroque era left a significant imprint on the world of art, particularly in the shape of magnificent palaces and churches that continue to enthrall visitors to this day. Baroque art and music are known to have had a long-lasting impact on future artistic movements due to the intense feelings they evoke and the dynamic compositions they feature. In addition, the breakthroughs in philosophy and science that occurred during this time period laid the groundwork for the Enlightenment and the Scientific Revolution that followed.

Interactions and their Repercussions

In spite of the fact that the Renaissance and the Baroque periods are easily distinguishable from one another in terms of the characteristics and artistic expressions of their respective times, they were not isolated from one another. The Renaissance created the groundwork for the Baroque period, which expanded upon those foundations and was influenced by the intellectual and creative advancements that occurred during the Renaissance.

Continuity in the Methods of Artistic Creation:

The importance placed on perspective, proportion, and naturalism during the Renaissance era had a profound effect on the art created during the Baroque period. These concepts were incorporated into the works of artists like Caravaggio, who also added a heightened sense of drama and emotion to his creations.

The Advancement of Science:

The scientific quest for knowledge and exploration of the world got its start during the Renaissance and carried on into the Baroque period. Galileo and Kepler, two prominent figures who were active throughout the later part of the Renaissance, made substantial contributions to the field of astronomy during the early part of the Baroque period.

Transitions in Philosophical Thought:

A paradigm shift occurred in philosophical thought during the transition from the Renaissance to the Baroque period. The humanism of the Renaissance, which placed an emphasis on rationality and individuality, gradually gave way to the baroque worldview of the late renaissance and early baroque periods, which embraced the irrational and the strange.

The relationship between religion and the Counter-Reformation:

The religious passion that characterized the Baroque period might be understood, at least in part, as a response to the theological conflicts that characterized the Renaissance. The Counter-Reformation, which aimed to restore the power of the Catholic

ART AND ARCHITECTURE

Church, was a key driving force behind the construction of great Baroque churches and the production of religious art. This movement began in the 15th century and lasted until the 16th century.

Influence from Literature:

The literary accomplishments of the Baroque period can be traced back to the foundation that was established by Renaissance literature with its investigation of humanism and classical ideals. Authors such as Cervantes and Milton built upon the humanist heritage while imbuing their works with the intricate details of the baroque style.

Both the Renaissance and the Baroque periods were crucial in the development of Western culture during their respective epochs. A new period of art, culture, and intellectual inquiry was ushered in with the beginning of the Renaissance. The Renaissance was marked by its celebration of human potential and its resurrection of classical learning. Following the Renaissance was the Baroque period, which is known for the addition of a sense of drama, emotion, and complexity to creative expression as well as continuing the advancement of scientific and philosophical ideas.

Although they are separate epochs, the growth and influence of these two time periods are intricately connected. The intellectual and creative roots upon which the Baroque period was created were provided by the Renaissance, and the transitions between the two periods reflect the growing ideals and values of the time.

It is clear that the Renaissance and Baroque periods left an indelible mark on our world, as evidenced by the art, music, literature, and scientific achievements that continue to have an impact even in the modern era. These eras serve as a reminder of the power that lies inside the creative potential of humans as well as the ever-changing nature of culture and knowledge.

4.1 Italian Renaissance Art and Architecture

The art and architecture of the Italian Renaissance are widely regarded as the zenith of human invention and inventiveness. The creative norms of the medieval period, which immediately preceded the Renaissance period, were radically upended when the Renaissance first appeared in Italy in the 14th century. The art and architecture of the Italian Renaissance were influential in altering the cultural environment and laying the groundwork for the growth of Western art. Renaissance art and architecture were characterized by a renewed interest in classical antiquity, humanism, and a concentration on realism. In this essay, we will look into the fundamental characteristics, important artists, and famous works that defined Italian Renaissance art and architecture, thereby shaping the aesthetic and cultural identity of the time period.

Before we begin:

The Italian Renaissance was a time of unmatched creativity and the regeneration of cultures all across the world. It is commonly referred to as the "golden age" of artistic excellence. It was a time when painters and builders, influenced by the ideals of humanism and ancient antiquity, endeavored to capture both the splendor of the natural world and the breadth of the human experience in their work. The Italian Renaissance left an unmistakable effect on the history of Western civilization, leaving behind works of art and architecture that continue to evoke feelings of awe and adoration.

Renaissance art in Italy: its defining characteristics
The Naturalism and Realist Viewpoints:

Naturalism and realism were given a significant amount of consideration in the works of art produced during the Italian Renaissance. The human figure and the natural world were both depicted with a level of accuracy and delicacy that had never been seen before by artists. In order to achieve a feeling of depth, three-dimensionality, and lifelikeness in their works, they utilized methods such as linear perspective, chiaroscuro, and sfumato in their artwork.

Individualism and Humanism: Neither

Art throughout the Renaissance was heavily inspired by humanist principles, which placed a strong emphasis on the importance of human potential and individuality. Artists paid homage to the human body and all that it was capable of by investigating topics such as human feelings, intellectual capacity, and aesthetic appeal. The art of portraiture developed into an important genre because it gave painters the opportunity to capture the personalities and qualities of their subjects.

The impact of classical music:

One of the most distinguishing characteristics of Italian Renaissance art is its emphasis on the rebirth of classical antiquity. The artwork, literature, and philosophy of ancient Greece and Rome served as a source of inspiration for artists, who then incorporated classical motifs, themes, and forms into their own creations as a result. In art and architecture during the Renaissance period, the employment of classical features like symmetry, proportion, and an idealized version of beauty became increasingly common.

In terms of viewpoint and composition:

The use of linear perspective, which artists like as Filippo Brunelleschi and Leon Battista Alberti were among the first to pioneer, completely changed the way that artists represented space and depth in their work. This method gave painters the ability to construct compositions that were both realistic and spatially coherent, which led to a substantial improvement in the way that architectural spaces and landscapes were portrayed.

Artists of Importance during the Italian Renaissance
Leonardo da Vinci lived from 1452 to 1519:

The spirit of the Italian Renaissance can be said to be best encapsulated by Leonardo da Vinci, the typical Renaissance polymath. His wide range of skills included painting, sculpting, building, engineering, anatomical research, and general scientific investigation. His mastery of technique, composition, and the expression of human emotion can be seen in iconic works such as "Mona Lisa" and "The Last Supper," both of which he created.

Michelangelo Buonarroti was active from 1475 until 1564:

Michelangelo was a towering figure in Italian Renaissance art, famed for his mastery of sculpture, painting, and architecture. He was born in Florence in 1475 and died in Rome in 1564. His enormous masterpieces, such as "David," the ceiling of the Sistine Chapel, and the dome of St. Peter's Basilica, illustrate his great skill in portraying the human form, conveying emotion, and building architectural creations that inspire awe and reverence.

Raphael, active from 1483 to 1520:

Raphael was lauded for his contributions to the artistic movement known as the Italian Renaissance and was admired for his beautiful and harmonious compositions. His paintings, such as "School of Athens" and "Sistine Madonna," are examples of his mastery of balance, proportion, and the beauty of an idealized form. The legacy he left behind as an artist continues to have an impact on succeeding generations of artists.

Sandro Botticelli, who lived from 1445 until 1510:

The paintings of Sandro Botticelli are some of the most iconic examples of Italian Renaissance art because they epitomize the era's hallmark qualities of refinement, grace, and ethereal beauty. Both "Birth of Venus" and "Primavera" are excellent examples of his use of delicate lines, brilliant colors, and mythological themes. These characteristics are a reflection of the humanist ideals and classical influences that were prevalent during the time period.

Titian, who lived around 1488-1576:

During the time period of the Italian Renaissance, Titian was a notable artist in the Venetian school of painting. He is best recognized for his color and compositional ability. His use of rich, brilliant colors and energetic brushwork helped to the development of the Venetian Renaissance style. This can be seen in works such as "Assumption of the Virgin" and "Bacchus and Ariadne," both of which feature examples of his work.

The Architecture of Italy During the Renaissance

Revival of the Classics:

The resurrection of ancient architectural forms and principles had a significant impact on the architecture of the Italian Renaissance. Ancient Roman and Greek structures served as a source of creativity for architects, who took aspects such as columns, arches, and domes and incorporated them into their own designs. In the course of the Renaissance, symmetry, proportion, and the application of mathematical concepts became defining characteristics of architectural style.

Architecture within the Home:

Renaissance architects used elements of classical architecture into the design of private dwellings as well as palaces, resulting in the creation of structures that were harmonious and exquisite. The Palazzo Medici Riccardi in Florence, which was constructed by Michelozzo di Bartolomeo, is a famous example of Renaissance domestic architecture. It showcases a balance of classical elements and innovative design, and it was built for the Medici family during the Renaissance period.

Architecture in the Service of Religion:

The religious zeal of the Renaissance period is reflected in the extravagant and artistically stunning churches and cathedrals that Renaissance architects produced during this time period. The erection of the dome of Florence Cathedral, which Filippo Brunelleschi was responsible for designing, is regarded as a major achievement in Renaissance architecture because it demonstrates the technological inventiveness and engineering prowess of the Renaissance period.

Planning of Cities:

The urban planning of the Italian Renaissance was centered on the building of cityscapes that were both harmonious and visually beautiful. Michelangelo was responsible for the remodeling of Rome's Piazza del Campidoglio, which demonstrates the Renaissance emphasis on spatial organization, geometric perfection, and the integration of architectural elements to create a unified and visually impressive urban environment. The Piazza del Campidoglio is located in the center of Rome.

Treatises on Architectural Design:

During the time period known as the Italian Renaissance, numerous prominent treatises on architecture were written and published, which encouraged the spread of architectural knowledge and concepts. Both Leon Battista Alberti's "De re Aedificatoria" and Andrea Palladio's "Four Books of Architecture" provided extensive insights into architectural philosophy, design, and construction. As a result, these works influenced the practice of architecture not just in Italy but far beyond its borders.

Art and architecture of Italy's Renaissance Period Left an Inheritance and Had an Influence Abroad

The legacy of Italian Renaissance art and architecture is significant and extensive, and it continues to motivate painters, architects, and academics all around the world. The naturalism, humanism, and classical revival tenets that were prioritized throughout this time period laid the groundwork for the evolution of the artistic and architectural traditions of the West. The level of expertise that Renaissance painters, sculptors, and architects attained in terms of technique, composition, and aesthetic principles established a benchmark of excellence that has persisted throughout the years.

It is possible to observe the impact of Italian Renaissance art and architecture in subsequent artistic periods such as Mannerism and the Baroque, both of which expanded upon the innovations and aesthetic principles that were established during the Renaissance. In addition, the resurgence of classical forms and the investigation of humanistic topics have had a significant and long-lasting influence on the evolution of intellectual thought as well as the development of art and architecture in the modern era.

4.2 Baroque Splendor in Europe

ART AND ARCHITECTURE

In Europe, the late 16th century and the early 18th century include the time period known as the Baroque era, which was characterized by a significant shift in the region's artistic and cultural practices. Baroque is a style of art, architecture, and music that is famous for the grandeur, drama, and opulence it embodies. This style has left an enduring effect on society as a whole. throughout this essay, the idea of "Baroque Splendor" will be investigated throughout Europe. Particular attention will be paid to the defining characteristics, significant artistic developments, and the cultural effect of this prosperous and opulent time period.

Introducing the Characteristics of Baroque Splendor

Originally, the term "baroque" referred to a particular style of pearls with asymmetrical shapes. Over time, however, the phrase grew to represent an artistic movement that was typified by lavish adornment and dramatic intensity. Baroque Splendor is a notion that emphasizes the extravagance, emotional depth, and sensory richness of the art and culture of the Baroque period. It captures the essence of this artistic and cultural epoch. It was a period in which artists and architects sought to provoke powerful feelings, incite wonder, and create immersive, over-the-top experiences in their works.

The Aspects That Constitute Baroque Splendor

Feelings and excitement:

The artistic expression of the time known as the Baroque period was characterized by a heightened feeling of emotionalism and drama. The goal of many artists was to provoke robust feelings of feeling in those who viewed or listened to their work. Baroque art, whether it was painting, sculpture, or music, placed a strong emphasis on depicting powerful feelings that were frequently accompanied by turbulence.

Compositions that are both ornate and dynamic:

Compositions in baroque art and architecture were defined by being particularly intricate and active. The majority of the items had characteristics such as ornate ornamentation, detailed workmanship, and an excess of embellishments. Forms that twisted and spiraled were frequently used in baroque art, which contributed to an overall sense of motion and drama in the works.

Tenebrism and the use of chiaroscuro:

Chiaroscuro and tenebrism are two artistic methods that put an emphasis on the contrast between light and shade. The Baroque style utilized both techniques extensively. Not only did this make the dramatic effect stronger, but it also gave the artwork more depth and made it appear more three-dimensional.

The Naturalism:

Even though Baroque art was known for its predilection for grandeur and excess, it nevertheless

remained committed to naturalism throughout its history. The human form and the natural world continued to be depicted by artists with a high degree of realism, which made the emotional impact all the more powerful.

Utilization of Light:

In both art and architecture, the utilization of light was an essential component of the baroque style. Light was employed not just to generate contrast but also to bring attention to particular elements or figures in a composition. This was accomplished by casting shadows on those objects or figures. This contributed to the overall feeling of beauty and spectacle that was present.

Important Steps Forward in Artistic Developments

Painting in the Baroque Style:

Caravaggio, whose works such as "The Calling of Saint Matthew" and "Judith Beheading Holofernes" epitomize the use of chiaroscuro and tenebrism, is an example of an artist who contributed to the development of Baroque painting. Another well-known painter from the Baroque period was Peter Paul Rubens, who is known for his lively and active compositions. The intensity of feeling that he conveys in his masterwork "The Descent from the Cross" is unmatched.

Sculpture of the Baroque:

One of the most important figures in Baroque sculpture, Gian Lorenzo Bernini was an Italian sculptor and architect who lived during the Baroque period. His masterpiece, "The Ecstasy of Saint Teresa," is an excellent illustration of the dynamic and emotive elements that are characteristic of Baroque sculpture. His talent for capturing motion and resembling lifelike forms established a new benchmark in the realm of art.

Architecture of the Baroque Period:

The goal of baroque architecture was to produce structures that were ornate, ornately decorated, and visually appealing. Both the Church of the Gesù in Rome and the Palace of Versailles are excellent examples of the beauty that can be achieved through the use of baroque architecture. The Church of the Gesù in Rome is particularly well-known for the elaborate front as well as the interior of the building.

Music of the Baroque Era:

During the time period known as the Baroque, numerous novel musical styles and forms began to emerge. During this time period, substantial contributions to the musical canon were made by composers such as Johann Sebastian Bach, George Frideric Handel, and Antonio Vivaldi. The vibrant concertos of Vivaldi, the complicated fugues of Bach, and the huge oratorios of Handel are some of the most famous examples of Baroque music.

The Influence of Baroque Splendor on Culture

The relationship between religion and the Counter-Reformation:

There is a strong connection between the Baroque style and the Counter-Reformation, which was the response of the Catholic Church to the Protestant Reformation. Art and architecture from the Baroque period were utilized as potent elements in the process of reigniting religious zeal. The magnificence of Baroque buildings, with its elaborate altars, statues, and frescoes, was intended to inspire piety and devotion in the worshipers who entered them.

Patronage of the king:

The sponsorship of kings and other members of the nobility led to the flourishing of baroque art and architecture. It was common practice to adopt the grandiosity of the baroque style in order to depict the wealth and authority of ruling elites. Royal luxury was sometimes displayed through the construction of extravagant palaces, such as the Palace of Versailles in France and the Hofburg Palace in Vienna.

Both the Stage and the Opera:

The period known as the Baroque was a prosperous time for the performing arts. The essence of Baroque splendor was captured through the creation of grandiose and immersive theater shows, in addition to the birth of opera as a separate art form. The dramatic power of Baroque opera was brilliantly displayed in works such as "L'Orfeo" by Monteverdi and "Armide" by Lully.

Poetry and prose literature:

The intricate and ornate style of writing that was prevalent throughout the Baroque period was reflective of the aesthetic tendencies of the time. Baroque grandeur can be seen in its literary forms in works such as John Donne's metaphysical poetry and the intricate conceits of the baroque sonnet, to name just two examples.

The following are developments in science and philosophy:

During the time period known as the Baroque, tremendous scientific discoveries were being made, particularly in the sciences of astronomy and physics. The likes of Galileo Galilei and Johannes Kepler made vital contributions to our current state of knowledge regarding the cosmos through their work. In the field of philosophy, the writings of René Descartes and Blaise Pascal posed new questions concerning commonly held beliefs regarding knowing and reason.

The Inheritance of Baroque Beauty

The heritage of Baroque beauty continues to exert an impact and inspiration on contemporary art, architecture, and audiences. The modern visual arts, musical compositions, and architectural designs all make use of it because of its dramatic and emotive aspects. The emphasis on theatricality and spectacle has found a home in the realm of entertainment, from the extravagance of big theater shows to the dazzling visuals of contemporary film.

The enormous palaces and churches built during the Baroque period continue to serve as examples of architectural luxury even today. The utilization of light and shadow, in addition to the development of immersive settings, continues to serve as a source of motivation for architects and designers working in modern times.

The preoccupation with human emotion and the portrayal of profound psychological states that was prevalent during the Baroque period has left an indelible effect on the art of writing, drama, and film. It established the foundation for the growth of psychological realism in the arts and has had an impact on the portrayal of complicated characters in contemporary narratives.

4.3 Mesoamerican Art and Architecture

Mesoamerican art and architecture represent a rich cultural history that flourished in the pre-Columbian era in what is now Mexico and Central America. Mesoamerican art and architecture represent a rich and diversified cultural heritage. This legacy covers the creative output of civilizations such as the Olmec, Maya, Aztec, and Zapotec, and it is distinguished by a vast diversity of artistic styles, ranging from enormous pyramids and temples to detailed pottery and murals. It was prevalent in Central and South America during the Late Pre-Columbian and Early Colonial periods. This article is a thorough investigation into the art and architecture of Mesoamerica, delving into the history, primary characteristics, artistic evolution, and cultural relevance of this magnificent heritage.

Before we begin:

A great number of technologically powerful indigenous civilizations once flourished in Mesoamerica, which is an area that stretches from the middle of Mexico into parts of Central America. Long before European explorers and invaders arrived, these societies had already matured into complex civilizations, complete with highly developed artistic and architectural traditions. The distinctive cosmologies, religious practices, and ways of life of the people who lived in Mesoamerica are reflected in the region's art and architecture.

Mesoamerican Art and Architecture: Where Did They Come From?

The ancient Olmec civilization, which originated approximately 1400 BCE in what is now southern Mexico, is considered to be the progenitor of Mesoamerican art and architecture. This may be demonstrated by tracing the history of these two fields. The Olmec are frequently referred to as the "mother culture" of Mesoamerica. This is because they are credited with laying the groundwork for a variety of artistic and architectural aspects that were subsequently adopted and adapted by future civilizations.

The impact of the Olmec culture:

The Olmec culture is well-known for its gigantic stone heads, which are enormous basalt sculptures depicting human faces and are sculpted in the form of human faces. These heads, together with other Olmec artifacts and religious symbols, laid the groundwork for the creation of Mesoamerican iconography, particularly the jaguar, snake, and other animal and human motifs. This iconography includes the jaguar, serpent, and other animal and human motifs.

The Origin and Evolution of Ceramics:

The Olmec period is considered to be the beginning of one of the most enduring and productive art forms in the world: ceramics from Mesoamerica. They were skilled potters who made work with sophisticated designs, including the use of symbolic themes and complex decorative patterns, which were incorporated into their work.

Planning of Cities:

ART AND ARCHITECTURE

In addition, the Olmec culture is credited with laying the foundation for urban planning in Mesoamerica by constructing ball courts and ceremonial sites. Later Mesoamerican civilizations would come to place a significant emphasis on the idea of the sacred city, which consisted of plazas and buildings specifically designed for ceremonial purposes.

Principal Characteristics of Mesoamerican Art and Architecture
Utilization of Natural Components:
Stone, clay, and wood were common building materials used by Mesoamerican artists and architects because these materials were readily available in the region. In particular, stone was selected for use in the construction of monumental architecture, while clay was the material of choice for pottery and sculptures.

The use of Symbolism and Iconography:
Iconography and symbolism, which are frequently connected to a culture's religious or cosmological ideas, are abundant in Mesoamerican art. The feathered serpent (Quetzalcoatl/Kukulkan), the jaguar, and the holy calendar are some repeating themes that can be found in Mesoamerican art. Symbols and motifs are also common in Mesoamerican architecture.

Ceramics:
Ceramics from Mesoamerica were highly developed and included intricate designs along with a broad variety of shapes, sizes, and purposes. Pottery had both practical and ceremonial uses, and the vessels frequently featured elaborate histories or religious symbols. Pottery was utilized for both everyday items and in ritual settings.

Paintings on Walls:
Paintings on walls, sometimes known as murals, played a key role in Mesoamerican art and architecture. Murals were used to decorate the interiors of palaces and temples. These murals showed a variety of scenes, including as religious rites, conflicts, and everyday life. Sites such as Bonampak and Teotihuacan are home to some of the murals that have been kept in the best possible condition.

Architecture of Monumental Significance:
The creation of enormous pyramids, temples, and palaces is one of the defining characteristics of Mesoamerican architecture. In many cases, these buildings took the form of steep, tiered pyramids that were topped by temples and featured staircases going up to them. The worship of particular deities and the performance of rituals were the primary functions of temples, which also served as community gathering places.

Mesoamerican Art and Architecture, as well as the Civilizations That Created It
The Civilization of the Maya:
The Maya were noted for their spectacular buildings and pyramids, as well as the development of elaborate hieroglyphic writing, calendar systems, and a pantheon of gods. Temples built by the Maya were characterized by their towering height, exquisite

stucco artwork, and corbelled vaults. Chichen Itza, Palenque, and Tikal are three of the most famous Maya archaeological sites.

The Empire of the Aztecs:

The Aztecs were a fierce people who founded the city of Tenochtitlan, which became their capital. There, they constructed impressive pyramids, temples, and an intricate network of causeways and canals. One of the most well-known examples of Aztec architecture is the Templo Mayor, which is located in Tenochtitlan and serves as the city's primary temple. Intricate codices and colorful featherwork were frequently included in Aztec artwork.

The Civilization of the Zapotec:

The city of Monte Albán served as the cultural epicenter for the Zapotec people, who were responsible for the development of a particular architectural style that was characterized by plazas, ball courts, and a hieroglyphic script. They also manufactured a wide range of ceramics, which included effigy jars, incense burners, and urns, all of which were ornamented with elaborate motifs.

The culture known as Teotihuacan:

The ancient city of Teotihuacan was a hub of artistic and cultural activity. It is most known for the gigantic pyramids that dominated its landscape, including the Pyramid of the Sun and the Pyramid of the Moon. Deities, animals, and religious rituals were frequently represented in the pottery and murals of Teotihuacan.

Architecture and Art in Mesoamerican Civilizations Bearing Religious Significance

Both their art and architecture represented the importance of religion in Mesoamerican society, which was reflected in their religious practices. Mesoamericans held a polytheistic worldview, and their religious rituals were an essential part of their day-to-day lives. Artwork frequently featured major deities, such as the feathered serpent Quetzalcoatl, the rain god Tlaloc, and the goddess of fertility. These deities were honored with complex rituals and celebrations.

The Pyramids and the Temples:

In order to pay homage to these gods and to provide a place of worship for the people, temples and pyramids were built. Their buildings frequently used astronomical alignments and sacred geometry, which reflected the Mesoamerican belief in the interdependence of the physical and spiritual worlds.

Observances and Acts of Sacrifice:

In Mesoamerican art, rituals and sacrifices were frequently shown because they played an important role in religious activity. In an effort to placate the gods and assure the continued fertility of the land, human and animal victims were offered as sacrifices. Murals and sculptures frequently include depictions of these religious rites in their scenes.

The Codices:

Codices, also known as pictorial manuscripts, were an essential component in the process of documenting historical events, calendar systems, and religious information. The Dresden Codex and the Codex Borbonicus are two of the most well-known manuscripts that have been found to date.

Mesoamerican Art and Architecture: Their Heritage and Their Influence

Mesoamerican cultures' contributions to the world of art and architecture have had a significant and enduring influence on the artistic practices of following civilizations. Their complex use of symbols and iconography has had an impact on contemporary art, especially in the areas of symbolism and abstraction. Ceramics and murals from Mesoamerican cultures continue to serve as a source of motivation and ideas for contemporary artists and crafters.

The idea of the enormous pyramid and temple complex may be found in the design of many contemporary buildings. This notion comes from the field of architecture. Corbelled arches, which were used by the Maya, have made their way into modern architecture for a variety of reasons, including those related to aesthetics as well as the building's functionality.

In addition, the Mesoamerican worldview, which places a strong emphasis on the interdependence of the physical and spiritual realms, has played a role in the development of holistic and environmentally conscious approaches to building and design in modern times.

The art and architecture of Mesoamerica are representative of a cultural heritage that is both rich and complex. This heritage is distinguished by its profound symbolism, religious significance, and mastery of a variety of artistic forms. Mesoamerican art and architecture continue to attract and amaze spectators due to their beauty and the depth of their cultural traditions.

This can be seen in everything from the massive pyramids and temples to the vivid pottery and murals. Mesoamerican art and architecture continue to be a source of astonishment and appreciation because they demonstrate the eternal power of human imagination and expression. They are also a monument to the inventiveness and intellect of the indigenous peoples who inhabited the region.

Chapter 5

The Age of Enlightenment and Neoclassicism

In the history of the Western world, the period that is known as the Age of Enlightenment and Neoclassicism was an important one for the region's cultural and intellectual development. These movements began in the 18th century and were characterized by a significant shift in both the intellectual ideas and creative expression of their time. This essay presents a comprehensive analysis of the Age of Enlightenment and its influence on the creation of Neoclassical art and architecture, diving into the origins, significant aspects, major artists, and the lasting impact of these interconnected epochs. The Age of Enlightenment and Neoclassical art and architecture were both heavily influenced by the Enlightenment.

Before we begin:

The Age of Enlightenment, also known as simply the Enlightenment, was a time of intellectual ferment and cultural revolution that swept over Europe in the 18th century. It is commonly referred to as "the Enlightenment." It was marked by a deep dedication to reason, empiricism, and skepticism, which led to a reevaluation of established authorities and ideas. During this time, there was also a shift away from religious dogmatism. This intellectual revolution had a significant effect on many facets of society, including politics, science, philosophy, and the arts, to name a few. In the sphere of creative expression, the Enlightenment was responsible for the birth of a new artistic movement known as Neoclassicism. Neoclassicism was an artistic movement that attempted to recreate the classical ideals of ancient Greece and Rome.

The Beginnings and Defining Characteristics of the Age of Enlightenment Structures Based on Intellectual and Philosophical Principles:

The Enlightenment was influenced by earlier developments in philosophy and science, notably the writings of philosophers and scientists such as René Descartes, John Locke, and Isaac Newton, amongst others. These historical personalities placed a strong emphasis on the importance of using powerful tools, like as reason, empiricism, and the scientific method, in order to get a better understanding of the world.

ART AND ARCHITECTURE

Skepticism and Rationalism Rationalism:

The strength of human reason and the ability to think critically was championed by philosophers of the Enlightenment. They questioned the conventional authorities of the day, such as the church and the monarchy, and they worked toward the goal of establishing a society based on the values of individual rights, freedom, and equality.

Coffeehouses and Hairdressing Parlors:

Intellectual and philosophical arguments took place in the salons of important women as well as at coffeehouses, which were gathering places for people from a wide range of socioeconomic strata who wanted to have interesting conversations. These environments had an important role in the development of Enlightenment thought and the dissemination of ideas.

The Encyclopaedia:

The Encyclopédie was a gigantic work that was edited by Denis Diderot and Jean le Rond d'Alembert. Its purpose was to collect and spread knowledge in a fashion that was organized and understandable to the general public. This grandiose endeavor served as a demonstration of the Enlightenment's dedication to the spread of knowledge and education.

Influence on Societies and Governments:

The political and social landscape of the 18th century was significantly altered as a direct result of the Enlightenment's influence. The concepts of the Enlightenment inspired political reform movements, such as the American and French Revolutions, which aimed to replace absolute monarchy with more democratic systems of governance. These movements were influenced by the Enlightenment.

Manifestation of the Arts:

The Enlightenment was also a movement that had a significant impact on the arts. The creative trend known as neoclassicism arose from a desire to express the principles of rationality, order, and harmony in one's work. The art and culture of ancient Greece and Rome served as a source of inspiration and direction for artists working in the neoclassical style.

The Enlightenment as an Inspiration for Artistic Expression in Neoclassicism
The Historical and Conceptual Origins of:

As an artistic movement, neoclassicism can be traced back to the Enlightenment's emphasis on reason and a return to classical values.

This was the movement's inspiration. It favored the restraint, balance, and simplicity of ancient Greek and Roman art above the extravagant, elaborate, and passionate excesses of the Baroque and Rococo forms. This was due to the fact that it believed these earlier styles were more authentic.

Revival of the Classics:

The aesthetics of antiquity served as a source of inspiration for neoclassical artists and architects as they strove to create works that imitated the classical world. The purity, proportion, and idealized forms of classical sculptures and architecture were revered by artists, and these qualities inspired them to seek ways to incorporate them into their own work.

Characteristics Observable to the Eye:

The focus that is placed on order, symmetry, and clarity are defining characteristics of neoclassical art. Linear perspective, exact representation, and the utilization of classical forms such as columns, arches, and pediments were some of the techniques that were utilized by the artists. These characteristics contributed to the works of the neoclassical period having a feeling of balance and logic.

Taking a portrait:

Neoclassical portraiture was a popular genre in which artists portrayed their sitters as having an idealized version of their natural beauty and frequently dressed them in clothing from antiquity. The moral and intellectual attributes of the sitter were also communicated through the sitter's portrait in addition to their physical likeness.

The following articles cover historical and mythological topics:

As a means of conveying moral and intellectual issues, neoclassical painters frequently turned to historical and mythical subjects as their subject matter of choice. These narratives served as a platform for investigating experiences that are both timeless and universal to the human condition.

Important Artists from the Neoclassical Period

Jacques-Louis David, who lived from 1748 until 1825:

The great Neoclassical painter Jacques-Louis David was noted for his dedication to classical principles as well as his involvement with the French Revolution. Jacques-Louis David was born in 1730 and died in 1825. His works, such as "The Death of Sardanapalus" and "The Oath of the Horatii," are excellent examples of the Neoclassical style, which places a strong emphasis on themes related to heroism, civic virtue, and sacrifice.

Antonio Canova, who lived from 1757 until 1822:

Antonio Canova was a well-known Neoclassical sculptor who is most recognized for his sculptures that are known for their elegance and emotional reserve. The sculpture he created, titled "Psyche Revived by Cupid's Kiss," is a masterwork of the Neoclassical style. It depicts a classical subject with elegance and an idealized version of beauty.

Angelica Kauffman was born in 1741 and died in 1807.

Angelica Kauffman was a well-known Neoclassical painter who was noted for her historical and mythological settings, which frequently featured powerful and virtuous women as subjects. Her piece titled "Cornelia Pointing to Her Children as Her Treasures" is an example of how well she is able to communicate instructive and moral ideas through the medium of art.

The Influence of Neoclassicism on Culture

The 18th and 19th centuries were marked by a significant cultural shift brought on by the Neoclassical movement. It was in line with the emphasis that the Enlightenment placed on reason, order, and the search of knowledge, and it was a crucial factor in the development of the aesthetics of the time period.

The Architectural Era Leaves Behind:

The neoclassical style of architecture left an indelible impression on the urban landscapes of many European and American towns. The United States Capitol and the British Museum are two examples of neoclassical architecture, which may be identified by its use of columns, pediments, and symmetrical design. Neoclassical architecture can be seen in governmental buildings, museums, and monuments.

Themes Relating to Education and Ethics:

Neoclassical art frequently transmitted educational and moral themes, as painters strove to inspire audiences with narratives of valor, sacrifice, and virtue. Neoclassical art was popular during the 18th and 19th centuries. It was believed that exposing people to these works would improve their aesthetic sensibilities and teach them important life lessons.

Classical Revival as an Emerging Style:

The neoclassical style even made its way into the world of fashion, where it inspired a movement known as "neoclassical dress." This style was influenced by classical antiquity, and it was characterized by loose-fitting clothing, traditional draperies, and clean, uncomplicated lines.

The Greek and Roman cultures are experiencing a renaissance

The revival of interest in ancient Greek and Roman culture that was spurred by neoclassicism led to a significant number of intellectuals and artists devoting their time to the study of the classics as well as the archaeological findings of the era. This preoccupation with ancient times was a major driving force behind the creation of classical education as well as classical archaeology.

Influence that Lasts Forever and a Legacy

An indelible mark was left on the Western world by the Enlightenment and Neoclassicism, which had a profound effect on the development of history, art, and culture. The foundation for contemporary democratic nations was built by the intellectual currents of the Enlightenment, which placed an emphasis on reason, liberty, and human rights. Neoclassical art and architecture continue to serve as a source of inspiration for current architects, designers, and artists due to their emphasis on harmony, order, and the reintroduction of classical principles.

The Neoclassical renaissance that occurred in the 18th and 19th centuries had a significant impact on academic art, which in turn affected creative training and aesthetics. There are many different types of public and civic architecture, and some of them feature characteristics of the neoclassical style. Some examples are government buildings, museums, and university campuses. The relationship that neoclassicism has to ageless and all-encompassing values such as beauty, order, and the quest for knowledge is the source of the movement's continuing allure.

5.1 Enlightenment Ideals in Architecture

The Enlightenment was an intellectual and philosophical movement that swept over Europe in the 18th century. This movement had a major impact on many parts of society, including politics, science, and the arts. The ideals of the Enlightenment signaled a substantial break from the ornate and extravagant styles of the Baroque and Rococo eras that were prevalent in the field of architecture. The pursuit by architects and thinkers of harmonizing architecture with the rational and reformative concepts of the Enlightenment resulted in the development of a specific architectural style that mirrored these objectives, and this style is known as the Enlightenment style. In this essay, the influence of the Enlightenment on architecture, as well as the essential characteristics of Enlightenment architecture, and its long-lasting impact on the built environment, will be investigated.

The Age of Enlightenment and the Impact It Had on Architectural Design
Reason and rationality are highlighted with an emphasis:
An unwavering dedication to reason, empiricism, and the scientific method was one of the defining characteristics of the Enlightenment. René Descartes, John Locke, and Voltaire are just a few examples of the Enlightenment thinkers that championed the power of human reason as a method for gaining a better understanding of the world. The logical method was one that many philosophers and architects of the period attempted to apply to architectural design.

Elimination of Extraneous Decoration and Effort:
The ornate and excessive styles of the Baroque and Rococo periods were rejected by intellectuals of the Enlightenment period because they were considered to be extravagant and irrational. They advocated simplicity, clarity, and functionalism in architecture rather than the traditional styles.

Reform of the social system and the common good:
Philosophers of the Enlightenment period advocated for individual rights, liberty, and equality during this period of social and political transformation known as the Enlightenment. Architects traditionally viewed their work as a way to make a positive contribution to society by creating environments and structures that encouraged logical living and societal advancement.

Effects of the Neoclassical Movement:
Architecture of the Enlightenment period was inextricably linked to the aesthetics of the Neoclassical movement, which drew its motivation from the aesthetics of ancient Greece and Rome. The return to classical values of logic and order, as expressed through the resurrection of classical ideals, forms, and principles.

Important Characteristics of Enlightenment-Era Architecture
Clarity and ease of understanding:
Architecture during the Enlightenment period was distinguished by its simplicity, clarity, and concentration on rational structure. The exteriors of the buildings were built to have symmetrical facades, clear lines, and an overall sense of order. In order to prioritize functionality in the design, excessive decoration was avoided.

ART AND ARCHITECTURE

The Proportions of Geometry:

In order to design harmonious and aesthetically beautiful constructions, architects utilized geometric proportions in their work. This included the utilization of the golden ratio as well as the application of mathematical principles. The use of these proportions helped to create a sense of balance and rationale in the construction of architectural structures.

Utilization of Traditional Forms:

The classical architecture of antiquity served as a source of creativity for Enlightenment architects, who included aspects like as columns, arches, and pediments into their designs. This classical revival attempted to evoke the ideals of ancient Greece and Rome, with a concentration on the beauty of idealized forms and ideas that have stood the test of time.

The pursuit of Order and Symmetry:

The Enlightenment placed a strong emphasis on order and symmetry in its architectural designs. The majority of the facades were symmetrical, and the floor plans adhered to a logical and sensible arrangement. The commitment of the Enlightenment to reason and clarity is mirrored in the movement's emphasis on order.

Brightness and breeze:

In their designs, architects of the Enlightenment period placed a significant emphasis on making use of natural light and ventilation. A living atmosphere that was healthy and reasonable was contributed to by the presence of ample natural light and fresh air, which was made possible by large windows, openings that were strategically located, and open floor designs.

Famous Architects and the Works That They Have Created

Étienne-Louis Boullée, who lived from 1728 to 1799:

Étienne-Louis Boullée was a forward-thinking French architect who is most renowned for his ultra-rational and utopian architectural concepts. Even though it was never built, his design for the cenotaph that was to be built in honor of Sir Isaac Newton epitomizes the principles of Enlightenment architecture through its utilization of geometric forms and mathematical precision.

Claude-Nicolas Ledoux, who lived from 1736 until 1806:

Another notable French architect connected to the Enlightenment period of architecture was Claude-Nicolas Ledoux. The Saline Royale that he designed and built at Arc-et-Senans is a well-known example of his work. It is known for its distinct geometric layout and its emphasis on functional design for the production of salt.

Thomas Jefferson, who lived from 1743 till 1826:

Thomas Jefferson, the third President of the United States of America, was both an architect and an advocate for the architectural style known as neoclassicism. His design for Monticello, his personal mansion, illustrates his dedication to the principles of the Enlightenment with its rational layout and classical elements.

Influence on Culture Caused by Enlightenment Architecture

Planning for the city and designing public buildings:

The principles of the Enlightenment period in architecture had an impact on urban planning, which led to the building of cities that were rational and well-organized. In the construction of public structures like government offices, libraries, and universities, an emphasis was placed on reason and order, and classical architectural aspects were frequently used.

The Importance of Education in Public Places:

The emphasis placed on education and the dissemination of knowledge during the Enlightenment may be seen mirrored in the architecture of educational institutions and public libraries during this time period. These structures frequently featured classical facades and floor plans, which communicated the significance of education and intellectual endeavors to those who passed by.

The Planning and Landscaping of Parks:

The design of parks and landscapes became an integral part of Enlightenment architecture, with the primary goal being the production of green areas that are both aesthetically beautiful and logical. The use of geometric patterns and classical elements in the design of parks and gardens became a defining characteristic of this time period.

Residences & Decorative Arts:

The architecture of private dwellings was influenced by the ideas of the Enlightenment, which placed an emphasis on the creation of living spaces that were rational, well-lit, and well-ventilated. Classical motifs and decorative features, which gave the impression of order and sophistication, were frequently used to embellish the interiors of buildings.

Influence that Lasts Forever and a Legacy

The influence of Enlightenment architecture can be seen in the layout of many contemporary public structures, such as museums, libraries, and university campuses. The tenets of rationality, clarity, and classical inspiration continue to play a significant role in determining both the current trends in architecture and the aesthetics of the built environment.

The modern sustainable and green architectural methods have a lot in common with the

Enlightenment architecture's emphasis on natural light, ventilation, and the logical organization of space. A guiding element in contemporary architecture and urban planning continues to be the dedication to the creation of living environments that are useful and sensible.

5.2 Neoclassical Revival

The Neoclassical Revival is a trend that evolved in the 18th and 19th centuries and is characterized by an increased interest in the art and culture of ancient Greece and Rome. This interest can be seen in the architecture and artwork that came out of this movement. The Neoclassical Revival was a movement that had a significant impact on Western architecture, art, and culture. This movement had its origins in the rationalism of the Enlightenment and a desire to regain the classical ideals of beauty and order. This essay dives into the roots of the Neoclassical Revival as well as its main characteristics, famous instances, and the lasting influence that it has had.

Before we begin:

The Neoclassical Revival, also known as Neoclassicism, was a cultural movement that tried to recover the aesthetics and ideas of ancient Greece and Rome. It is also known by its shorter form, the Neoclassical Revival. It developed as a reaction to the opulent and frivolous forms that prevailed throughout the Baroque and Rococo periods. Additionally, it was closely associated with the emphasis that the Enlightenment placed on reason and order. The classical world was viewed by architects, artists, and thinkers of the 18th and 19th centuries as a source of inspiration that would remain relevant across time and might guide the development of a logical and harmonious modern society.

The Beginnings of Neoclassicism and Its Principal Characteristics
Inspiration from the Classics:

The art, architecture, and philosophy of ancient Greece and Rome were significant sources of motivation for the development of neoclassicism. The classical world served as a model for clarity, proportion, and an idealized version of beauty that was turned to for inspiration by artists and architects.

The pursuit of simplicity and rationality:

The principles of reason and rationality, which were important to Enlightenment thought, were at the heart of neoclassical architecture. The excessive ornamentation that was common in earlier architectural styles was avoided in favor of neoclassical architecture's emphasis on clean lines, simple shapes, and geometric proportions.

Elements of the Classical Period:

Classical architectural details, such as columns, pediments, arches, and friezes, were strongly included in neoclassical architecture. These components were utilized so that the finished compositions would be symmetrical and balanced.

Utilization of Traditional Orders:

The Doric, Ionic, and Corinthian orders were utilized as fundamental components in the architectural designs created by Neoclassical architects. Each order had its own one-of-a-kind column and capital design, which enabled architects to express themselves in a wide variety of ways.

Mythology and historical accounts:

Themes from classical literature, mythology, and history were frequently depicted in neoclassical artwork. These narratives were not there for the sole purpose of decoration; rather, they were used as vehicles for imparting intellectual and moral concepts.

Notable Architects and the Works They Created
Andrea Palladio was active from 1508 until 1580:

One of the key figures in the development of the neoclassical style of architecture was Andrea Palladio, an Italian architect active during the Renaissance. His treatise entitled "The Four Books of Architecture" was a significant contributor to the revival of the ancient orders. His Villa Rotonda, which was designed in a symmetrical fashion and had classical columns and a central dome, is considered an outstanding example of Neoclassical architecture.

Étienne-Louis Boullée, who lived from 1728 to 1799:
French architect Étienne-Louis Boullée was noted for his highly rational and utopian Neoclassical designs. He was a visionary. Even though it was never built, his design for the cenotaph that was to be built in honor of Sir Isaac Newton epitomizes the principles of Enlightenment architecture through its utilization of geometric forms and mathematical precision.

Thomas Jefferson, who lived from 1743 till 1826:
Thomas Jefferson, the third President of the United States of America, was both an architect and an advocate for the architectural style known as neoclassicism. His design for Monticello, his personal mansion, illustrates his dedication to the principles of the Enlightenment with its rational layout and classical elements.

Notable Illustrations of the Neoclassical Style of Architecture

William Thornton, Benjamin Henry Latrobe, and Charles Bulfinch were the architects that designed the United States Capitol in Washington, D.C.: The United States Capitol building is often regarded as the most iconic example of Neoclassical architecture in the country. A sense of order and reason is conveyed by the structure's symmetrical layout as well as by its classical columns and central dome.

Jacques-Germain Soufflot's design for the Panthéon in Paris An outstanding example of Neoclassical architecture in France is the Panthéon, which was initially constructed as a church. It has a dome, pediment, and classical columns as its architectural highlights. The architecture of the building is a representation of the Enlightenment's values of rationalism and civic virtue.

Sir Robert Smirke, Director of the British Museum in London: In the United Kingdom, one of the most well-known examples of Neoclassical architecture is found in the British Museum. A huge collection of art and antiquities are stored behind its classically designed front, which features columns and pediments.

The ancient Greek temple in Athens known as the Parthenon, which was devoted to the goddess Athena, was an important direct source of inspiration for Neoclassical architects. Numerous Neoclassical structures have adopted the usage of pediments and Doric columns as a result of its popularity.

Influence on Culture Caused by the Neoclassical Revival

The 18th and 19th centuries were marked by a significant cultural shift brought on by the Neoclassical Revival. Beyond the realm of architecture, its influence was felt in other realms as well, including art, fashion, education, and even political thought. The following are important features of its influence on culture:

Art and Education in the Academic World:

The neoclassical style eventually came to predominate in academic art, where it significantly influenced both creative instruction and aesthetics. Students attending art academies were instructed to model their work after that of the great classical masters and to incorporate ethical and intellectual ideas into their creations.

Education in the Classical Tradition and Archaeology:

As a result of the Neoclassical renaissance, there was a resurgence of interest in archaeology and classical education. This preoccupation with ancient times was a major factor in the emergence of the academic fields of classical education and classical archaeology.

Dress and Fashion of the Neoclassical Era:

A style that became popular in the 18th and 19th centuries was called "neoclassical dress." This style was influenced by classical antiquity, and it was characterized by loose-fitting clothing, traditional draperies, and clean, uncomplicated lines.

A Return to the Ideals of the Classical Era:

Additionally, classical principles in politics and society were resurrected as a result of neoclassicism's influence. In particular, the American and French Revolutions had the goal of reestablishing the values that were prevalent in ancient Greece and Rome. These values included concepts such as liberty, equality, and civic virtue.

Influence that Lasts Forever and a Legacy

The Neoclassical Revival is still influential on contemporary architectural design, interior decorating, and artistic expression. The focus it places on simplicity, clarity, and classically-inspired design makes it compatible with the ideas of modernist architecture as well as contemporary sustainable design. The relationship that neoclassicism has to ageless and all-encompassing values such as beauty, order, and the quest for knowledge is the source of the movement's continuing allure.

5.3 Colonial Architecture

The cultural integration, assimilation, and adaptation that took place throughout the age of global discovery and colonialism is exemplified in the architectural styles that were prevalent during that time period. Colonial architecture contains a rich tapestry of forms that vary across regions and reflect the complexity of colonial history. These styles are the result of a combination of indigenous traditions and European influences and represent a merger of those two. This essay presents a comprehensive investigation into colonial architecture, diving into its roots, primary characteristics, regional differences, and continuing influence in today's world. Specifically, the essay examines these topics.

Before we begin:

As a result of European colonization of many parts of the world, including the Americas, Africa, and Asia, a distinct style of architecture known as "colonial architecture" came into being. It is a representation of the architectural legacy left behind by colonial powers like as Spain, Portugal, Britain, France, and the Netherlands, amongst others. These powers took their own architectural traditions with them when they founded colonies in new countries. These traditions were frequently combined with local building methods and materials. The combination of different styles and techniques resulted in the development of a wide variety of colonial architectural forms, many of which are still influential in the built environment of many different regions today.

The Beginnings and Defining Characteristics of Colonial Architecture
European influences can be seen in:

Colonial architecture was greatly influenced by the architectural styles that were common in the countries that had ruled the colonies at the time of colonization. For example, the impact of Moorish and Gothic styles can be seen in Spanish colonial architecture, whilst Georgian and Victorian styles can be seen in British colonial architecture. Both forms were influenced by European architecture.

Adaptations of the Indigenous Peoples:

In many cases, parts of indigenous building traditions, material selections, and aesthetic preferences were incorporated into colonial architecture. This integration occurred as a direct result of the requirement to adjust to the prevailing climatic conditions, cultural norms, and resources in the area.

Capabilities of Operation and Flexibility:

Adaptability and functionality were frequently considered during the design process of colonial building. Buildings were designed and erected to endure the local natural conditions, such as tropical climates, earthquakes, or monsoons, while also catering to the functional requirements of the colonial administration and the local populace.

Syncretism across Cultures:

Colonial architecture reflected a process of cultural syncretism, in which European and native architectural forms merged to create novel hybrid styles. This process resulted in the creation of distinct hybrid styles. This combination resulted in the development of new architectural vocabularies that merged aspects of colonial architecture with those of indigenous practices.

Differences in the Colonial Architecture of Different Regions
Architecture of the Spanish Colonial Era:

The adobe structure, clay tile roofs, central courtyards, and ornate facades that are characteristic of Spanish colonial architecture in the Americas and the Philippines may be found in both of these regions. The missions of California and the colonial cities of Mexico are two notable examples of this style of architecture because of the baroque and neoclassical elements present in each.

Architecture of the British Colonial Period:

Georgian and Victorian influences can be seen in the architecture that was built during the British colonial period in areas such as India and parts of Africa. This style of architecture frequently featured red-brick facades, colonnaded porches, and wide windows, all of which were reflective of the formal and symmetrical styles that were prominent in Britain during the time of the colonial rule.

Architecture of the Dutch Colonial Period:

Dutch colonial architecture, notably in places such as Indonesia and South Africa, integrated
characteristics of Dutch design, such as gabled roofs, huge verandas, and tall, narrow windows. This was particularly prevalent in the architecture of buildings that were constructed during the Dutch colonial period. These structures frequently made use of native building materials like brick and wood, fusing Dutch architectural principles with traditional indigenous construction practices.

Architecture of the French Colonial Period:

French colonial architecture in regions such as Vietnam and the Caribbean mixed indigenous architectural traditions with aspects of French classicism. The beauty and grandeur of French design was often reflected in the architecture of these structures through the use of steeply pitched roofs, wrap-around balconies, and intricate wrought-iron features.

The Influence of Colonial Architecture on Society

The following is a symbol of power and authority:

Colonial architecture frequently acted as a symbol of colonial power and authority. Monumental
government buildings, churches, and fortresses were sometimes constructed in an effort to impose control over newly acquired areas through the use of colonial architecture. These buildings were a visual representation of the colonial powers' cultural, political, and economic superiority in the region.

The mixing of cultures and the sharing of practices:

The intricate and multifaceted process of cultural interchange and hybridization that took place throughout the colonial period was reflected in the architecture of the time. Not only did the combination of European and native architectural styles result in the creation of distinctive building forms, but it also encouraged the mixing of different cultural traditions and facilitated cultural exchanges.

Planning of Cities in Colonial Times:

Colonial architecture frequently served as a major inspiration for the general plan and style of colonial cities and towns. Under colonial authority, urban planning was focused on constructing administrative centers, commercial hubs, and residential quarters that followed to the hierarchical and functional requirements of the colonial administration. These requirements included the separation of public and private functions inside the city.

Repurposing and conserving in an Adaptive Manner:

During the post-colonial era, many colonial buildings have been preserved and repurposed through a variety of adaptive reuse projects. Some buildings have been transformed as museums, cultural centers, or government agencies; these establishments serve both as reminders of the colonial past and as repositories of cultural history.

Colonial architecture's Inheritance and Enduring Impact on the Built Environment

Tourism and the Protection of Cultural Heritage:

Colonial architecture has emerged as a big draw for vacationers and a source of cultural pride for a great deal of the world. Visitors who are interested in examining the architectural, historical, and cultural legacies left behind by colonialism are frequently drawn to old colonial buildings and neighborhoods.

Conservation and Restoration of Architectural Elements:

In recent years, there has been a rising realization of the necessity to maintain colonial architecture as part of a shared global history. This has led to an increase in the number of efforts that are being made to conserve and repair colonial architecture. The goal of preservation efforts is to ensure that colonial structures will be around for future generations and to foster a greater comprehension of the historical and cultural relevance of these buildings.

Revival and Continuity in Architectural Design:

In places that were formerly under colonial rule, elements of colonial architecture continue to have an impact on the design and construction of modern buildings. There is a continuing admiration for the aesthetic and functional features of colonial architecture, which is shown in the widespread use of colonial design motifs, materials, and spatial layouts in contemporary building construction.

The Relationship Between Cultural Identities and Nationalism:

Colonial architecture has contributed in some way to the formation of post-colonial societies' cultural identities as well as their sense of national pride. In several instances, colonial structures have been transformed as symbols of national pride. These buildings now serve as reminders of the struggles for independence and as testimonials to the tenacity of local cultures.

Chapter 6

The 19th Century and Industrialization

The 19th century was a time in human history that was marked by significant upheaval and change. The process of industrialization was the primary impetus behind this transition. The swift transition from agricultural and craft-based economies to industrial and urban ones had far-reaching repercussions for society as a whole, as well as for the economy and culture specifically. This essay dives into the 19th century and industrialization, investigating the origins and repercussions of this critical era that transformed the globe in ways that could not have been imagined at the time.

1. **The Beginnings of the Industrial Revolution**
   1.1. The Revolution in Agricultural Practices
   Before we can have a handle on the industrialization of the 19th century, we need to look at what came before it. The Agricultural Revolution of the 18th century served as the foundation for the Industrial Revolution, which is frequently seen as the defining characteristic of this time period. Increased agricultural output had resulted from the use of new farming techniques and the enclosure movement, which had led to the liberation of labor from the countryside.
   1.2. The Development of New Technologies
   Additionally, the technological advances made in the 18th century, such as the steam engine and mechanized textile production, paved the way for industrialization and set the foundation for its development. For example, James Watt's improved steam engine would become the core of many different industries in the 19th century, resulting in a dramatic improvement in the effectiveness of power generation.
2. **The Beginning of the Industrial Revolution**
   2.1. The Textile Manufacturing Sector
   The textile industry was a significant driving force in the process of industrialization.

The mass manufacturing of textiles was made possible by the mechanization of the textile production process, which was demonstrated by inventions such as the spinning jenny and the power loom. Not only did this result in an increase in productivity, but it also led to a shift in the nature of the labor, with skilled artisans being replaced by factory workers.

2.2. Ferrous Metals and Steel

During this same time period, the iron and steel industry went through a period of profound change. The Bessemer method, which was invented to make steel, brought about revolutionary changes in the fields of construction, transportation, and manufacturing. Steel supported the creation of railroads, ships, and many other machines during the Industrial Revolution, making it an essential component of the revolution.

2.3. Methods of Transport

Additionally, the transportation industry underwent a sea change during the 19th century. The introduction of the railroad system and the building of huge canal networks both contributed to a major reduction in the amount of money and time needed to carry both people and commodities. This development is best illustrated by George Stephenson's "Rocket," which depicts a locomotive. Trade and urbanization were both helped along by the development of transportation networks that were both quicker and more efficient.

3. The Effects of Migration and Urbanization

3.1. The Destruction of the City

The rise of industrialization resulted in a significant population shift away from rural areas and toward urban cores. As a result of the higher pay offered by factories compared to those of traditional agricultural work, many people moved from the countryside to the developing cities. This massive movement led to the quick expansion of urban regions and the emergence of factory towns, which ultimately resulted in the creation of a new urban working class.

3.2. Conditions of Working and Living Arrangements

The rise of industrial capitalism occurred concurrently with the urbanization process. Despite the fact that it created economic opportunities, it also resulted in many people being forced to live and work in deplorable conditions. Workers in industries frequently had to put up with excessive hours, little pay, and hazardous working conditions. Because there were no regulations in place, there was widespread use of child labor and exploitation.

4. Developments and Advancements in Technology

4.1. The Use of Steam

James Watt was a significant contributor to the development of the steam engine, which was an essential component in the process of industrialization. It had a transformative effect on a number of different industries, including the production of textiles, mining, and transportation. Steam engines provided power to companies, which allowed for the uninterruptible running of machinery and increased the overall efficiency of output.

4.2. The Digitalization of Communication Revolution

In addition to the industrial and transportation revolutions that took place in the 19th century, important advances in communication technology also took place during this time period. Samuel Morse's invention of the telegraph made it possible for people to communicate quickly across large distances, linking previously isolated areas and making it easier to share information. This innovation had a significant effect not only on business but also on diplomacy and journalism.

4.3. Power and Energy

At the tail end of the 19th century, electricity emerged as a force capable of bringing about fundamental change. The creation and delivery of electrical power both trace their origins to the pioneering efforts of inventors such as Thomas Edison and Nikola Tesla. Lighting, transportation, and a plethora of other new technologies were all made possible thanks to the advent of electric power, which not only revolutionized industry but also everyday life.

5. Alterations to the Economic System

5.1. The Capitalist Economy and Independent Business

The transition from feudalism to capitalism was the driving force behind the 19th century's rapid industrialization. Entrepreneurs who invested in and managed the newly formed industrial businesses emerged alongside the rise of industrial capitalism. The pursuit of profit in a capitalist economy, together with intense rivalry, fueled innovation and efficiency.

5.2. The Growth of the World Economy

The process of industrialization was not exclusive to any one country; rather, it extended across the entire world. In particular, the European powers engaged in a period of imperial expansion during which they established colonies and trading networks in other parts of the world, including Africa, Asia, and the Americas.

The globalization of industry and trade had significant repercussions, both economically and socially, for both the colonizers and the people who were colonized.

6. Repercussions on Society

6.1. The Differences Between Social Classes and Inequality

The growth of industry in the 19th century gave rise to a complex social structure that was characterized by clear divisions between social classes. An elite class was developed by affluent industrialists and business owners, while the working class toiled away in mines and factories. This schism gave rise to social tensions, which in turn led to the formation of labor movements that campaigned for workers' rights and improved working conditions.

6.2. The Function of Women

Although their contributions to the industrialization of the 19th century are frequently neglected, women played a vital role in the process. They entered the labor force in significant numbers, the majority of them finding work in textile mills. The work that women did, despite its importance to the financial well-being of families, was typically underpaid and underestimated. In spite of this, the time period also witnessed the beginning stages of the women's rights movement, during which women started fighting for equal opportunity.

7. Reactions in the Fields of Culture and the Arts

7.1. The Age of Romanticism

The revolutionary period of industrialization sparked a wide range of responses in the fields of culture and the arts. The rise of Romanticism in literary and artistic production can be seen as a pushback against the increasing automation and urbanization of society at the time. Romantic authors and artists, such as Caspar David Friedrich and William Wordsworth, praised nature, emotion, and individualism as a reaction to what they saw as the dehumanizing impacts of the industrial age.

7.2. Being Realistic

On the other hand, the goal of the Realist movement in art and literature was to reflect the harsh, everyday realities of industrial civilization. Writers such as Charles Dickens highlighted the difficult lives of the urban poor, and painters such as Gustave Courbet created scenes of laborers and everyday life in the time period. The goal of realism was to bring attention to the socioeconomic inequities and injustices that existed during that era.

8. Shifts in Political Stability

8.1. Working-Class Movements

The 19th century was also characterized by the proliferation of labor movements, which were characterized by workers organizing themselves to seek greater wages, shorter working hours, and improved working conditions. The establishment of labor unions and the promotion of workers' rights were two of the primary driving forces behind the development of labor laws and safeguards in the 20th century.

8.2. Ideologies Regarding Politics

The era of industrialization provided the ideal conditions for the development of several political philosophies. Workers who were disenchanted with the disparities of industrial capitalism were receptive to the ideas of socialism, which centered on the collective ownership of the means of production. Socialism gained popularity among these workers. Classical liberalism and the laissez-faire economics school of thought, on the other hand, emphasized the significance of individual liberty and advocated for limited state intervention.

9. Repercussions on the Environment

9.1. Utilization of Available Resources

The consumption of natural resources skyrocketed as a direct result of the industrial revolution. The extraction of coal and iron ore, in addition to the cutting down of trees, had considerable negative effects on the surrounding ecology. The contamination of the air and water caused by factories and other industrial operations contributed further to the degradation of the ecosystem.

9.2. Early Concerns Regarding the Environment

Early warnings that there might be a problem with the environment appeared alongside the expansion of industrialization. The writings of environmental forefathers such as John Muir and Henry David Thoreau brought attention to the critical importance of preserving natural settings. These worries served as a precursor to the contemporary environmental movement, which began to gain traction in the 20th century.

The 19th century was a time of unparalleled change as a result of the widespread impact that the industrial revolution had on every aspect of human life. It resulted in dramatic changes not only in the technological landscape but also in the economic landscape and cultural responses. However, in addition to this, it worsened existing socioeconomic inequities and had major impacts on the surrounding ecosystem.

The legacy of the industrialization of the 19th century continues to this day, continuing to shape the world in which we live. While the social and political movements of this era set the stage for ongoing fights for workers' rights and environmental preservation, the breakthroughs of this era lay the groundwork for the current industrial and technical landscape. To know the world we live in and the issues we continue to confront, it is necessary to have a firm grasp of the 19th century and the industrialization that took place during that era.

6.1 Victorian Architecture

The reign of Queen Victoria, which began in 1837 and ended in 1901, was marked by an extraordinary revolution in architecture. This transformation took place during the Victorian era. The architecture that was prevalent throughout this time period, known as Victorian architecture, is a complex tapestry that represents the social, political, and technological advancements that were taking place at the time. This essay goes into the world of Victorian architecture, examining its most prominent qualities, styles, and the ongoing influence it has had on the built environment.

1. **Setting the Scene in Time**

    Significant political, social, and economic shifts occurred during the time period known as the Victorian era. The British Empire had reached its pinnacle, and the Industrial Revolution was in full gear, both of which contributed to a dramatic shift away from agricultural and rural lifestyles and toward urban and industrialized societies. The Victorian age was distinguished by a stringent moral code, the growth of the middle class, and an obsession with history and exoticism.

These underlying historical influences have a significant impact on the built environment, particularly on architecture. The physical environment of the Victorian era was a reflection of the intricate fabric of Victorian society, which resulted in a diverse array of architectural styles and expressions. This was because the Victorian era was characterized by a wide range of social classes.

2. **Principal Traits of the Architecture of the Victorian Era**

   A eclectic approach

   Eclecticism is often considered to be one of the distinguishing qualities of Victorian architecture. Architects and builders took their cues for new designs from a diverse assortment of architectural styles from throughout history and around the world. This eclecticism resulted in a wonderfully varied combination of Gothic, Classical, Italianate, and other styles of architecture. It was not unusual for a single structure to incorporate a number of different artistic aspects, which resulted in the illusion of being visually intricate and frequently adorned.

   Decorative element

   Ornamentation plays a significant role in Victorian-era building design. The majority of the buildings have elements such as elaborate detailing, exquisite ironwork, and ornamental façade. The Victorian mentality, in which ostentation was typically connected with riches and respectability, was reflected in the love of adornment that existed throughout that time period.

   The lack of symmetry

   Asymmetry is yet another essential trait that distinguishes Victorian architecture. The façade of many Victorian buildings featured an uneven and asymmetrical design, with projecting bays, towers, and turrets that gave visual interest and complexity to the structures' exteriors. Many people looked to asymmetry in art as a way to express their individuality and stand out from the crowd.

   Very Steep Roofs

   A defining characteristic of Victorian architecture is steeply sloping roofs, which are frequently embellished with architectural features such as gables, dormers, and finials. A tribute to the Romantic rebirth of medieval architecture, particularly in the Gothic rebirth style, these roofs allowed more space for attics while also paying homage to that style.

3. **Principal Types of Architectural Construction**

   The Gothic Revival style

   During the Victorian era, one of the most popular architectural trends was known as the Gothic Revival style. This design was influenced by the Gothic architecture of the Middle Ages, which was recognizable by its pointed arches, ribbed vaults, and exquisite tracery. The Palace of Westminster in London, which was designed by Charles Barry, as well as a number of churches and cathedrals are both examples of this architectural style.

   Italicize (also italic)

The architecture of the Italian Renaissance served as a source of influence for the Italianate style, which is where the style gets its name. The stately villas of Italy served as inspiration for the design of the Italianate style of architecture, which is recognizable by its low-sloped roofs, wide eaves adorned with ornate brackets, and tower-like components in many cases. Osbert Lang, an architect who is famous for his work in this style, created many public and private structures as well as homes in the Italianate aesthetic.

Anne, Queen

Asymmetry, intricate detailing, and heavy use of timbering and decorative shingles are key features of the Queen Anne style, which can be recognized by its name. Although it was called after the English monarch Queen Anne, the fashion was more prevalent in the United States than in England at the time. The Victorian homes in San Francisco that became famously known as "painted ladies" are excellent examples of this style.

After the First Empire

The mansard roof, which consists of a steep double-pitched roof with dormer windows, is a readily recognizable characteristic of the Second Empire style of architecture. This style, which was heavily influenced by French architecture, was widely used for public buildings, great palaces, and municipal halls. The Royal Exhibition Building in Melbourne, Australia, is an outstanding example of the architectural style known as the Second Empire.

Romanesque with Richardsonian Influence

This architectural style was developed in the United States and was given its name after the architect Henry Hobson Richardson. It is distinguished by its use of huge stone structure, rounded arches, and heavy, rugged masonry. The incorporation of Romanesque details into building design imparted a sense of enduring strength and a connection to the past. The Trinity Church in Boston is a well-known building that was built in this style.

Stick-Eastlake is an example.

The Stick-Eastlake style was distinguished by its open wooden framing, which was commonly referred to as "stickwork." It was distinguished by straightforward, geometric shapes, as well as the employment of ornamental elements in the Eastlake style, which was influenced by the designs of Charles Eastlake. This design became a forerunner of the Arts and Crafts movement and was popularly employed in the construction of homes in the middle class.

4. **Differences Across Geographies**

It is important to note that the influence of Victorian architecture was felt not only in the United Kingdom but also in the British colonies and the United States. There were variances in the application of Victorian styles based on regional preferences and the materials that were readily available, despite the fact that the fundamental traits remained the same.

For instance, the Queen Anne architectural style became very popular in the United States, where it was modified to suit regional tastes by frequently combining characteristics of the Shingle architectural style. The accessibility of timber and the requirement for structures that could resist the severe weather of the time period both had an impact on the development of Victorian architecture in Australia. The end result was an amalgamation of Victorian fashions and Australian variations on those styles.

5. **Influence That Will Last Forever**

The influence of Victorian architecture can be seen in buildings constructed far after the 19th century. Many aspects of Victorian architecture and interior design continue to have an influence on contemporary architecture and interior design. The employment of ornate ornamentation, steep-pitched roofs, and asymmetrical facades can still be observed in modern residences, particularly in the resurrection of "Victorian-inspired" architecture. This is especially true in the case of homes built in the last few decades.

In addition, the eclecticism of Victorian architecture has been a source of inspiration for architects and designers, leading them to combine historical and contemporary aspects in novel ways. The concept of blending several architectural styles may be seen in the designs of today's urban landscape, which results in a distinctive architectural personality for cities all over the world.

The imaginative and intricate designs of the 19th century are on full display in the form of Victorian architecture. It exemplified the Victorian era's love of adornment, its embracing of eclecticism, and its interest with the past. The architectural styles that were popular throughout this time period, such as the Gothic Revival and the Queen Anne, continue to enchant us with their one-of-a-kind combination of historical influences and enduring appeal from an aesthetic standpoint.

Although the Victorian era has been and gone for quite some time, its architectural heritage lives on and continues to influence the towns and houses that we live in today. The ornate facades, distinctive rooflines, and one-of-a-kind embellishments of Victorian architecture continue to captivate the imagination. They also remind us of a period that honored individuality, craftsmanship, and the synthesis of tradition and innovation in the built world.

6.2 Art Nouveau and the Belle Époque

From the late 19th century up until the beginning of World War I, a period known as the Belle Époque, often known as the "Beautiful Era," was characterized by significant shifts in societal norms and artistic practices. During this time period, the prominent artistic movement known as Art Nouveau came into being. This essay investigates the connected history of Art Nouveau and the Belle Époque, focusing on the characteristics, significant people, and long-lasting impact of these two artistic movements on the world of art, design, and culture. Art Nouveau and the Belle Époque were both artistic movements that emerged in the late 19th century.

1. **The Opening Statements**
   The Belle Époque was a time marked by optimism, creativity, and the exploration of various artistic mediums. An era of relative peace, economic prosperity, and cultural vitality, it was defined by the end of the Franco-Prussian War in roughly 1871 and the beginning of World War I in 1914. It was during this time that the Industrial Revolution took place. The Belle Époque was a period of time in France, particularly in Paris, that was characterized by grandiosity, an explosion of artistic expression, and rapid technological innovation. It was during this time period that the art movement known as Art Nouveau thrived. Art Nouveau is distinguished by its use of organic and decorative motifs.
2. **The Evolving Historical and Cultural Landscape**
   2.1 The Age of Flamboyance
   The tumultuous events of the 19th century, such as the aftermath of the French Revolution, industrialization, and the Franco-Prussian War, were a direct cause for the emergence of the Belle Époque as a cultural movement. It was a time of political stability and expansion of the French colonial empire, with economic prosperity allowing for increased opportunities for leisure and cultural activities. During this time, the French colonial empire also expanded. During this time period, there was an intersection of high culture, mainstream entertainment, and the advancement of science.
   2.2 Trends in the Visual Arts and the Literary Arts
   The Belle Époque was a period that saw a lot of artistic and literary genres coming together and experimenting with new ideas. The quest for more profound and illusive meanings gave rise to the literary and artistic movement known as symbolism, which arose as an expression of that quest. In painting, Impressionism was a movement that questioned traditional modes of representation, while Post-Impressionism was a movement that stretched Impressionism's already expansive boundaries even farther. These movements laid the groundwork for Art Nouveau's emphasis on the discovery of decorative and sensual forms, which was a central tenet of the style.
3. **Art Nouveau: Traits and Sources of Inspiration**
   Art Nouveau was an artistic movement that aspired to break away from the previous styles and embrace a new, innovative approach to design. The word "Art Nouveau" was taken from the French phrase "New Art," and it was used to describe this artistic trend. It developed as a reaction to the academic and historical styles of the 19th century, including Neoclassicism and the academic art fostered by institutions like the Académie des Beaux-Arts. In other words, it was a reaction to the academic and historical styles of the 19th century.

3.1 Curves and Forms Found in Nature

The use of organic forms and sinuous, curved lines was one of the distinguishing features of Art Nouveau, which is also known as the Art Nouveau period. The natural world and the natural world itself served as inspiration for many artists and designers, who integrated natural aspects like tendrils, flowers, and vines into their work. In contrast to the rigid, geometrical forms of previous styles, this emphasis on organic shapes and asymmetry was prevalent in later styles.

3.2 An Accentuation of the Sensual

Sensuality and the human form were frequently celebrated throughout Art Nouveau's history. Images of graceful, elongated women, frequently referred to as "femmes fatales," with flowing hair and flowing clothing were prominently featured in the work. Not only was an emphasis placed on sensuality in the visual arts, but also in architecture, fashion, and interior design.

3.3 Utilization of Emerging Materials

The Art Nouveau movement was open to using contemporary materials and methods. In several instances, iron, glass, and ceramic tiles were utilized in conjunction with one another to produce creative designs. The use of new materials made it possible to create more detailed and delicate detailing, which is one of the defining characteristics of Art Nouveau.

3.4 A Consolidation of the Arts

The Art Nouveau movement was an attempt to develop an aesthetic that was more in tune with its surroundings. It incorporated a wide range of artistic practices, including sculpting, painting, architecture, and decorative arts, among others. The works of architects such as Hector Guimard and designers such as Louis Comfort Tiffany are excellent examples of this confluence of the arts.

4. Art Nouveau's Most Influential Artists and Designers

4.1 Hector Guimard

Hector Guimard was a French architect and designer who is best remembered for his significant contributions to the Art Nouveau style. He is possibly most known for his designs of the entrances to the Paris Métro, which demonstrate the use of organic, curved shapes in architectural design. His work is renowned worldwide. The work of Guimard was an essential component in the formation of the aesthetically distinctive characteristics of the Belle Époque in Paris.

4.2 The works of Alphonse Mucha

The Czech artist Alphonse Mucha was a prolific figure in the development of the Art Nouveau style. He was also an influential person. The posters he created brought him a lot of attention; they typically depicted ethereal women with long hair and intricate designs. The sensual and decorative components of the movement were beautifully encapsulated in Mucha's paintings.

4.3 The Louis C. Tiffany and Company

Louis Comfort Tiffany was a prominent participant in the Art Nouveau style in the United States.

He was known for his stained glass windows. He was well-known for his work with stained glass, producing pieces of glass that were both detailed and iridescent. The global influence of Art Nouveau is reflected in the breadth of Tiffany's achievements, which include both interior design and jewelry design.

5. **Art Nouveau in Different Parts of the World**

Art Nouveau was not exclusive to France; rather, it was a global movement that took diverse forms in each country where it was practiced. In Belgium, it was known as "Sécession" or "Sezessionstil," in Germany as "Jugendstil," in Spain as "Modernisme," and in Great Britain as the "Arts and Crafts Movement." Each variant had its own set of identifying qualities, but they all had one thing in common: they all sought to incorporate novel and forward-thinking design elements.

5.1 Art Nouveau from Belgium

The works of architects Victor Horta and Paul Hankar epitomized the "Sécession" style of Art Nouveau that flourished in Belgium in the early 20th century. Horta's work, which includes the design of the Hôtel Tassel, is widely regarded as a masterpiece of the style. The emphasis was placed on the creation of a whole art setting, and it featured organic forms and exquisite ironwork.

5.2 The Style of the German Jugend

People like as Peter Behrens and Richard Riemerschmid were influential figures in the Jugendstil movement in Germany. This particular iteration of Art Nouveau placed an emphasis on geometric forms, simpler designs, and a focus on usefulness, all of which impacted subsequent modernist movement.

5.3 Craftsmanship from the United Kingdom

An extension of Art Nouveau may be found in the United Kingdom in the form of the Arts and Crafts Movement. This movement was spearheaded by individuals such as William Morris and Charles Rennie Mackintosh.

It placed an emphasis on hand craftsmanship over mass production and favored simple forms over complex ones. This method set the way for subsequent movements such as Art Deco and modernism in the art world.

6. **Inheritance and Influence**

The Art Nouveau movement only lasted for a brief period of time, but its influence on the visual arts, design, and architecture persisted much beyond the Belle Époque. Its emphasis on inventive design and the integration of the arts helped pave the way for succeeding modernist movements, such as Art Deco and the Bauhaus, which placed greater importance on these aspects.

Art Nouveau can be observed as an influence in many different elements of current design, such as graphic design, fashion, and interior décor. Artists and designers all over the world continue to draw inspiration from its organic shapes and colorful features. In particular, Art Nouveau's emphasis on the synthesis of the arts remains a potent and enduring concept, as can be seen in the interdisciplinary nature of current design. This concentration on the synthesis of the arts was one of Art Nouveau's defining characteristics.

In the latter half of the 19th century and the early 20th century, an era characterized by inventiveness, optimism, and artistic exploration was known as the Belle Époque and Art Nouveau. The elegance of the natural environment, sensuality, and the coming together of the arts were all honored throughout this time period. Even though it was only there for a short period of time, the Art Nouveau style managed to capture people's imaginations and continue to have an impact on contemporary design. This is a monument to the ever-present power that beauty and innovation possess. In times of social and political upheaval, the Belle Époque and Art Nouveau serve as a useful reminder of the potential transformative power that art and culture possess.

6.3 Impact of Industrialization on Cities

The trend of industrialization, which gathered substantial steam in the 18th and 19th centuries, was responsible for bringing about significant shifts in society, the economy, and the built environment of urban areas. As a result of the transition from agricultural to industrial economies, large numbers of people moved to urban areas in pursuit of jobs and other possibilities. This led to a surge of urbanization. This essay investigates the myriad ways in which industrialization had an effect on urban regions, focusing specifically on the ways in which it altered the physical, social, economic, and cultural landscapes of metropolitan areas.

1. **The Rise of Urbanization and the Industrial Revolution**

   1.1 The Industrial Revolution as a Trigger for the Beginning of Urbanization

   The beginning of extensive mechanization and the shift from agricultural to industrial economies both coincided with the beginning of the Industrial Revolution. It was at this time that machinery, steam engines, and factory management systems were developed and put into use, which revolutionized manufacturing and transportation. This time period, which began in the latter half of the 18th century, was pivotal in establishing the groundwork for the massive scale of urbanization that was to follow.

   1.2 Concentration of the Population in Urban Areas

   As a result of the growth of various industries, urban centers became a magnet for workers. People moved away from rural areas and toward urban ones because cities offered better job opportunities, greater pay, and higher overall standards of living. This rural-to-urban migration was a distinguishing feature of industrialization, which resulted in the explosive growth of urban populations.

2. **The Evolution of the Built Environment in Cities**

   2.1 Urbanization and the Development of Infrastructure

ART AND ARCHITECTURE

The development of industry resulted in the growth of urban centers to significant proportions. Cities were forced to adapt in order to handle the growing number of workers and industries. This expansion required the construction of brand new infrastructure, such as roads, bridges, sewage systems, and public transportation systems, among other things. To accommodate the requirements of the industrial revolution, the topography of urban areas was significantly altered.

2.2 Breakthroughs in Building Construction

During the period of industrialization, cities went through enormous transitions in terms of their built environments. The rise of industry and commerce brought in the rise of tenement buildings, warehouses, and factories as significant characteristics of urban environments. These buildings were distinguished by their functional architecture, which was frequently devoid of ornate embellishment of any kind. The demand for speedy and inexpensive building techniques drove the adoption of innovative building materials such as iron and steel, which in turn changed the architectural industry.

2.3 Planning for the City

Urban planning became an absolute necessity as a result of the fast growth of cities. Planners
and architects started designing cities with efficiency, hygiene, and safety in mind from the beginning of the process. Some of the results of urban planning carried out during this time period include the establishment of grid layouts, public parks, and the segmentation of residential, industrial, and commercial areas.

3. ## The Financial Influence Local Economies Have

   ### 3.1 Important Economic Hubs

   Cities evolved become the principal centers of economic activity in nations that later became industrialized. They served as locations for manufacturing facilities, workshops, and commercial hubs. These metropolitan centers acted as important contributors to the expansion of the national economy because they concentrated economic activity.

   ### 3.2 Potential Employment Situations

   The industrialization of cities resulted in the creation of new job opportunities. Manufacturing facilities, mines, and factories all offered employment opportunities, which resulted in a significant rise in the number of people living and working in metropolitan areas. On the other hand, these chances typically involved working long hours for a poor income in difficult working circumstances.

   ### 3.3 The Class Structure of Society

   The industrialization of labor led to a distinct chasm in social status amongst residents of metropolitan centers. Although there were economic opportunities, not everyone took advantage of them, and a sizeable percentage of the population was forced to suffer difficult working circumstances and was forced to live in poverty as a result. The rise of a working class, which is also commonly known as a "proletariat," brought attention to the differences in income and living standards that existed at the time.

4. **Alterations in Societies and Cultures**

    4.1 Urbanization and the Shifting Social Order

    Significant societal shifts were brought about as a result of the process of urbanization. The growing concentration of ethnic groups in urban centers facilitated the sharing of cultural traditions and contributed to their integration. This mixing of people from various origins resulted in the development of novel concepts, artistic practices, and cultural manifestations.

    However, the intimate living quarters and hard urban conditions also contributed to the development of social problems, such as overcrowding and worries for public health.

    4.2 Social and Cultural Revolutions

    During the time of the industrial revolution, cities were not only hubs of production; they were also the incubation grounds for various cultural and artistic trends. The urban experience and the difficulties experienced by the working class were mirrored in the emergence of literary movements such as realism and naturalism during this time period. Visual arts and music also developed to capture the industrial landscape and the human condition inside it as it grew throughout time.

    4.3 Entertainment in the City

    The development of cities resulted in the emergence of novel forms of entertainment and activities for leisure time. People who lived in cities had access to a wide range of leisure opportunities, such as going to the theater, going to amusement parks, attending sporting events, and participating in other types of recreational pursuits. The growth of urban entertainment districts highlighted the shifting preferences of the public with regard to how they choose to spend their leisure time.

5. **Modes of Transport and Methods of Communication**

    5.1 The Awakening of the Transportation Revolution

    The rise of industry ushered in a transportation revolution that had enormous repercussions for urban areas. The creation of railroads as well as the expansion and improvement of road networks made it easier to transport both commodities and people. This not only boosted economic activity but also made it simpler for people to go to and from their jobs in the city cores.

    5.2 Developments in Methods of Communication

    The nineteenth century saw a surge in urbanization at the same time that advances were being made in communication technology. While the printing press and newspapers were responsible for the dissemination of information, the telegraph made it possible to communicate quickly over large distances. These

developments in communication helped further connect cities not only with one another but also with the rest of the world.
6. **Sanitation and the Public Health System**
   6.1 The Problems Caused by Urbanization
   The urbanization of a region presented considerable difficulties to the fields of public health and sanitation. Overcrowding, inadequate housing, and poor sanitation were the direct results of the rapid migration of people into cities. These circumstances created an environment that was ideal for the proliferation of diseases like cholera and typhoid fever.
   6.2 Municipal Reorganization and Community Health
   The issue in public health prompted the emergence of urban reform movements as a solution. These movements worked toward the goal of bettering living conditions and sanitation in urban areas. To reduce the risk of disease transmission, reformers advocated for the building of public parks, the installation of sewage systems, and the upgrading of housing standards.
7. **The Impact of the Industrial Revolution on Towns and Cities**

   7.1 The Process of Urbanization Proceeds
   The beginning of the urbanization process may be traced back to the advent of industrialization, and this pattern has persisted into the 21st century. Cities have expanded to become megacities, and urban populations are continuing to grow, both of which are reflections of the enduring attractiveness of cities as centers of opportunity and economic activity.
   7.2 Heritage of the Industrial Age
   The legacy of architecture and industry from the 19th century continues to have an impact on the appearance of cities. Old factories and warehouses in many cities are being preserved and repurposed as residential lofts, cultural centers, and museums thanks to urban revitalization efforts. This preservation not only serves as a testament to the era of industrialization, but it also makes a significant contribution to the singular personality of today's metropolitan settings.
   7.3 Community Development and Physical Infrastructure
   The importance of urban planning and the development of infrastructure, both of which rose to prominence during the industrial age, continues to be critical to the operation of modern cities. Urban planning efforts that attempt to create efficient, sustainable, and livable urban settings still place a significant emphasis on the importance of concepts such as zoning, public transportation, and green spaces.
   7.4 Differences in Socioeconomic Status
   There has not been a complete elimination of the socioeconomic disparities that arose as a result of the industrialization process. Cities continue to struggle with issues of wealth inequality, unequal access to educational options, and opportunity gaps.

The efforts that are being made to alleviate these imbalances continue to be a primary focus of urban policy and development.

7.5 Obstacles Regarding the Environment

In addition, industrialization left its mark on urban areas by contributing to pollution and the degradation of the natural environment. The environment in urban areas continues to be negatively impacted by issues such as air and water pollution, which calls for continual efforts to minimize and address these issues.

The process of industrialization had a profound and far-reaching effect on cities, one that was intricate and multi-faceted, and it was felt in virtually every area of urban life. It resulted to congestion, social inequities, and environmental issues, despite the fact that it brought about economic possibilities, cultural interaction, and technical improvements. The continual growth of cities, the protection of industrial history, and the ongoing efforts to solve urban concerns like as inequality and environmental sustainability are all legacies that may be recognized as a result of industrialization.

The power that industrialization has had and continues to have to change society as well as the built environment is powerfully demonstrated by the transformation of urban landscapes that took place during the industrial era. It is vital to have an understanding of this historical process in order to manage the issues that come along with urbanization in the 21st century as well as the opportunities it presents.

Chapter 7

Modernism and the Avant-Garde

In the latter half of the 19th century and the early part of the 20th century, the globe went through a period of profound change in many spheres, including the arts, literature, music, and philosophy. This transformative period, known as Modernism, was witness to the rise of the Avant-Garde movement, which altered old artistic traditions and challenged the status quo. During this time, the status quo was questioned by the artists who participated in the movement. Both modernism and the avant-garde were movements that represented a departure from the traditional norms and values of the past. As a result, they helped to pave the way for a new period of artistic experimentation, innovative thinking, and intellectual inquiry. This essay goes deep into the complexities of Modernism and the Avant-Garde, assessing their significant influence on the cultural landscape and their ongoing legacy in today's modern society.

Acquiring Knowledge of Modernism:

As an artistic and literary movement, modernism spanned a vast variety of fields, including the written word, the visual arts, architecture, and design, to name just a few. It was distinguished by a fundamental rejection of established forms, with an emphasis placed instead on experimentation, individualism, and a heightened awareness of the world's fast changing environment. Artists who adhered to the modernist movement attempted to express the essence of the modern experience via their work, which was meant to depict the turbulent social, political, and technological transformations that characterized the early 20th century. The modernist movement was distinguished by a number of key qualities, including an emphasis on fragmented form, a concentration on subjective experience, and an investigation of the unconscious mind. This movement radically challenged the standard conceptions of representation and interpretation, which resulted in the emergence of a wide variety of inventive forms of artistic expression.

The Beginning of the Age of the Avant-Garde:

The word "avant-garde," which comes from a French military expression that translates to "advance guard," referred to a vanguard of artists and intellectuals who were the driving force behind the Modernist movement. Artists who created in an avant-garde style were at the vanguard of experimental inventiveness, pushing the boundaries of creative rules and conventions that had previously been established. They rejected the restrictions of traditional aesthetics and instead embraced radical techniques and uncommon subject themes in an effort to inspire cultural revolution, question established standards, and provoke thought.

The term "avant-garde" does not refer to a specific artistic subgenre; rather, it refers to a movement that included many other types of artistic expression, such as the visual arts, literature, music, theater, and performance art.

Important Ideas and Subject Matter Expressed by Modernism and the Avant-Garde

Subjectivity and Perception: Modernist painters placed a high value on the artist's own subjective experience and interpretation of the work. These artists frequently used abstract and symbolic representations to depict the intricacies of human awareness and emotion.

Experimentation and Fragmentation: Two important characteristics of modernist artworks were the fragmentation of form and the experimentation with new techniques. These characteristics reflected the dissolution of old narrative structures and artistic traditions.

Social Criticism and Political Activism: The Avant-Garde movement, in particular, was profoundly based in social critique and political activism. It challenged preexisting notions and advocated for societal change via works of art that were provocative and frequently contentious.

Interdisciplinary Collaboration: Modernist artists regularly engaged in interdisciplinary partnerships, blurring the barriers between different art forms and integrating diverse disciplines to create works of art that were complex and dynamic in nature.

Innovation and Technological Advancement: Modernism and the Avant-Garde were tightly connected with the rapid breakthroughs in technology and the industrial revolution. These two movements inspired artists to experiment with new materials, techniques, and mediums to reflect the changing modern world.

Important People and Events that Influenced Movements:

Cubism was a pioneering movement that changed the portrayal of form and space through the use of geometric shapes and fractured perspectives. It was pioneered by Pablo Picasso and Georges Braque, who are considered to be the style's pioneers.

T.S. Eliot and Virginia Woolf: Both of these writers are renowned for their contributions to Modernist literature. They explored the complexity of human awareness as well as the fragmented character of reality, so paving the way for new narrative strategies and literary experimentation.

The provocative artworks of Marcel Duchamp and the Dadaist movement as a whole questioned the conventions of art and society by embracing absurdity, nihilism, and anti-establishment feelings.

Wassily Kandinsky and the development of Abstract Expressionism: Kandinsky's investigation of abstract shapes and the spiritual essence of art had a profound impact on the development of Abstract Expressionism, an art movement that emphasized emotional intensity and the spontaneous expression of the artist's psyche. Abstract Expressionism was a movement that began in the early 20th century.

Igor Stravinsky and Arnold Schoenberg are two of the most influential composers of the modern era. They revolutionized the sound of contemporary music by introducing dissonance, atonality, and intricate rhythmic frameworks. As a result, modernist musical styles such as expressionism and serialism came into existence.

Legacy and Repercussions:

The legacy of modernism and the avant-garde continues to reverberate in contemporary art and culture, exerting an influence on succeeding generations of artists and helping to shape the trajectory of artistic innovation. Abstract expressionism, pop art, and postmodernism are just few of the artistic forms that were able to flourish as a direct result of the focus placed on independence, creative freedom, and the unrelenting desire of novelty during this time period. In addition, the Avant-Garde's emphasis on social critique and political activism established a precedent for artists to utilize their artistic platforms as a method of lobbying for social change, encouraging greater awareness of important socio-political concerns, and promoting cultural debate. This was made possible as a result of the Avant-Garde's contribution to the cultural movement known as the Modernist movement.

Both modernism and the avant-garde were important movements that were responsible for redefining the bounds of creative expression and radically altering the aesthetic landscape. They forced audiences to confront the difficulties of the modern world, which led to a significant reevaluation of cultural values and societal paradigms. Their extreme departure from existing standards challenged audiences to confront the complexities of the modern world. The everlasting legacy of modernism and the avant-garde highlights the ongoing impact that these movements had on the development of art, literature, music, and philosophy. This heritage serves as a witness to the power that artistic innovation and creative rebellion continue to have even after they have passed.

7.1 The Bauhaus Movement

Walter Gropius, an architect, established the revolutionary Bauhaus school of art, design, and architecture in Weimar, Germany in 1919. The institution was named after Gropius himself. The original focus of the school was on the incorporation of art, craft, and technology into the design and construction of buildings; the name "Bauhaus" literally translates to "Building House" in German. Nevertheless, the influence of the Bauhaus movement was felt across a far wider spectrum of artistic practices than just architecture, and its importance to the development of contemporary design and education is still widely acknowledged. This essay dives into the history of the Bauhaus movement as well as its guiding ideas, prominent people, and enduring legacy.

1. **Setting the Scene in Time**
   1.1 The devastation left behind by World War I
   In 1919, amid a period of significant social and political upheaval in Germany, the Bauhaus school of architecture and design was established. Following World War I and during the turbulent time of the Weimar Republic, a fertile ground was established for artistic experimentation, as well as a desire to rethink the institutions of society, including design and education. This ambition was fueled by the conditions of the time.
   1.2 The Impact of the Modernist Movement
   The modernist movement as a whole, which strove to distance itself from the historical and ornamental styles of the past, had a significant impact on the Bauhaus school of design and architecture. The pursuit of new forms that were pertinent to contemporary life and technology was at the heart of the modernist movement, which advocated for minimalism, functionalism, and a rejection of excess.
2. **The Bauhaus School's Guiding Ideas**
   2.1 Incorporation of Artistic Pursuits and Handicrafts
   By putting an emphasis on the oneness of art and technology, the Bauhaus tried to close the gap that existed between fine art and craft. This philosophy represented the early ideals of the school, which was built on the premise that artists, designers, and craftsmen could work together to develop items that had both artistic value and utilitarian worth. This principle reflected the early ideals of the school.
   2.2 Function Determines the Form
   The concept that form should follow function was one of the most important tenets of the Bauhaus philosophy. The modernist movement is strongly related with this concept, which emphasized that the design of an object should be informed by its intended purpose rather than the other way around. The emphasis was placed on functionality and efficiency rather than an excessive amount of adornment.
   2.3 The Art of Minimalism
   The Bauhaus school of architecture and design was also an early proponent of minimalism, which advocates stripping down design features to their most fundamental constituents. This method placed an emphasis on clarity and straightforwardness in its design, with the goal of doing away with superfluous adornment and complication.

2.4 Utilization of Emerging Materials
In accordance with the tenets of modernism, the Bauhaus investigated and enthusiastically embraced the use of newly developed technology and materials. This featured the use of materials such as steel, glass, and concrete in design and architecture, which led to the development of novel and effective methods of building.

3. Prominent Members of the Bauhaus Community
3.1 The architect Walter Gropius
Walter Gropius was the man responsible for establishing the Bauhaus and serving as its first director. In his capacity as an architect, he made substantial contributions to the development of the Bauhaus's pedagogical approach and course offerings. Gropius had a vision for the Bauhaus that it would be a place where the arts and crafts could join together to generate works that were works that were both artistic and utilitarian.

3.2 The Count of Johannes Itten
Johannes Itten was a significant character at the Bauhaus. He was in charge of the foundational course, which introduced pupils to the fundamentals of form, color, and materials. Itten was also a significant figure in the Bauhaus. The early method of teaching art that was developed at the Bauhaus was profoundly influenced by Itten's emphasis on spirituality and symbolism in design, as well as the use of color.

3.3 Moholy-Nagy, László László
At the Bauhaus, one of the most influential instructors and artists was László Moholy-Nagy. In the fields of art and design, he promoted the utilization of industrial materials as well as photography and film. His forward-thinking approach to many kinds of materials and media was an essential factor in the development of the educational curriculum at the Bauhaus.

3.4 Regarding Josef Albers
In his time at the Bauhaus, Josef Albers served first as a pupil and then as a professor. His contributions to color theory and the study of the relationships between colors had a profound effect on the development of modern art and design. The lessons that Albers taught about color and abstraction continue to have an impact on today's art and design education.

4. The Instructional Methods and Study Materials
4.1 The Vorkurs [The Vork]
The "foundation course," also known as the "Vorkurs," was an essential component of the Bauhaus education program. Students were given a solid grounding in the fundamentals of design, such as form, color, and materials, under the direction of Johannes Itten, who was succeeded in the role by Josef Albers. The course was designed to challenge conventional ideas about artistic education and to foster creative thought.

4.2 The System of the Workshop

The educational model pioneered by the Bauhaus was centered on the use of workshops, in which students gained knowledge by assisting master artisans and artists in their daily labor. The workshops offered a wide variety of activities, including but not limited to painting, weaving, metallurgy, and woodworking. This method placed an emphasis on hands-on, practical experience as well as the blending of artistic and artisanal practices.

4.3 The Working Relationship

The cooperative spirit of the Bauhaus was one of the most important factors in its overall success. In the spirit of the belief that creativity might be fostered through multidisciplinary cooperation, the educational institution fostered an environment in which designers, artists, and craftspeople could come together to collaborate on projects together. The application of this strategy resulted in the development of designs that were original and forward-thinking.

5. Transferring and Ending Operations

Throughout the entirety of its life, the Bauhaus was met with hostility by conservatives who were also politically motivated. The school relocated from Weimar to Dessau in 1925, where Walter Gropius was commissioned to build a brand new campus for the institution. This action signaled a change in the Bauhaus's approach, which resulted in a greater focus being placed on industrial design and architecture.

In spite of this, the political situation in Germany continued to deteriorate, and in 1933, the Nazi administration exerted enough pressure to compel the closure of the Bauhaus school of design. Many of the school's instructors and students moved to other countries, taking the Bauhaus's philosophies and methodologies with them. As a result, the Bauhaus's influence can now be seen all over the world.

6. The Influence of the Bauhaus

6.1 The Contemporary Style

Many people believe that the Bauhaus was the institution that laid the groundwork for modern design. Product design, architectural design, and graphic design are just few of the areas that have been profoundly influenced by the ideals of usefulness, simplicity, and the merging of art and technology that it espouses.

6.2 Instruction in Art and Design

The method of teaching design that was pioneered at the Bauhaus has left an indelible mark on art and design schools all around the world. Students are encouraged to explore the borders of art, craft, and technology through a method that has been adopted by many educational institutions and is based on the workshop model pioneered by the Bauhaus.

6.3 The Role of Architecture in Influencing

The architectural practices of the time and the growth of the modernist architectural style were profoundly impacted by the Bauhaus school of design. Both the "form follows function" philosophy of the Bauhaus and the incorporation of innovative materials are still essential tenets of today's architectural practice.

6.4 Aspects Relating to Culture

Artists, designers, and cultural institutions continue to draw motivation from the Bauhaus's insistence on the need of innovation, experimentation, and the integration of art into everyday life. A basic concept of modern art and culture is the notion that works of art and design have the potential to influence how people live their lives and interact with the outside world.

The Bauhaus movement, which emerged in the wake of World War I and flourished during a period of political and social turmoil, is a living example of the power of creative thinking in the face of adversity. The Bauhaus is credited with fostering ideas that are still influential in the contemporary fields of art, design, and education. These ideas include a focus on minimalism, functionality, and multidisciplinary cooperation. The long legacy of the Bauhaus serves as a reminder that individuals who are innovative and forward-thinking may affect the course of history, leaving a tremendous impact on the way in which we live, work, and interact with the world around us.

7.2 Frank Lloyd Wright and Organic Architecture

The term "organic architecture" was used to describe Frank Lloyd Wright's groundbreaking approach to building design. Wright is widely regarded as one of the most innovative and influential architects of the 20th century. This ideology has as its foundation the idea that architecture should be in harmony with its natural surroundings, should embrace the principles of organic growth, and should serve the need of the people living in the structure. In this essay, we examine the life and work of Frank Lloyd Wright, as well as his organic architectural principles and the lasting influence that his vision has left in the fields of design and architecture.

1. **A Life of Frank Lloyd Wright, by I. Frank Lloyd Wright**

   1.1 Childhood and Formative Years of Education

   On June 8, 1867, Frank Lloyd Wright was born in Richland Center, which is located in the state of Wisconsin, in the United States. His mother pushed him to pursue creative endeavors, and from an early age he showed early interest in architecture. Wright's formal education consisted of time spent at the University of Wisconsin and an apprenticeship with the well-known Chicago architect Louis Sullivan. During his time with Sullivan, Wright was exposed to the growing design theories of the time. Wright is credited with revolutionizing the field of architecture.

   1.2 The Prairie School and the Beginning of Your Career

   Wright's early career was distinguished by his involvement with the Prairie School, which was a group of architects in the Midwest who shared a common vision for developing structures that merged with the flat, broad terrain of the region. Wright's early career was marked by his association with the Prairie School. During this time period, he developed a style that became identified with his work. This style is marked by horizontal lines, flat roofs, and overhanging eaves.

1.3 Taliesin's Private Life and Other Aspects

Taliesin, Wright's home and studio, was established in Spring Green, Wisconsin, near the year 1911 by Wright. This architectural wonder served as a tribute to the organic design principles that he adhered to, and it blended in well with its natural surroundings. His personal life was marked by turbulent relationships and several marriages, notably his second wife, Mamah Borthwick Cheney, whose murder in 1914 at Taliesin stunned the nation. Wright's personal life was distinguished by multiple marriages and violent relationships.

1.4 Later Years in His Career and the Guggenheim Fellowship

Wright's career extended several decades, during which he was responsible for designing some of the most recognizable structures in the world. In the 1930s, he was responsible for designing Fallingwater, a house that was constructed in Pennsylvania over a waterfall, as well as the Johnson Wax Headquarters in Racine, which is located in the state of Wisconsin. In the latter part of his career, he was responsible for establishing the Solomon R. Guggenheim Museum in New York City. This museum is a demonstration of his dedication to organic principles.

1.5 Our Heritage and Our Influence

The work and guiding concepts of Frank Lloyd Wright have indelibly influenced the fields of architecture and design. His theories continue to have an impact on modern architecture and have had a significant impact on the way we think about the connection between man-made surroundings and the natural world.

2. Organic Architecture, with an Emphasis on Principles and Philosophy

2.1 Harmony with the Natural World

The idea that man-made structures and natural environments are inextricably linked was central to the organic architectural concept developed by Frank Lloyd Wright. He emphasized the importance of harmony with the natural environment by viewing buildings as extensions of their natural surroundings. His designs frequently used components of nature, such as stone, wood, and water, so blurring the lines between the natural world and the man-made world.

2.2 Growth of Organic Material

Wright was a firm believer in the organic growth principles and tried to model his design processes after the natural occurrences he observed. This idea was frequently referred to by him as "form follows function," and he emphasized that the design of a structure should be molded by both the purpose for which it was constructed and the natural materials that were used in its creation. This strategy resulted in buildings that had the appearance and feel of having grown out of the earth themselves.

2.3 The Style of the Prairie

The Prairie Style is one of the most prominent examples of the organic architecture that Frank Lloyd Wright created. This architectural style intended to blend structures with the landscape around them by employing low, horizontal lines, flat roofs, and extended eaves on the buildings it commissioned. It was meant to evoke a feeling of openness and vastness, and it was inspired by the vast stretches of land that characterize the American Midwest.

2.4 The Usonian Residence

In the 1930s, Wright invented the idea of the "Usonian" house, which was a term he coined to characterize dwellings that were affordable, functional, and organic for the American middle class. Wright's vision for the "Usonian" house was to create buildings that were organic in their design. These houses typically have open floor plans, flat roofs with overhanging overhangs, and a robust connection to the natural environment in their locations. For decades, the Usonian notion was a significant factor in the construction of suburban dwellings.

3. The Most Recognizable Examples of Organic Architecture

3.1 The Fallingwater (novel)

One of the most well-known and admired examples of Frank Lloyd Wright's architecture is Fallingwater, sometimes called the Kaufmann Residence. The structure was finished in 1939 and may be seen in the woods of southern Pennsylvania. It is perched dramatically above a waterfall in the region. The house is a stunning example of organic architecture, with terraces that are perfectly integrated with the surrounding natural rock formations and a cantilevered design that gives the impression that it is floating on the water.

3.2 The Area of Taliesin West

The home and studio that Frank Lloyd Wright used during the winter was called Taliesin West, and it was situated in Scottsdale, Arizona. It is a tribute to his organic architecture ideals, with a design influenced by the desert, the use of local materials, and integration with the terrain that surrounds it. The structure is filled with various elements, such as reflecting ponds, gardens, and open courtyards, that demonstrate Wright's attention on achieving harmony with nature.

3.3 The Solomon R. Guggenheim Museum

One of Frank Lloyd Wright's most well-known and groundbreaking creations is the Solomon R. Guggenheim Museum, which can be found in New York City. The museum was finished in 1959 and has a design that resembles a spiral ramp that allows visitors to navigate the museum's collection of artwork in a seamless manner. The Guggenheim Museum is an excellent illustration of Wright's organic architectural ideas because of its curved design and its use of natural light to create a sense of openness and connection to the exterior of the building.

3.4 The Johnson Wax Corporate Offices

Another famous building that was designed by Wright late in his career is the Johnson Wax Headquarters in Racine, Wisconsin. It wasn't finished until 1939, but it already had a dendriform column system that was constructed out of dendritic concrete and Pyrex glass tubing. The design is an example of organic architecture, which is characterized by a focus on functionality, harmony with natural surroundings, and the use of novel materials.

4. The Influence That They Have Had On Modern Architecture And Design

4.1 Design that is Eco-Friendly

Contemporary sustainable design approaches can be said to be influenced by Wright's emphasis on the integration of architecture with the natural environment. Today's architects and designers strive to create structures that have as little of an adverse effect on the natural world as possible by making use of components and innovations that cut down on the amount of energy used and the amount of waste produced.

4.2 Floor Plans With Open Spaces

Wright's ideas continue to have an influence on residential and commercial architecture thanks to the open floor plans and flexible interior spaces that he included in his creations. These characteristics contribute to contemporary living and working settings by making the most efficient use of available space and fostering a feeling of openness.

4.3 New and Pioneering Materials

Modern architects have been encouraged to experiment with new building materials and technology by Frank Lloyd Wright's use of forward-thinking materials such as steel, glass, and concrete in his buildings. These advancements have led to the creation of ecologically friendly materials as well as environmentally friendly ways of building.

4.4 A Construct That Is Harmonious

In contemporary architecture and design, one of the most important fundamental principles remains to be the integration of man-made environments with natural ones, as well as an emphasis on maintaining harmony with the surrounding natural world. The goal of architectural design and interior design is to create environments that foster well-being and a sense of connection to the natural world.

5. Obstacles and Rebuttals to Criticisms

The organic architectural concepts developed by Frank Lloyd Wright have left an unmistakable effect on the world of design; nonetheless, they were not without their share of difficulties and critics. His detractors asserted, however, that his ideas could not be put into practice and would be too expensive to create. In addition, his emphasis on form and aesthetics frequently took precedence over concerns regarding

ART AND ARCHITECTURE

functionality and comfort. On the other hand, it is precisely these issues that have inspired continuous discussions about the balance between form and function in architectural design and design more generally.

The profound and everlasting legacy that Frank Lloyd Wright's innovative approach to design, which came to be known as organic architecture, has left behind. His devotion to organic growth, his emphasis on practical design principles, and his view that architecture and nature are one helped him transform the world of architecture and design. His most well-known buildings, including Fallingwater, Taliesin West, and the Guggenheim Museum, continue to motivate and enthrall architects, designers, and fans of his work.

Modern architectural practices can largely be traced back to the organic architecture concepts developed by Wright, as well as to his use of novel materials and his dedication to environmentally responsible design. His vision of harmony between the natural world and the constructed environment is still an influential and everlasting concept. It serves as a reminder of the potential for architecture to create spaces that improve our lives and connect us to the world around us.

7.3 Post-World War II Architectural Innovations

The years immediately following field War II were characterized in the field of architecture by a degree of change and turmoil that had never been seen before. As architects embraced new materials, construction processes, and design philosophies, this era experienced a departure from the historical and opulent designs of the past. This era witnessed a departure from the historical and extravagant styles of the past. The pursuit of modernism, when paired with the impact of social, political, and technological elements, resulted in a vast number of advancements in architectural design. In this essay, we will investigate the architectural innovations that came to define the era following World War II and the impact those innovations have had on the built environment of the contemporary day.

1. **The Environment After the War**

    1.1 Reconstruction After Devastation and Destruction

    The devastation that was left in its wake across Europe and Asia as a result of World War II led to the destruction of many cities and the architectural legacy of those towns. The immediate time period following the war was characterized by the requirement for reconstruction, which paved the way for innovative architectural concepts and strategies.

    1.2 The Growth of the Economy

    In the years immediately following World War II, the economy of the United States experienced a period of unprecedented growth that has come to be known as the "Post-War Economic Miracle." The rapid growth of the American economy, in conjunction with the baby boomer generation, resulted in an increase in the need for housing, public buildings, and other forms of infrastructure.

1.3 The Origin and Growth of New Nations

The decades immediately following World War II saw the birth of numerous new nations, particularly in Asia and Africa, all of which were intent on developing their own distinct architectural styles. In order to develop a style that is all their own, architects and designers in these areas drew inspiration from both the local customs and the architectural trends of the modern day.

2. The Modernist Movement and the Effects It Had

2.1 The Style Adopted Around the World

After the war, the International Style, which had its beginnings as a modernist architectural movement in the early part of the 20th century, continued to have a significant impact on architectural design. The International Style, which is characterized by a design that is efficient and minimalistic, clean lines, and the use of industrial materials, found fertile ground in the architectural landscape that emerged after the war.

2.2 Brutalism and the Contribution of Le Corbusier

Le Corbusier, a leading modernist architect who was also a pioneer, made a substantial contribution to the architectural scene after the war. His theories on functionalism and urban planning, in addition to the idea of "Unite d'Habitation," had a significant impact on the architectural design of housing complexes all over the world. The brutalist architectural movement was significantly influenced by Le Corbusier's use of concrete in unrefined, angular forms.

2.3 Modern of the Mid-Century

After the war, one of the most famous trends in architecture was the mid-century modern style, which was distinguished by its focus on clean lines, organic shapes, and the utilization of natural materials. The classic furniture and interior designs created by designers such as Charles and Ray Eames, Eero Saarinen, and Arne Jacobsen have had a long-lasting effect on the design world.

3. Developments in Methods and Components of Technology

3.1 Construction Methods Utilizing Prefabrication and Modularization

Following the end of World War II, architects began investigating prefabrication and modular construction techniques as potential ways to increase both efficiency and speed. This strategy entailed producing building components away from the actual construction site and then assembling them at the site. Buckminster Fuller's geodesic domes and the Case Study Houses in California are two notable examples of this type of architecture.

3.2 Utilization of Emerging Materials

During and during World War II, scientists made significant advancements in material science, which paved the path for architects to experiment with novel materials. Steel, glass, concrete, and polymers all played a vital role in the development of creative post-war buildings. These materials enabled architects to explore new structural possibilities, which led to the creation of some truly remarkable structures.

3.3 The Engineering of Structures

The development of structural engineering opened up new opportunities for architects to explore the limits of design. Iconic buildings like the Sydney Opera House and the John Hancock Center in Chicago were made possible by advancements in the use of reinforced concrete, steel frames, and tension structures. The Sydney Opera House is known for its expressive shell-like forms, and the John Hancock Center in Chicago is known for its distinctive X-bracing system.

4. Architectural Developments Specific to Each Region

4.1 The Europe

In Europe, architects tried to find a way to satisfy both the requirement for post-war reconstruction and the demand for modernity in their designs. During this time period, a number of different architectural styles emerged, ranging from the brutalism that was popular in the United Kingdom to the organic architecture that was prevalent in Scandinavia.

The Ronchamp Chapel in France, designed by Le Corbusier, and the Sydney Opera House in Australia, designed by Jorn Utzon, are two instances of iconic architecture.

4.2 United States of America

The United States experienced a building boom in the decades following World War II, during which time notable modernist architects such as Ludwig Mies van der Rohe, Philip Johnson, and Richard Neutra were active in the field. Initiated by Arts & Architecture magazine, the Case Study House initiative led to the creation of housing prototypes that were both forward-thinking and accessible to a wide range of budgets.

4.3 Asia

To forge a style all their own, architects in Asia drew inspiration from both the region's indigenous practices and the region's modernist movements. The Hiroshima Peace Memorial Park designed by Kenzo Tange and other significant examples of Metabolist architecture can be found throughout Japan. Le Corbusier was commissioned to develop the city of Chandigarh in India, which features a mix of modernist ideals with traditional Indian culture.

4.4 South and Central America

Oscar Niemeyer and Lina Bo Bardi were two Latin American architects who made significant contributions to the growth of the modernist architectural movement. Niemeyer's design of Brasil, the new capital of Brazil, is lauded for its forward-thinking approach to urban planning and its overall sense of ambition.

4.5 Africa

Emerging nations across Africa have been quick to embrace architectural innovation, frequently striking a balance between modernism and traditional design aspects. Hassan Fathy's New Gourna Village in Egypt is one example of a building that utilizes local materials and vernacular architecture while still incorporating modernist design concepts, producing a structure that is one of a kind.

5. **Movements in Societal and Cultural Aspects**

   5.1 Housing Assistance Programs

   Following the end of World War II, there was a significant increase in the building of social housing to meet the growing need for homes. Innovative communal housing projects such as Le Corbusier's Unite d'Habitation in Marseille and Alison and Peter Smithson's Robin Hood Gardens in London tried to produce housing that was both affordable and efficient while adhering to the principles of modernist architecture.

   5.2 Experimental and Countercultural Communities and Movements

   In the 1960s and 1970s, there was a proliferation of counterculture movements and experimental communities that searched for alternative ways of life. Architectural initiatives such as Drop City in the United States and the commune movement in Denmark reflected a desire for more communal and environmentally responsible ways of living.

   5.3 Conservation and Adaptive Reuse of Existing Materials

   An increasing number of people were interested in historic preservation and creative reuse as modernist architecture continued to develop over time. The preservation of historic buildings, like the renovation of London's Battersea Power Station, brought to light the necessity of fusing the old with the new and repurposing industrial structures for more modern applications.

6. **Contemporary Inheritance and Obstacles to Overcome**

   6.1 A Design That Is Eco-Friendly

   In the 21st century, environmentally responsible design has emerged as a primary motivator in contemporary architectural practice. construction on the modernist ideas of functionality and form following function, more and more architects and designers are placing an emphasis on environmentally responsible practices like as energy efficiency, the use of green construction materials, and ecological responsibility.

   6.2 Developments In The Field Of Technology

   The architectural profession has undergone significant change as a result of the digital revolution and other technological breakthroughs. The design and construction processes have been changed thanks to developments in computer-aided design (CAD), Building Information Modeling (BIM), and parametric design. These developments have made it possible for architects to create structures that are both complicated and inventive.

   6.3 Internationalization

   The sharing of different architectural ideas and influences has become much easier as a result of globalization. A landscape of architecture that is often characterized by its eclecticism is the result of architects frequently drawing influence from a wide variety of cultures and traditions. The architecture of today is a reflection of the mixing and matching of different styles and ideas.

6.4 The Obligation Towards Society

Architects nowadays are faced with a number of social and ethical challenges, including the construction of environmentally friendly and resilient structures, as well as the problem of urban sprawl and the rising cost of housing. The postwar era placed a strong emphasis on social housing and experimentation, both of which continue to have a significant impact on conversations that take place today regarding the function of architecture in society.

After World War II, there was a period of tremendous architectural innovation that was defined by a departure from historical styles and an embrace of modernist ideas. This departure from historical styles was one of the defining characteristics of this period. The rich architectural landscape of the era was contributed to by architects and designers from all over the world, including Europe, the United States, Asia, Latin America, and Africa. The pursuit of modernity, in conjunction with advances in material science, technological innovation, and social movements, created the groundwork for the development of contemporary architecture.

Today, the legacy of the architectural breakthroughs that occurred after the war is visible in the dedication to environmentally responsible design, technical progress, and social responsibility. The challenges posed by the built environment continue to be a point of contention for architects, who, at the same time, look to the past for inspiration and forward to a future that will be defined by innovation and adaptability. The architectural changes that took place after World War II continue to serve as a witness to the power of architecture to represent the spirit of its time and to shape the way in which we live, work, and experience the world.

Chapter 8

Contemporary Trends in Art and Architecture

The fields of art and architecture have, since the beginning of time, been in a condition of perpetual change, adapting to reflect the shifting cultural, social, and technological landscapes of each era. In the 21st century, contemporary art and architecture are characterized by a wide variety of tendencies that subvert conventional ideas, experiment with novel materials and technology, and provide responses to urgent problems on a global scale. This article sheds insight on the dynamic and ever-evolving nature of creative expression in our time by investigating some of the most significant and influential contemporary trends in art and architecture.

1. **Current Art Movements and Their Influence**
   1.1 The Field of Conceptual Art
   Since the middle of the 20th century, conceptual art has been a trend that has had a significant impact on the art world and is still thriving in the 21st century. Instead of placing a premium on aesthetics or skilled craftsmanship, this artistic practice lays significant significance on ideas and concepts. Artists frequently make use of a diverse array of media, such as literature, performance, and installation, in order to communicate the ideas behind their work and encourage intellectual participation. Prominent conceptual artists like as Jenny Holzer and Sol LeWitt push the limits of what is considered to be "traditional" art by placing a greater emphasis on the significance of ideas than on traditional materials.
   1.2 Graffiti and Other Forms of Urban Art
   Graffiti and street art are no longer considered to be on the periphery of the art world; instead, they have made their way into the center of attention thanks to artists such as Banksy. These art forms, which are frequently connected with urban landscapes as well as social and political criticism, are continuously developing. Street artists frequently experiment with new approaches and mediums, fusing classic graffiti with muralism, stencils, and even digital interventions.

They do this by merging these styles. It is becoming increasingly common for artists to use the medium of street art as a tool to communicate with the general public and discuss topics like as social justice, gentrification, and public space.

1.3 Art Using New Media

The development of new technologies has resulted in the emergence of a new artistic movement known as new media art. This art investigates how technological developments intersect with artistic expression. This movement encompasses digital art, interactive installations, and experiences of virtual reality as well as artworks generated by algorithms. Innovative technologies are being used by artists such as Olafur Eliasson and Ryoji Ikeda to create works of art that are interactive and immersive. These works of art question conventional ideas of space and perception. The topics of surveillance, identity, and the blurring of the virtual and actual worlds are regularly addressed in new media art, which frequently explores concerns relating to the digital age.

1.4 The Art of the Environment

Environmental art, also known as eco-art or land art, addresses current environmental challenges and our relationship with the natural world. Environmental art also goes by the names "land art" and "eco-art." Artists like Maya Lin and Richard Long produce large-scale installations and landscape interventions to bring attention to environmental concerns and advocate for sustainable practices. The purpose of environmental art is to act as a visual and symbolic reminder of our duties to the environment and the necessity of maintaining a harmonious relationship with the world.

1.5 Art That Is Engaged In Society

Art that is socially involved, commonly known as "artivism," is art that attempts to solve social and political issues by actively engaging with communities and cooperating with others who are not artists. Tania Bruguera and Theaster Gates are two examples of artists that use their creative practices to promote social change, empower underrepresented communities, and encourage conversations about critical social concerns. This current movement highlights the potential for art to be a driving force behind the transformation of society.

1.6 The Value of Difference and Acceptance

Both the artists who create contemporary art and the subjects it portrays are increasingly reflecting the importance of diversity and inclusivity in their work. This is true of both the artists and the subjects represented. The art world is gradually becoming more accepting of works created by artists hailing from historically marginalized groups, such as people of color, LGBTQ+ folks, and women. This movement is about more than just representation; it's about artists using their work to challenge prejudices, celebrate their identities, and push for social justice. Not only are inclusion and diversity essential components of the work of art itself, but they are also essential components of the art institutions, galleries, and museums that promote and showcase the work of these artists.

2. **Modern Developments in the Field of Architecture**

   2.1 Environmental Responsibility and Eco-Friendly Buildings
   The concept of sustainability is at the forefront of today's architectural practices, and there is a significant emphasis placed on the construction of structures that are both energy-efficient and kind to the environment. A defining characteristic of this movement is the incorporation of environmentally friendly technologies, as well as renewable energy sources and sustainable materials. Jeanne Gang and Bjarke Ingels are just two examples of architects who are known for their innovative approaches to environmentally friendly architecture. These approaches put an emphasis on energy efficiency and sustainable building practices.

   2.2 Digital Fabrication and the Use of Parametric Designs
   The process by which architects imagine, design, and build buildings has been revolutionized as a result of the usage of tools for parametric design and digital manufacturing. The adjustment of design factors in real time is made possible by parametric design, which ultimately results in the creation of highly complex and uniquely crafted structures. The advent of digital fabrication technologies such as 3D printing and robotic assembly has made it possible for architects to construct forms that were previously impossible to achieve but are now complicated and carefully engineered. Iconic buildings have been produced as a result of the utilization of these technologies by architects such as Frank Gehry and Zaha Hadid.

   2.3 Creative Repurposing
   Repurposing and refurbishing existing structures, frequently those with historical or architectural significance, so that they can be used for modern purposes is an example of adaptive reuse. This strategy prioritizes the conservation of cultural assets while also promoting environmentally responsible behaviors. Adaptive reuse projects have been taken on by architects and designers such as Herzog & de Meuron. These projects have provided older buildings with a new lease on life and given them a second chance in a world that is always evolving.

   2.4 Biophilic Design and Biomimetic Engineering
   The latest trend in architecture is called biomimicry, and it takes its cues for design and construction from elements of nature and the functioning of natural systems. A related trend known as "biophilic design" places an emphasis on the incorporation of natural components into man-made spaces with the goal of enhancing one's sense of well-being and connection to the natural world. Michael Pawlyn, an architect, is well-known for his work in the field of biomimicry, and the concepts of biophilic design have been implemented in a number of recent projects, including Amazon's Spheres in Seattle.

   2.5 Modern and High-Tech Buildings

ART AND ARCHITECTURE

High-tech architecture, which is distinguished by the application of cutting-edge technology and materials, has emerged as a dominant style in today's architectural landscape. Architects such as Norman Foster and Richard Rogers have been at the forefront of technological innovation, incorporating cutting-edge HVAC systems, energy-efficient building designs, and intelligent facades into their work. In high-tech architecture, innovation and functionality are frequently given precedence.

2.6 Architecture that is Both Responsive and Intelligent

Architecture that is both responsive and smart makes use of technology to create places that are both dynamic and adaptable. Structures that are outfitted with sensors, robotics, and artificial intelligence are able to adapt to shifting climatic circumstances and user preferences. An example of a "smart building" is the "The Edge" in Amsterdam, which was designed by PLP Architecture. This building makes use of data and technology to maximize user experiences as well as energy use. This trend draws attention to the fact that intelligent design has the potential to improve both the comfort and the efficiency of architectural spaces.

3. Points of Confluence Between Art and Architecture

In modern practice, the lines that once delineated art and architecture are becoming increasingly blurry and hazy. Together, artists and architects may create works that are immersive, push the limits of what's possible, and question the validity of established categories. Installation art, architectural exhibitions, and public art projects that interface with architectural contexts are examples of how installation art and architecture may work well together. This convergence of art and architecture may be seen in projects such as the Serpentine Pavilion in London, which was designed by a number of different artists and architects.

4. Obstacles and Causes for Concern

4.1 Redevelopment of Urban Areas and Gentrification

Gentrification and the eviction of long-term residents can be caused by the growing urbanization of cities and the development of upmarket, design-focused areas in those cities. In many different metropolitan centers, one of the most important concerns is how to manage the conflicting goals of architectural innovation and the preservation of existing neighborhoods.

4.2 The Balance Between the Appropriation of Other Cultures and Authenticity

In this day and age of increased global connectivity, there is a heightened awareness of the cultural appropriation that occurs in the fields of architecture and art.

Questions of cultural sensitivity and authenticity in design and construction are raised as a direct result of the requirement to both respect and appreciate cultural heritage while simultaneously promoting innovation.

4.3 Provision of Access and Encouragement of Inclusion

The fields of contemporary art and architecture are tasked with tackling the challenges of accessibility and inclusivity, ensuring that their designs are warm and inviting to people from a wide range of backgrounds. These concerns transcend beyond the realm of physical access and include the sociocultural, economic, and political spheres as well.

4.4 Application of Technology in an Ethical Manner

The incorporation of cutting-edge technologies like artificial intelligence and facial recognition into creative and architectural projects poses ethical problems around monitoring, privacy, and the protection of sensitive data. The creative industries are becoming increasingly concerned about the responsible and ethical utilization of technology.

Trends in contemporary art and architecture reflect the intricacies of our current environment, which is undergoing tremendous change. Approaches that are innovative and forward-thinking are being utilized by artists and architects as a means of responding to global concerns, advances in technology capability, and evolving cultural standards. These themes emphasize the flexibility and adaptability of creative expression in the 21st century. From the blurring of boundaries between art and architecture to the emphasis on sustainability, technology, and social involvement, these trends show how art and architecture are becoming increasingly intertwined.

Contemporary art and architecture not only serve as a reflection of the moment we live in but also as a wellspring of ideas for the foreseeable future as the globe continues to advance. These trends demonstrate the limitless potential that is available to creative minds to alter the way in which we live, engage with one another, and experience the world, while also providing solutions to the most important problems of our day. The ever-shifting environment of contemporary art and architecture is defined by the dynamic interaction between established norms and newly developed practices, aesthetics and practicality, and inventiveness and social responsibility.

8.1 Sustainable and Green Architecture

Architecture that is sustainable and green, also known as architecture that is eco-friendly or architecture that is environmentally conscious, is a design approach that places a priority on the health and happiness of both the inhabitants of the world and the planet itself. The way that buildings are conceived of, created, and operated is being reimagined by architects and designers as a response to the growing environmental concerns that are being presented, such as climate change, the depletion of resources, and urbanization. This essay investigates the ideas, methods, and innovations that underpin sustainable and green architecture. It also highlights the critical role that sustainable and green architecture plays in lessening the impact that human activities have on the environment.

ART AND ARCHITECTURE

1. **The Foundational Ideas Behind Eco-Friendly and Energy-Saving Architecture**

   1.1 Our Responsibilities to the Environment

   The concept of environmental responsibility is at the heart of sustainable and green architecture, which lays a great emphasis on its implementation. Throughout the entirety of a building's life cycle, architects and designers take into account the influence that their projects will have on the environment. This includes the phases of planning and construction, as well as operation, eventual demolition, and reuse. This requires minimizing resource use, avoiding waste, and taking into consideration the built environment's potential long-term effects on the surrounding ecosystem.

   1.2 Effective Use of Energy

   Efficiency in the use of energy is one of the core tenants of environmentally responsible
   architectural design. Because buildings are such large consumers of energy, architects work hard to cut down on building energy consumption by improving insulation, designing more effective heating and cooling systems, and incorporating renewable energy sources such as solar panels and wind turbines into their designs. The orientation and layout of buildings are another emphasis of sustainable design. The goal is to optimize the amount of natural light and ventilation that enters the building, hence lowering the need for artificial lighting and mechanical cooling.

   1.3 Utilization of Eco-Friendly Materials

   The practice of sustainable architecture encourages the employment of materials that are less harmful to the environment and that are supplied locally. Materials having a minimal carbon footprint, such as bamboo or recycled steel, as well as building components that are non-toxic and do not pollute the environment are included in this category. One of the most important tenets of green building methods is reducing the amount of materials that are used, particularly those that deplete natural resources or contribute to pollution.

   1.4 The Effective Use of Water

   The responsible use of water is yet another essential component of environmentally friendly and sustainable building. In order to cut down on the amount of water that is used, architects and designers will add low-flow plumbing fixtures, rainwater harvesting systems, and effective wastewater treatment. Innovative techniques, such as green roofs and permeable pavement, are useful for managing rainwater and reducing the load that is placed on urban drainage systems.

   1.5 The Protection of Natural Habitats and Biological Diversity

   The goal of green architecture is to preserve and improve the biodiversity of the surrounding area through the integration of natural habitats, green spaces, and vegetation into the constructed environment. Rooftop gardens, vertical gardens, and green walls not only add to a building's curb appeal, but they also generate unique microclimates, mitigate the impact of urban heat islands, and provide essential habitat for native plant and animal species.

1.6 Sense of Belonging and Community

The health and happiness of people living or working in a structure is given equal weight to the preservation of its natural surroundings in sustainable and green architecture. This strategy takes into account aspects such as the quality of the air indoors, the amount of natural lighting, and the level of thermal comfort, so producing environments that are better for the people who live there. Incorporating the ideas of biophilic design, which aim to reconnect people with the natural world, is an essential component of improving people's well-being.

2. Certifications and Standards for Eco-Friendly Buildings

2.1 This building has achieved a LEED (Leadership in Energy and Environmental Design) rating

One of the green building certification systems with the most widespread recognition is called LEED, and it was developed by the United States Green Building Council (USGBC). It assesses the performance of the building in a number of different areas, such as energy efficiency, water conservation, indoor environmental quality, and sustainable site development.

2.2 The Building Research Establishment's Energy and Environmental Assessment Method, or BREEAM for short

The British Environmental Assessment Method, or BREEAM, is a well-known and widely used green building certification system. The environmental impact of a building, from its design through its construction and operation, is evaluated using this process. The BREEAM rating system assesses a number of different aspects, including health and well-being, energy efficiency, materials, and waste management.

2.3 Out of 5 Green Stars

Green Star is a certification system that is founded in Australia and focuses on environmentally responsible and sustainable building methods. It evaluates buildings based on a variety of criteria, including management, the quality of the internal environment, energy consumption, and emissions. In addition, Green Star provides a selection of tools that are adapted to the needs of particular kinds of buildings, such as schools, residential complexes, and commercial establishments.

2.4 Passivhaus in German

The Passive House Standard, often known as Passivhaus, is an energy efficiency benchmark that buildings can voluntarily adhere to. In order to achieve great energy efficiency and occupant comfort, this design places a strong emphasis on superinsulation, airtightness, and mechanical ventilation. In spite of the fact that it was designed in Germany at first, the Passivhaus Standard has garnered acclaim all over the world.

2.5 The Challenge of Living Buildings

One of the most rigorous environmental certification schemes for buildings is called the Living Building Challenge, and it was developed by the International Living Future Institute. It places an emphasis on the construction of structures that behave as though they are "living" systems by producing more energy than they use up and making use of only non-toxic materials that are acquired from the immediate area.

3. Innovations in Environmentally Responsible Building Design

3.1 Design for Passive Solar Energy

Buildings can be heated, cooled, and lit using energy from the sun if they have been designed with passive solar architecture. It entails planning the construction of buildings in such a way as to maximize the amount of solar gain experienced during the winter and minimize the amount of heat experienced during the summer. In order to maximize a building's energy efficiency, passive solar design elements like big windows that face south, thermal mass, and shading devices are typically incorporated into the construction process.

3.2 Vegetation Coverage on the Roof and Walls

Green roofs and living walls (also known as green walls) are examples of sustainable design features that can be used to bring more flora into urban settings. Green roofs lessen the urban heat island effect while also providing insulation and reducing the amount of stormwater runoff. Living walls not only improve the beauty of a space but also the quality of the air around it and provide a habitat for various types of wildlife.

3.3 Buildings That Use No Energy At All

Buildings that create the same amount of energy in a year as they use are said to have achieved "net zero energy." In most cases, achieving net zero energy consumption requires a mix of energy-efficient design, on-site generation of renewable energy (such solar panels), and energy storage devices. These structures are a big step toward a more environmentally responsible and sustainable future.

3.4 Intelligent Building Control Systems

The administration and operation of buildings have been drastically altered as a result of developments in smart building systems and technology. These systems make use of sensors, automation, and data analytics to maximize the efficiency with which energy is used, increase the comfort of building occupants, and strengthen building security. The construction of intelligent buildings is vital to the achievement of environmentally responsible and economically sound operations.

3.5 High-Performance Front and Rear Facades

The effectiveness of a building's facade in controlling energy consumption and the quality of the inside environment is directly correlated with its level of performance. Enhancing thermal insulation, controlling solar gain, and reducing heat loss or gain can be accomplished with the help of novel materials, coatings, and design solutions. Facades that have a high level of performance contribute to the energy efficiency and occupant comfort of a building.

3.6 Construction Methods Including Prefabrication and Modularization

The use of modular and prefabricated construction systems offers a more cost-effective and environmentally responsible approach to the building process. These systems provide for the construction of individual building components away from the actual construction site, followed by the on-site assembly of those components. This not only lessens the amount of garbage produced during building, but it also speeds up the construction process, which in turn causes less interruption to the surrounding environment.

4. Examples of Eco-Friendly and Sustainable Buildings in Practice

4.1 One Angel Square, also known as the headquarters of the Co-operative Group

One Angel Square in Manchester, United Kingdom, is one of the office buildings in the world that is considered to be among the most environmentally sustainable. It received an Outstanding rating from the BREEAM certification program and is powered by a trigeneration plant that supplies heat, cooling, and electricity. In order to cut down on the amount of energy needed to run the building, innovative lighting and heating systems, in addition to a natural ventilation system, have been incorporated.

4.2 At Deloitte's headquarters, known as "The Edge"

The Edge, which is located in Amsterdam and serves as the headquarters for Deloitte, is frequently referred to as the "greenest office building in the world." Solar panels, a rainwater collection system, and other cutting-edge Internet of Things (IoT)-based smart building technologies are included in its energy-efficient design, which has earned it an Outstanding certification from BREEAM. The app for the building gives residents the ability to manage the temperature, lighting, and ventilation of their individual workspaces, as well as locate open parking spots.

4.3 The Bullitt Center (Bullitt Center)

The Bullitt Center, located in Seattle, Washington, is a commercial office building that has been awarded certification from the Living Building Challenge. It does this by installing solar photovoltaic panels, composting toilets, and rainwater collection systems, which together provide more energy than the building needs. The Bullitt Center makes use of healthy and non-toxic building materials throughout its construction and makes the most of the available natural light.

4.4 The City of Masdar

Masdar City is a planned sustainable city located in Abu Dhabi, United Arab Emirates (UAE). It is home to a number of cutting-edge sustainable and environmentally friendly architectural projects. The city is planned to have zero net emissions of carbon dioxide and will have an emphasis on sustainable transportation, waste reduction, and the utilization of renewable energy. Its structures incorporate innovative waste management systems, green roofs, and passive solar architecture to reduce their environmental impact.

4.5 Rating For The Crystal

The Crystal, which can be found in London, operates as a center for the promotion of environmentally responsible urban development. The structure is an example of environmentally responsible architecture; it is equipped with a cutting-edge water management system, energy-efficient lighting, and a variety of renewable energy technology. The Crystal is an educational and exhibition center that encourages people to engage in environmentally responsible building techniques.

5. Obstacles and Rebuttals to Criticisms

5.1 Exorbitant Beginning Prices

One of the most significant arguments against sustainable and environmentally friendly building approaches is that they can result in increased initial construction costs.

It is possible for environmentally friendly materials, energy-efficient technology, and certification procedures to have a higher initial cost, which may discourage investors and customers. However, it is essential to keep in mind that these costs are frequently compensated for by long-term savings on energy costs and benefits to operations.

5.2 The restricted availability of environmentally friendly materials

In some areas, the selection of environmentally friendly and sustainable building materials may be limited, which may provide logistical issues and lead to higher expenses. In addition, the fact that certain environmentally friendly materials might not be compliant with certain legal criteria might make it difficult to employ them in building.

5.3 Complicated Procedures for Certification

Certification systems such as LEED and BREEAM demand in-depth paperwork and evaluation, which can add extra time and money to the process of completing a project. These certification methods have been criticized for being overly bureaucratic and for producing results that may not always be representative of a building's actual environmental performance.

5.4 Striking a Balance Between Aesthetics and Environmental Impact

It can be difficult to design structures that are ecologically responsible while still satisfying aesthetic and cultural needs at the same time. Finding a happy medium between environmentally responsible architecture and aesthetically pleasing design can be challenging at times, and may call for inventive problem-solving on the part of architects and designers.

5.5 Modifications Made to Already-Existing Buildings

It can be difficult and expensive to modify old buildings so that they comply with green building standards, despite the fact that there is a growing emphasis on the sustainable design of newly constructed buildings. The problem comes in retrofitting older structures with contemporary methods and technologies for environmental sustainability.

Architecture that is both sustainable and environmentally friendly represents an important and game-changing trend in the design and construction of buildings. It does so by using environmentally friendly ideas, forward-thinking technologies, and ethical design methods in order to meet the significant concerns of resource conservation, climate change, and human well-being. The environmental crisis is becoming more widely known around the world, which has led to the continued development of sustainable design, which provides a model for a more sustainable and resilient future.

The concepts and ideas that underpin sustainable and green design are not restricted to a single structure's confines; rather, they extend beyond urban planning, infrastructure, and even entire cities. It is abundantly evident that the direction in which architecture is headed is toward a harmonious coexistence with the natural environment. This will need the creation of spaces that are not just attractive and useful, but also responsible and regenerative. Architecture that is sustainable and environmentally friendly is not just a trend; it is a must for our planet and the generations to come.

8.2 Postmodernism and Deconstructivism

Postmodernism and deconstructivism are two important architectural styles that developed in the latter half of the 20th century, challenging the modernist principles that had dominated the architectural scene for decades. Both of these major movements emerged in response to the modernist ideas that had dominated the architectural landscape. While the goal of postmodernism was to escape the strictures of modernist ideals and investigate historical allusions, the objective of deconstructivism was to dismantle established architectural conventions and challenge conventional concepts of form and structure. This essay investigates the fundamental ideas, defining traits, and significant impacts of both postmodernism and deconstructivism, focusing on the roles that these ideologies played in the development of contemporary architecture.

1. ### The Postmodern Approach to Architecture
   1.1 **Contextualism and Historical References in the Text**

   Postmodern architects frequently drew ideas for their designs from previous eras' architectural styles and incorporated components from a variety of eras' worth of history into their creations. A humorous and eclectic architectural language was created through the reinterpretation and juxtaposition of traditional vernacular building techniques, historical references, and classical design themes. Buildings that were more visually engaging and responsive to their surroundings were the consequence of contextualism's emphasis on the importance of

ART AND ARCHITECTURE

adapting to the surrounding environment and cultural context. Contextualism was a movement that began in the 1960s.

1.2 Irony with a sense of playfulness

Irony, comedy, and a sense of playfulness were incorporated into postmodern architecture as a means of posing a challenge to the solemnity and perceived rigidity of modernist architecture. In order to create visually arresting and unique designs that frequently contradicted standard assumptions, architects utilized techniques such as juxtaposition, pastiche, and exaggeration in their work. This method promoted an interpretation of architectural shapes and symbolism that was more subtle and open to individual interpretation.

1.3 The Refusal to Acknowledge Universal Truths

Postmodernism was a philosophical movement that advocated for several points of view rather than accepting the idea that there are any absolute truths. This rejection may be seen reflected in the architectural form through the utilization of asymmetry, broken geometries, and eclectic design features. Postmodern architecture frequently featured an intentional flattening of hierarchical relationships, calling into question the notion that there is a unique and best way to construct and experience buildings.

1.4 An Extravagant and Eclectic Appearance

Postmodern architecture promoted diversity and eclecticism in design, incorporating a wide range of materials, colors, and textures to produce structures that were visually dynamic and lively. Architects were able to experiment with unique and expressive design choices thanks to the use of bright colors, exaggerated forms, and unconventional materials, which resulted in structures that were visually exciting as well as cognitively rich.

2. Deconstructivist Approaches in the Field of Architecture

2.1 The Breaking Up and Moving Around of the Pieces

The fragmentation and dislocation of architectural elements is a defining trait of deconstructivist architecture. This style of architecture seeks to challenge conventional ideas of form and structure. In order to create visually complex and dynamic compositions that challenged conventional spatial assumptions, architects frequently disassembled and reconfigured the various building parts in their designs. This fragmentation enabled a new way of viewing space and shape, encouraging spectators to challenge their expectations about the architectural stability and coherence they were accustomed to thinking about.

2.2 Geometries That Aren't Based on Euclid

Deconstructivist architects embraced non-Euclidean geometries and used complicated and irregular forms that were a departure from the standard rectilinear shapes used in modernist architecture. They experimented with asymmetry, distorted planes, and skewered angles, which led to the creation of visually stunning and dynamic spatial compositions that defied the restrictions of classical geometry. Because of this deviation from traditional geometric principles, there was a need for a reconsideration of the spatial relationships and architectural limits.

2.3 Expressionism in Structural Form

The aesthetic movement known as deconstructivism placed an emphasis on the expressive potential of structure, frequently exposing the aspects of structure that lie beneath the surface in order to generate a feeling of visual mystery and complexity.

The structural components of the structures were brought to the forefront by the architects, who presented beams, columns, and trusses in novel and visually arresting configurations. This emphasis on structural expressionism attempted to challenge conventional assumptions of architectural stability and develop a deeper knowledge of the relationship between form and function. The goal of this emphasis was to inspire structural expressionism in architecture.

2.4 Experimentation with Various Materials

Deconstructivist architects were noted for their inventive use of materials and building processes; in order to realize their design ambitions, they frequently pushed the boundaries of what was possible with the materials at their disposal. They tried out uncommon building materials, such titanium, glass, and steel, in order to design structures that had a visually adventurous appearance and appeared to be technologically advanced. This focus on material experimentation brought to light the significance of materiality in terms of determining the overall aesthetic as well as the spatial experience provided by a structure.

3. Influence and Obligation

3.1 The Changing Conversation Regarding Architecture

A movement in architectural discourse was prompted by postmodernism and deconstructivism, which encouraged a more nuanced and critical study of architectural theory and practice. These groups posed opposition to the predominately modernist ideals of their day and paved the way for new paths of creative development and academic investigation. They advocated for architects to adopt a design philosophy that was more open-minded and diversified, and they suggested that architects incorporate a wider variety of cultural, historical, and philosophical elements into their projects.

3.2 Stress on Personal Perspective and Interpretation

Both postmodernism and deconstructivism placed an emphasis on the subjectivity of architectural interpretation. This encouraged viewers to interact with buildings in a manner that was more personally reflective. They inspired a reevaluation of the relationship between architecture and its social, cultural, and historical contexts, highlighting the necessity of different views and interpretations in the experience of built environments. This reevaluation was sparked as a result of the events that took place.

3.3 The Impact on Modern Methods of Design Practices
Contemporary design practices have been affected by the ideals and design tactics of postmodernism and deconstructivism. As a result, architects have been inspired to embrace an approach that is more experimental and original in terms of architectural form and expression.

Their continued emphasis on visual complexity, material experimentation, and spatial dynamism continues to influence modern design trends, so helping to cultivate a culture of architectural discovery and inventiveness.

3.4 Engagement with Architectural History from a Critical Perspective
A critical engagement with architectural history was motivated by postmodernism and deconstructivism, which encouraged architects to reevaluate the significance of previous architectural movements and its applicability to contemporary design practices. They emphasized how important a contextual understanding and historical awareness are in the process of determining the growth of architectural thought and practice, which helped to foster a more nuanced and multifaceted understanding of architectural history.

4. Contemporary Interpretations of the Text

Modern architects continue to reinterpret the tenets of postmodernism and deconstructivism,

incorporating the philosophies' ideals into fresh and forward-thinking design strategies. Reinterpretations of these trends that are prevalent in contemporary culture place an emphasis on the combination of innovation and tradition, the investigation of materiality and form, and the use of design techniques that are sustainable and mindful of the environment. In order to design structures that are reflective of the intricacies of the current built world, architects are increasingly drawing motivation from the theories of postmodernism and deconstructivism.

Postmodernism and deconstructivism are two significant architectural movements that have had a significant impact on the field and have redrawn the parameters of architectural practice and discourse. Their contributions to the development of contemporary architecture may be seen in the way that a focus is placed on contextualism, on the investigation of form and materiality, and on the celebration of diversity and complexity in design. All of these aspects are important. Deconstructivism encouraged a reevaluation of architectural stability and spatial coherence by challenging traditional conceptions of form and structure. Whereas postmodernism brought historical references and playful design aspects into architecture, deconstructivism attacked established notions of form and structure. These movements have, collectively, helped to cultivate a culture of architectural exploration and invention, which has shaped the way architects envision, design, and experience the built world.

8.3 Public Art and Urban Interventions

The use of public art and urban interventions as effective tools for altering the appearance of the urban landscape and engaging communities has become increasingly common. These creative expressions act as catalysts for change, boosting the aesthetic appeal of cities, strengthening the identity of communities, and tackling difficulties in the areas of culture, society, and the environment.

This essay investigates the significance of urban interventions and public art by focusing on the impact that these types of projects have on urban areas, communities, and the built environment.

1. **Comprehending the Concept of Public Art**
   1.1 The Availability of Access
   In order to make sure that it is accessible to a large and varied audience, works of public art are purposefully exhibited in public places. It eliminates the conventional obstacles that stand in the way of art by providing experiences that are both cost-free and accessible to people of any background or socioeconomic standing.
   1.2 Specificity to the Location
   Many works of public art are site-specific, meaning they are intended to engage with and respond to their immediate environment. Site-specific art is art that is created specifically for a location and integrates aspects of that location's history, culture, and environment. This creates
   a relationship between the artwork and its surroundings that is both distinctive and harmonious.
   1.3 Reflections on Society and Its Cultures
   Public art is frequently utilized as a forum for the expression of cultural and societal critique. Artists use their works to investigate a wide variety of topics, ranging from identity and diversity to social justice and environmental sustainability. Artists use their works in a variety of ways. These works encourage the public to participate in vital conversations and reflect the hopes and worries of the communities they serve.
   1.4 Participation and Active Participation
   The engagement and participation of viewers is encouraged through the use of public art. Whether it be through sculpture, murals, or installations, public art frequently urges viewers to participate with the artwork in some way, whether it be physically or emotionally. This engagement has the potential to heighten the overall effect of the work of art and instill a sense of ownership in the members of the audience.
2. **Different Categories of Public Art**
   2.1 Works of Sculpture
   Sculpture is one of the most common types of public art, and sculptors work with a wide variety of materials, including metal and stone as well as wood

and glass.

Sculptures, regardless of whether they are representational or abstract, frequently gain iconic status as landmarks in the cities in which they are located.

2.2 Paintings on Walls

Murals are large-scale paintings or other forms of artwork that are painted or otherwise applied directly to the walls of buildings or other types of surfaces. They are frequently utilized for the purpose of telling stories, commemorating cultural heritage, or enhancing the appearance of metropolitan areas. Murals have taken on many forms, including street art and graffiti, which have recently acquired popularity in metropolitan environments.

2.3 Assembly Procedures

Art installations can be either temporary or permanent works of art that are designed to interact with spectators in a specific setting. Changing one's perspective of space and place can be accomplished using a variety of mediums, including immersive and interactive installations as well as sculptures.

2.4 The Art of Performance

Live performances or interventions that engage the audience in a different way than usual are examples of performance art that can be found in public areas. The urban environment may serve as a stage for unplanned or planned creative expressions during these events, which may or may not be spontaneous.

3. The Effects That Public Art Has On Society

3.1 Improvements Made to the Appearance

The creation of visual attraction and an enhancement of the aesthetic appeal of public spaces are both results of the addition of public art to the urban landscape. It breathes new life into drab or neglected regions, transforming them into vivid, engaging environments that evoke feelings of awe and gratitude.

3.2 Artistic Expression of Culture

Communities are given a sense of cultural pride and identity when works of public art that celebrate their cultural heritage and variety are shown there. These artworks frequently communicate cultural narratives, historical references, and symbolic meanings that are meaningful to the inhabitants of the area in which they were created.

3.3 Participation in the Community

Engaging and interacting with the community is one of the goals of public art. It provides a stage for social events, as well as gatherings for the community and for cultural activities. It is common for communities to develop an emotional attachment to public art, which helps to build a sense of belonging and connection.

3.4 The Benefits to the Economy

The existence of public art has been shown to be associated with economic benefits for both cities and neighborhoods. It is beneficial to the local economy as it brings in tourists, which in turn enhances the value of property. Visitors who are interested in a city's creative and cultural attractions may be drawn there by the presence of public art, which can also encourage cultural tourism.

3.5 Social Movements and Political Activism

Activists and social change agents frequently utilize public art as a medium for their work. Artists utilize their work to bring attention to important social issues, to question the status quo, and to stimulate thinking and discussion. The fight for social justice, gender equality, and environmental sustainability has benefited greatly from public art's presence and participation.

4. Urban Interventions: Changing the Face of Cities

4.1 Provisional and Operational Measures

The nature of urban interventions is frequently one that is brief and strategic. Small, low-cost projects with the goal of testing ideas, gathering data, or addressing acute urban challenges can fall into this category. Pop-up parks and other temporary improvements to urban areas are examples of tactical urbanism's grassroots initiatives, which aim to make urban areas more livable on a short-term basis through the use of elements like street installations and pop-up parks.

4.2 Innovative Approaches to Solving Problems

Urban interventions require innovative approaches to problem-solving in order to successfully handle urban issues. They are looking for creative answers to problems such as the overcrowding of roads, the lack of available green space, and social isolation. These projects pose a challenge to the traditional methods that are used to plan and create cities by suggesting alternative strategies that put human well-being and interaction with their communities at the forefront.

4.3 Participation in the Community

Participation from the local community is an essential component of urban initiatives. In order to guarantee that the initiatives are responsive to the needs and wishes of the community, they frequently require collaboration with local citizens, businesses, and organizations. This strategy encourages participation from all members of the community, which helps to instill a sense of ownership and boosts pride.

4.4 Capacity for Adaptation and Flexibility

Urban interventions are adaptive and versatile, and they are able to evolve over time to suit the changing dynamics of urban environments. They are frequently conceived of as being able to be quickly modified, enlarged, or eliminated according to the requirements of the situation. Because of this versatility, urban interventions are able to respond to changing circumstances as well as feedback from the community.

5. Varieties of Urban Improvement Projects

5.1 Temporary Public Plazas and Parks

A pop-up park or plaza is a temporary installation that transforms underutilized locations, such as vacant lots or parking areas, into vibrant community meeting spots. Pop-up parks and plazas are also known as temporary public spaces. In order to make public places more inviting and interesting, these interventions frequently include the addition of landscaping, seating, and programming.

5.2 The Pedestrianization of Traffic

Pedestrianization schemes involve closing off roadways to motor vehicle traffic, either temporarily or permanently. This gives walkers and cyclists the opportunity to reclaim urban spaces. The purpose of this intervention is to increase the quality of public life while also reducing pollutants and promoting walkability.

5.3 The Practice of Guerrilla Gardening

Guerrilla gardening is the act of illegally cultivating urban sites that have been neglected or abandoned. Guerrilla gardeners are those who utilize their gardening talents to plant flowers, trees, and vegetables in areas that might use some additional greenery and could be made more aesthetically pleasing.

5.4 Graffiti and Other Forms of Urban Art

Graffiti and other forms of urban art have transitioned from being considered vandalism to being recognized as urban interventions that transform public spaces. The urban landscape serves as a canvas for artistic and social involvement in many of these creative manifestations, which frequently address social, political, and cultural issues.

5.5 Lanes for Tactical Biking

Tactical bike lanes are short-term installations that are relatively inexpensive and create dedicated cycling lanes on streets. This improves the riding environment for cyclists and encourages the use of active transportation. These interventions frequently involve the use of paint, barriers, or bollards that may be removed in order to build bike lanes in a hurry.

6. The Effects of Urban Interventions and Policies

6.1 An Increased Satisfaction with Life

The creation of urban areas that are more dynamic, accessible, and appealing is one of the many ways that urban interventions improve the quality of life in cities. They contribute to the overall well-being of the citizens by providing chances for social contact, cultural enrichment, and leisure activities for the community.

6.2 Overcoming Obstacles in Urban Areas

Specific urban problems, such as traffic congestion, a lack of green space, and social isolation are addressed by urban interventions. These projects contribute to the enhancement of urban infrastructure and the alleviation of urban problems by proposing creative solutions to the problems that are faced in urban areas.

6.3 Development of Community

Community development and social integration are encouraged by urban interventions. They inspire citizens to work together, get to know one another, and feel ownership over the urban environment in which they live. These projects frequently foster stronger social bonds and a greater sense of belonging among residents of areas.

6.4 Arenas for the Evaluation of Innovation

The urban interventions that are carried out act as testing grounds for new concepts in urban planning and design. They make it possible for cities to try out different solutions to urban problems before committing to making any changes that are long-term. This openness to experimentation is what supports a culture of constant innovation in urban planning.

6.5 Benefits to the Economy

Cities may stand to reap economic gains from urban reforms that are carried out successfully. They bring in tourists, which in turn helps local businesses thrive, and they open the door for a variety of cultural and social activities. These activities are important contributors to the expansion of the economy and to the vibrancy of metropolitan areas.

The use of urban interventions and public art are both transformative forces that help bring about the creation of cities that are more lively, engaging, and sustainable. Public art improves the aesthetic appeal of metropolitan surroundings, stimulates community participation, and honors the cultural diversity that exists in those environments. Urban interventions pose a challenge to established methods of urban planning and design by focusing on resolving particular urban issues while simultaneously encouraging community participation, adaptability, and creativity.

Both public art and urban interventions place an emphasis on the significance of community engagement, providing opportunity for locals to have a hand in shaping their urban environment and cultivating a sense of belonging in the process. These creative expressions will play an increasingly crucial role in determining the future of urban life and in inspiring positive change in our communities as cities continue to expand and face new challenges.

Chapter 9

Art and Architecture in Non-Western Cultures

The world is a patchwork of cultures, each with its own distinctive ways of expressing itself via art and architecture. These ways of expressing themselves in turn reflect the history, beliefs, values, and aspirations of the people who live in that culture. It is necessary to investigate the rich, varied, and frequently less well-known artistic traditions from non-Western nations, despite the fact that Western art and architecture have been thoroughly documented and praised for their beauty and complexity. This essay explores the art and architecture of a number of non-Western civilizations, focusing on their historical relevance, the cultural environment in which they existed, and the influence that they continue to have now.

1. **The Historical and Social Context of Art and Architecture in Non-Western Civilizations**
   1.1 The Diversity of Cultures
   The term "non-Western art and architecture" encompasses works from an incredible number of different cultures, each of which has its own set of defining traits. These civilizations can be found all throughout the world, including in places like Africa, Asia, the Middle East, Oceania, and the Americas. The great cultural diversity that exists within these countries has resulted in the development of a wide variety of artistic traditions. These artistic traditions range from the native arts of the Americas to the complex art forms of East Asia.
   1.2 Importance From a Religious and Spiritual Perspective
   Religion and other forms of spirituality are frequently given prominent placement in the visual arts and built environments of non-Western cultures. These forms of artistic expression serve the purpose of paying homage to deities, communicating spiritual narratives, and assisting in the performance of religious rites. In many instances, the cosmologies and belief systems of a society are intricately entwined with the art and architecture of that civilization. This is

especially true of non-Western cultures.

1.3 Functions of a Communal and Symbolic Nature

Symbolic and community purposes are typically served by works of art and architecture from non-Western cultures. They play an important role in rites of passage, in the coming together of the community, and in the commemoration of significant events in the life of a society. The importance of group identity and memory is frequently emphasized in non-Western art, which frequently makes use of symbolism to communicate stories, traditions, and moral lessons.

2. Works of Art and Buildings from Africa

Africa is a huge and diverse continent that is home to a plethora of artistic traditions. These traditions manifest themselves in the form of sculptures, masks, fabrics, and architectural wonders. The history of Africa, its many different civilizations, and the spiritual beliefs of its people all have a significant impact on the continent's art and architecture.

2.1 The Sculpture of Africa

The variety of styles and levels of skill found in African sculpture have earned it worldwide renown. For the creation of detailed figurative sculptures, wood, ivory, and bronze are three materials that are frequently used. Sculptures frequently depict ancestor figures, gods, or spirits, and each individual sculpture holds a special significance in the rituals, rites, and day-to-day activities of social life. The sculptures created by the Senufo people of Côte d'Ivoire and the Benin Bronzes from Nigeria are two examples that stand out as particularly notable.

2.2 Traditional African Masks

Masks play an important role in African art and may be found being used in a variety of religious and cultural ceremonies across the continent. They are frequently used as tools for transformation, allowing the wearers to connect with the spiritual world. They are manufactured in a variety of shapes and forms, and their appearance can vary greatly. Masks are traditionally worn by participants in rituals, dances, and other ceremonial activities. They are typically decorated with ornate patterns and vivid hues.

2.3 Architecture in African Countries

The wide variety of landscapes and cultural practices on Africa are reflected in the continent's architecture, which features a great deal of variety. In Africa, traditional architecture frequently makes use of materials that are found locally, such as mud, straw, and wood. The Great Mosque of Djenné in Mali is an excellent illustration of mud-brick architecture, which is a perfect example of sustainable building. Additionally, adobe construction, earthen homes, and open courtyards are all examples of unique components that can be found in African architecture. These components are a response to the climatic and sociological necessities of the regions.

ART AND ARCHITECTURE

3. **Art and Architecture from Asian Countries**
Asia is home to a diverse range of cultures and belief systems, and as a result, its art and architecture traditions include some of the world's oldest and most sophisticated examples of these fields. The people who constructed the many works of architecture in the region brought a wide variety of perspectives to their work.

3.1 Traditional Art and Architecture of China
The history of Chinese art and architecture dates back thousands of years and stretches across multiple continents. The Forbidden City in Beijing, which is included as a UNESCO World Heritage site, is an excellent illustration of the architecture of old China. Intricate calligraphy, silk paintings, and porcelain work are some of the most admired aspects of Chinese art. The Great Wall of China is a marvel of ancient architecture and a tribute to China's rich architectural heritage. It is over 13,000 miles long and covers a total distance of over 13,000 miles.

3.2 Traditional Art and Architecture of Japan
The elegance, simplicity, and focus on detail that characterize Japanese art and architecture have earned it a worldwide reputation for excellence. The wabi-sabi aesthetic is exemplified by traditional Japanese gardens, which are known for their precisely arranged landscapes, stones, and plants. Flooring made of tatami mats, sliding screens called shoji, and wooden constructions supported by post and beam are all elements of traditional Japanese architecture. The Kinkaku-ji, often known as the Golden Pavilion, can be found in Kyoto. The Ise Shrine, which is renovated every 20 years, is another notable example.

3.3 The Art and Architecture of the Indian Subcontinent
Rich cultural, religious, and creative influences from other countries have been exerting their effect on Indian art and architecture for hundreds of years. The temples of Khajuraho, which are well-known for the detailed erotic carvings they contain, are only one example of the architectural wonders that can be found in India. The ancient technique of henna tattoos and the contemporary utilization of elaborate patterns in fabrics and clothes are both examples of the vivid and detailed motifs that are characteristic of Indian art. The Taj Mahal is considered to be one of the most beautiful examples of Mughal architecture and is recognized as a UNESCO World Heritage site. It was built in the 16th century.

3.4 Art and Architecture in the Southeast Asian Region
The multifaceted history of Southeast Asia, which incorporates aspects of Indian and Chinese culture in addition to those of the region's indigenous peoples, has had an impact on the region's artistic and architectural traditions. One of the most well-known examples of architecture from Southeast Asia is found in Cambodia and is known as Angkor Wat. This complex of temples is a tribute to Khmer architecture. Angkor Wat is home to some of the most

elaborate sculptures and bas-reliefs in the world, and they tell stories from Hindu mythology.

4. **Works of Art and Architecture from the Middle East**

   The Middle East, which has been home to a number of different cultures and civilizations over the course of its history, is home to a significant creative and architectural legacy. In particular, Islamic art and architecture have left an everlasting impact on the area where they were practiced.

   4.1 The Art and Architecture of Islamic Countries

   In Islamic art and architecture, sophisticated geometric shapes, calligraphy, and patterns are frequently used in both religious and secular contexts. These elements can be seen in both religious and secular settings. The Alhambra in Spain, the Blue Mosque in Istanbul, and the Taj Mahal in India are only three examples of the prominent buildings that are built in the Islamic architectural style. The design of Islamic architecture is easily recognizable by its characteristic use of geometric tiling, elaborate domes, and pointed arches.

   4.2 The Art and Architecture of the Persian Empire

   The lavishness and intricacy of design that can be found in Persian art and architecture are two of its most lauded characteristics. The intricate designs and patterns seen on Persian carpets help to ensure their high value across the globe. The Imam Mosque in Isfahan is a great example of Persian architecture, as are the windcatchers, also known as badgirs, that are commonly used in traditional Persian buildings to facilitate natural ventilation.

5. **Art and Architecture from Oceania and Indigenous Peoples**

   The indigenous peoples of the Americas, Australia, and the Pacific Islands each have their own distinct creative traditions that are deeply ingrained in their particular environments and belief systems. These traditions have been passed down from generation to generation.

   5.1 Art from the Ocean

   Papua New Guinea, Hawaii, and Polynesia are examples of countries that contribute to what is known as "Oceanic art," which refers to the artistic expressions of cultures from across the Pacific Islands. Oceanic art is frequently characterized by ornate carvings, masks, and sculptures, with a special focus on the use of stone, shell, and wood in the creative process. Masks and sculptures are frequently utilized in a variety of rites and celebrations. These items frequently represent gods, ancestors, and other spirits.

   5.2 Art and Architecture Produced by Native Peoples in the Americas

   The native peoples of the Americas have a long and illustrious history of creative expression, which may be seen in their pottery, textiles, and sculptures. Native Americans from North America, for instance, are known for the beautiful basketry, beadwork, and totem poles that they produce.

   The Moai statues that may be found on Easter Island are some of the most well-known examples of indigenous sculpture in South America. Native American architecture frequently makes use of materials that are easily sourced in the surrounding area, such as adobe, thatch, and stone.

6. **Influence and Obligation**

6.1 **Intercultural Communication and Cooperation**

The global artistic landscape has been enriched as a result of the sharing of artistic ideas and practices between different cultures. Papermaking, printing, and pottery were only some of the artistic techniques that spread throughout the world as a result of Silk Road-facilitated cultural interaction, for instance.

6.2 **Sources of Inspiration for Artists Working Today**

The artistic traditions of non-Western cultures are frequently a source of inspiration for contemporary artists and architects. The use of themes, patterns, and cultural references originating from a variety of different cultures has become a defining characteristic of modern art. This has helped to promote an attitude of cross-cultural appreciation and collaboration.

6.3 **Preserving and Bringing Back to Life**

In recent years, there has been a growing movement toward the preservation and revitalization of historic artistic techniques. Traditional art forms have been protected thanks to the efforts of indigenous tribes and local craftspeople, which has ensured that these significant cultural manifestations will continue to flourish in the future.

6.4 **Diplomacy Through the Arts**

The fields of art and architecture are increasingly being used as instruments of cultural diplomacy, which helps nations better understand and appreciate one another. Building bridges between other cultures and fostering global cooperation have been made possible, in large part, by participating in cultural exchanges and collaborating on artistic projects.

Non-Western civilizations' artistic and architectural traditions present a rich and varied fabric of human ingenuity through their art and buildings. These expressions, which are profoundly ingrained in the history, beliefs, and values of their various cultures, shed light on the intricate web that is the human experience. It is necessary to identify and celebrate the equally rich, intricate, and meaningful artistic traditions of non-Western nations. Although Western art and architecture have frequently dominated the global discourse, it is essential to recognize and promote these traditions.

These artistic expressions not only contribute to the worldwide tapestry of art and architectural heritage but also serve as a testament to the resiliency and genius of human creation.

9.1 **Chinese Art and Architecture**

Art and architecture in China both have a long and illustrious history that can be traced back thousands of years; they are also essential parts of China's cultural legacy. This artistic heritage has affected artistic activities all around the world because it represents the values, beliefs, and social settings of the Chinese people. Art and architecture from China have left an unmistakable impression on the rest of the world, from the age-old statues of the Terracotta Army to the majesty of the Great Wall of China. This article delves into the history of Chinese art and architecture, charting its progression through a variety of dynasties and time periods to investigate its relevance and track its evolution.

1. **Traditional Art and Architecture of Ancient China**
   1.1 The Art of the Ancients
   There is evidence of prehistoric cave paintings and pottery in China that dates back as far as 20,000 years, indicating that the history of Chinese art can be traced back to the Paleolithic period. These artifacts shed light on the way of life and the beliefs of the ancient Chinese people, such as their veneration for animals and the spirits that inhabited them, as well as their relationship to nature.
   1.2 Dynasties of the Shang and the Zhou
   The Shang and Zhou dynasties (about 1600–1046 BCE) are generally regarded as the periods during which Chinese bronze casting was first developed. Artifacts made of bronze, such as ceremonial jars known as ding and jue, had complex patterns and inscriptions. The profound religious and spiritual ties that existed throughout this historical period are reflected in the ritualistic and ceremonial functions that these items played.
   1.3 Dynasty of the Qin
   The Qin Dynasty (221–206 BCE) is well known for the creation of the Terracotta Army, which is widely considered to be one of the most significant archeological finds ever made. To ensure that the first Emperor of China, Qin Shi Huang, would never be alone in the afterlife, he was entombed among thousands upon thousands of life-sized terracotta troops, horses, and chariots. Every one of these sculptures is intricately detailed in its own unique way, demonstrating a very high level of artistry and accuracy.
2. **Traditional Works of Art and Architecture from China**
   2.1 Dynasty of the Han
   The Han Dynasty, which lasted from 206 BCE until 220 CE, was a time of great artistic and architectural achievement in China. The development of new techniques for working with ceramics led to the creation of excellent porcelain pottery. The Silk Road was instrumental in promoting cultural interchange between China and other parts of the world, which ultimately resulted in the development of innovative artistic forms and methods.
   2.2 The Practice of Calligraphy as an Art Form
   The art of Chinese calligraphy, also referred to as "shufa," has a venerable and lengthy history. It is often regarded as one of the most accomplished methods of artistic expression. The art of calligraphy requires the careful execution of

brushwork as well as the utilization of a variety of styles, each of which possesses its own distinct personality and character. The evolution of this art form was significantly influenced by eminent Chinese calligraphers such as Wang Xizhi and Mi Fu, who are both examples of such artists.

2.3 Dynasty of the Tang

Many people consider the Tang Dynasty, which lasted from 618 to 907 CE, to be the golden age of Chinese art and culture. During this time period, poetry, art, and ceramics were at their creative peak. The excellent Tang tri-colored glazed ceramics and the development of landscape painting are two examples of the Tang artistic style, which is noted for its sophisticated and realistic qualities.

3. Chinese Art and Architecture from the Middle Ages

3.1 Dynasty of the Song

It was during the Song Dynasty (960–1279 CE) that significant advances were made in the fields of painting and ceramics. The "Shanshui" tradition of Song landscape painting, in particular, aimed to reflect the natural environment in a way that was expressive and passionate. During the Song dynasty, a style of porcelain known as "blue and white" was developed. This porcelain was distinguished by the application of a cobalt blue underglaze.

3.2 Dynasty of the Yuan

The Yuan Dynasty, which was governed by the Mongols and lasted from 1271 to 1368 CE, was distinguished by the influence of a wide variety of creative traditions from many places that were ruled by the Mongols. During this time period, the notion of "yuan blue and white" porcelain was introduced. This type of porcelain had exquisite designs and patterns with a lot of detail.

3.3 The Middle Ming Dynasty

The Ming Dynasty, which ruled China from 1368 to 1644 CE, is famous for its architectural accomplishments, the most notable of which being the building of the Forbidden City in Beijing. The "Longquan celadon" style of porcelain that was popular during the Ming dynasty is recognized for its elegant forms and understated green glaze. Shen Zhou and Wen Zhengming were two prominent artists working during the Ming dynasty who made important contributions to the evolution of Chinese art through their work in the landscape painting genre.

4. The Development of Contemporary Chinese Art and Architecture

4.1 Dynasty of the Qing

It was during the Qing Dynasty (1644–1912 CE) that traditional Chinese art and culture had a renaissance. At the same time, new artistic influences from other parts of the world were brought into China. The Qianlong Emperor, who was both a passionate art collector and a connoisseur, was an important contributor to the growth of art throughout the Qing dynasty. Porcelain that featured exquisite patterns and motifs, such as Famille Rose and blue and white ceramics, continued to be manufactured during this time period.

4.2 Gardens in the Traditional Chinese Style

Art, architecture, and the natural world come together seamlessly in traditional Chinese gardens. They are recognizable by the incorporation of water, rocks, pavilions, and vegetation into the design of their settings in order to achieve a sense of harmony and reflection. The classical gardens in Suzhou, which include the Humble Administrator's Garden and the Lingering Garden, are excellent examples of the intricacy that may be achieved in Chinese landscape architecture.

5. The Impact of Traditional Chinese Art and Architecture on the World

5.1 The Impact on Art of the East Asian Region

The arts and architecture of China have exerted a significant influence on the cultures of East Asia's bordering countries, most notably Japan and Korea. The artistic traditions of these countries have absorbed Chinese styles, techniques, and subjects, and have incorporated them into their own artistic canons. Chinese calligraphy and landscape painting have had a significant impact on Japanese and Korean art. This may be seen in both countries' artistic traditions.

5.2 Influence on Art Around the World

The aesthetic value of Chinese art and architecture is recognized and admired in regions

outside than East Asia. During the Age of Exploration, Europeans and people from other areas of the world had a strong need for Chinese porcelain in particular. As a result of China's sale of porcelain to other parts of the world, countries in Europe and the Middle East developed their own unique ceramic traditions.

5.3 Modern and Contemporary Art from China

The social, political, and cultural transformations that have taken place in modern China are reflected in the lively and varied realm of contemporary Chinese art. Because of their forward-thinking approaches to the artistic medium, artists such as Ai Weiwei and Xu Bing have garnered widespread acclaim around the world. The modern art scene in China continues to test the limits of tradition by investigating new forms of media and conceptual topics.

6. Conservation and Reconstruction

When it comes to protecting these cultural treasures, the preservation and restoration of Chinese art and architecture are absolutely necessary steps to take. UNESCO and the Palace Museum in Beijing are two examples of institutions that are actively engaged in efforts to preserve and protect important historical sites and artifacts. measures to preserve cultural heritage include structural repairs, artifact restoration, and measures to limit the influence of pollution and other environmental concerns.

The longevity of innovation, originality, and cultural depth can be seen in the art and architecture of China, which stands as a witness to the fact that China is one of the world's oldest civilizations. These artistic traditions reflect the complex history and

ART AND ARCHITECTURE

cultural wealth of China in a variety of forms, including porcelain, antique statues, and the vast palaces and gardens found throughout the country. Not only has the art of China shaped the visual language of East Asia, but it has also influenced the artistic traditions of other parts of the world. Along with China's ongoing modernization, the country's art and architecture are also undergoing transformations, ensuring that the legacy of this long-standing culture will continue to thrive in the contemporary world.

9.2 Japanese Traditional and Contemporary Design

Traditional elements and modern sensibilities are expertly incorporated into each and every piece of Japanese design. Japanese design, which has its origins in a deep cultural history, has developed over time to incorporate elements of modernism while retaining the features that make it unique. Japan has left an unmistakable influence on the landscape of global design, which can be seen in everything from classic architectural forms like shoin-zukuri to contemporary interiors that have a minimalist aesthetic.

This article delves into the history, fundamental characteristics, and persistent impact that Japanese design has had on the world of design. It examines the dynamic interplay that exists between traditional Japanese design and current Japanese design.

1. **Designs Inspired by Japanese Culture**

    1.1 The Philosophy of Aesthetics

    A profound reverence for brevity, the natural world, and the passage of time are the defining

    characteristics of traditional Japanese architecture and design. The concept of "Wabi-Sabi," which places an emphasis on the admiration of the natural world as well as the beauty that may be found in imperfection and transience, is fundamental to this school of thought. These principles are embodied in traditional Japanese design by characteristics such as subtle elegance, muted color palettes, and a stress on the compatibility of form and function.

    1.2 The Contribution of Shinto and Zen

    Shinto and Zen Buddhism are two prominent spiritual philosophies that have had a significant impact on traditional Japanese design. Shintoism, Japan's indigenous religion, places a strong emphasis on showing respect for the natural world and the spirits that inhabit it. This regard is reflected in the use of natural materials and motifs in design. On the other side, Zen Buddhism places a strong emphasis on simplicity and minimalism, which led to the development of Zen gardens, tea rooms, and temple architecture that exemplify these ideas.

    1.3 Architectural Styles Common in Traditional Japan

    1.3.1 Shinden-zukuri is a type of Japanese architecture that is distinguished by a central hall that is surrounded by wings on either side and a big open veranda that is frequently employed for religious and ceremonial purposes.

    1.3.2 This architectural style was developed during the Muromachi period and is marked by the use of shoji screens, tatami mat flooring, and an alcove called a tokonoma. Shoin-zukuri was named after the period in which it was developed. It is frequently connected to the tea ceremony as well as locations designed for introspection.

1.3.3 This style, known as sukiya-zukuri, places an emphasis on the aesthetics of the tea ceremony and places an emphasis on a rustic elegance that is subtle. It incorporates spaces for tea ceremonies and tea houses, both of which are intended to instill a sense of calm and awareness in their guests.

1.3.4 Minka are Japanese farmhouses built in the traditional style and often have thatched roofs and wooden beams in their construction. The history of agriculture in Japan's more remote regions is reflected in minka design.

2. **Modern and Contemporary Designs from Japan**

   2.1 The Influence of Modernism and the Bauhaus Movement

   The onset of modernism in Japan during the Meiji era (1868–1912) and the following openness of Japan to the Western world had a significant influence on the aesthetics of Japanese architecture and interior design. The Bauhaus school, which placed an emphasis on efficiency and minimalism, was a major contributor to the development of the "wa-yo-sei" or Japanese contemporary style. This design concept fuses the conventional aesthetics of Japanese culture with the fundamentals of modern design.

   2.2 Emphasis on Simplicity and Minimalism

   The terms "minimalism" and "simplicity" are frequently used to describe contemporary Japanese design. The philosophy that "less is more" can be seen reflected in both interior design and product design, as well as architecture. The impact of Zen ideas may be seen in the way that the use of neutral hues, clean lines, and uncluttered spaces generates a sense of peace and harmony.

   2.3 Innovation and Long-Term Sustainability

   The concepts of sustainability and innovation are given a significant amount of weight in contemporary Japanese design. In an effort to reduce their projects' overall impact on the environment, more and more designers and architects are turning to eco-friendly procedures and materials. These advancements can be seen mirrored in architectural designs that make the most of natural light and ventilation, as well as in product designs that place an emphasis on efficiency and sustainability.

   2.4 Kawaii, or Japanese Cuteness and Popular Culture

   The popularity of Japanese popular culture has spread throughout the world, which has a variety of effects on the design industry. The term "kawaii," which translates to "cute," is widely used in Japanese design and popular culture. Kawaii aesthetics are recognizable by their use of endearing characters and bright, cheerful colors. The youthful and upbeat spirit of Japanese culture is reflected in the aesthetic of kawaii, which is known as "cute" in Japan.

3. The Dynamic Relationship Between Classic and Modern Architecture and Interior Design

3.1 The Observance and Maintenance of Tradition
In spite of its openness to modern design, Japan continues to maintain a strong dedication to the preservation of its extensive artistic past. Ikebana, which is the skill of arranging flowers, tea ceremonies, and calligraphy are examples of traditional art forms that are still performed and appreciated today. Historic structures, such as Kyoto's Kinkaku-ji (also known as the Golden Pavilion) and Nijo Castle, serve as living examples of Japan's rich architectural history.

3.2 The Processes of Adaptation and Fusion
Japanese designers are highly talented in the art of adapting traditional features and merging them with more modern ones. For instance, traditional elements such as shoji screens and tatami flooring can be incorporated into contemporary architecture to maintain a link with Japanese culture while still embracing the benefits of modern living. In product design, fashion, and architecture, for example, classic materials and techniques are mixed with cutting-edge technology and innovation to create a fusion of the old and the modern.

3.3 The Impact on the World
The panorama of global design has been significantly altered as a result of the influence of Japanese design. It is possible to observe the impact that Japanese aesthetics, ranging from Zen simplicity to kawaii cuteness, have had on current trends in foreign design. Tadao Ando and Kengo Kuma are only two examples of the many Japanese architects who have gained international acclaim and made significant contributions to the development of contemporary architectural design.

4. The Application of Japanese Design in Everyday Life

4.1 The Structure of It
4.1.1 Tadao Ando's works include the Church of the Light and the Chikatsu-Asuka Historical Museum. Ando is well known for his minimalist use of concrete and his emphasis on the natural play of light and shadow in his architectural designs.

4.1.2 Kengo Kuma: Kuma is renowned for his use of natural materials and for putting an emphasis on linking architecture with the area in which it is located. Some of his most significant works include the Asakusa Culture and Tourist Information Center as well as the Suntory Museum of Art.

4.1.3 Shigeru Ban: Shigeru Ban is well-known for his humanitarian architecture and his designs that are environmentally friendly. He became famous all over the world for his ingenious use of paper tubes as temporary housing and constructions for those displaced by natural disasters.

4.2 Decoration of the Interior

The interior decor of Japanese homes frequently exemplifies a harmony between austerity, practicability, and attractiveness. The interiors of minimalist homes and businesses, like those found in Muji stores, place an emphasis on clean lines, neutral colors, and the effective use of space. Contemporary interiors frequently use traditional Japanese design elements such as fusuma (sliding doors), tatami floors, and shoji screens. In addition, tatami mats are frequently used as flooring.

4.3 Style and vogue

The art of Japanese fashion design is renowned worldwide for its forward-thinking aesthetics, cutting-edge innovations, and meticulous attention to detail. Issey Miyake, Yohji Yamamoto, and Rei Kawakubo are just a few of the Japanese fashion designers who have garnered international acclaim for their one-of-a-kind designs and approaches to the fashion industry. These designers push the frontiers of contemporary fashion while frequently drawing inspiration from traditional Japanese textiles and techniques and incorporating those influences into their creations.

4.4 The Design of Products

Form and function coexist harmoniously in Japanese product design, which is one of its defining characteristics. The design of the Muji brand, which places an emphasis on straightforwardness and practicability, is one example of an iconic design. Craftsmanship and attention to detail are typically exhibited in Japanese products, whether they are kitchenware, electronics, or furniture.

Traditional elements and contemporary sensibilities are able to coexist in perfect balance in Japanese design. It is a reflection of Japan's rich cultural past as well as the country's capacity to adapt to the shifting expectations of the modern world. Japanese design never ceases to enthrall and motivate members of the world's design community, whether they're drawn to the tranquil minimalism of Zen-inspired interiors or the carefree sweetness of kawaii culture.

The juxtaposition of traditional aesthetics with more modern approaches to design in Japan serves as a useful reminder that design is an art form that is ever undergoing change. When trying to solve the problems that will be faced in the 21st century, designers and architects look to the experiences of the past for guidance while also venturing into uncharted territory. The steadfast dedication to aesthetic principles and forward-thinking innovation that characterizes Japanese design is illustrative of the expansive scope of imaginative opportunities that can be realized when traditions and contemporary sensibilities are brought together in congruence.

9.3 African and Indigenous Architectural Styles

Architectural styles are a reflection of cultural diversity and distinctive ways of living in a place, and this is especially true of Africa's indigenous communities and other indigenous communities around the world. The history, beliefs, and values of the communities that gave rise to each of these architectural forms are strongly ingrained in the styles themselves. They behave in a manner that is consistent with the environmental, social, and cultural settings of the locales in which they are found.

ART AND ARCHITECTURE

This essay examines the different architectural traditions of Africa and indigenous civilizations, focusing on their historical relevance, the cultural environment in which they were developed, and their ongoing influence on modern architectural practice.

1. **Traditional Forms of African Architecture**
   1.1 The Wide Range of Architectural Styles in Africa
   Africa is a massive continent that is home to a diverse collection of architectural traditions. These traditions are a reflection of the enormous variety of cultures and surroundings that can be found on Africa. The term "African architecture" refers to a wide variety of structural styles, building methods, and building materials. For example, mud-brick homes can be found in the Sahel, whilst exquisite stone structures can be found in Ethiopia.
   1.2 Buildings Constructed Out of Earth
   The use of mud and straw as building materials is one of Africa's most widely practiced architectural styles. This architectural style is characterized by the use of readily accessible regional resources, such as mud, clay, and straw, in the construction of buildings that are ideally adapted to the environment and resources of the region. The Great Mosque of Djenné in Mali, which is listed on the UNESCO World Heritage list, is one of the most notable examples of earthen architecture. The ancient city of Timbuktu is also famous for the earthen architecture that can be seen there.
   1.3 The Architecture of the Vernacular
   The customs and rituals of various African groups have left an indelible mark on the continent's traditional architecture, known as vernacular architecture. These structures have been crafted to be in tune with their environments and to meet the particular requirements of the people who will be living in them. The towns of the Dogon people in Mali are excellent examples of how building can be harmoniously incorporated with its surrounding natural environment due to the way that their granaries and homes have been carved into the cliffs.
   1.4 Architectural Styles of the Swahili Coast
   The history of trade and cultural interchange has had a significant impact on the distinctive architectural culture that can be found throughout the Swahili Coast of East Africa. Typical components of Swahili architecture include inner courtyards, doors made of beautifully carved wood, and structures made of coral stone. Stone Town in Zanzibar is often considered to be the best example of Swahili architectural heritage anywhere in the world.
2. **Traditional Types of Native American Architecture**
   2.1 Traditional Building Practices Across the Americas
   2.1.1 Pueblo Architecture The Pueblo people of the American Southwest are responsible for the construction of multistory adobe buildings that serve as both homes and fortifications. Pueblos, like the Taos Pueblo in New Mexico, are still

used as living communities and as cultural landmarks today.

2.1.2 Longhouses Historically, indigenous peoples in the eastern woodlands of North America, such as the Iroquois, resided in structures called longhouses. Wood and bark were the primary building materials used in the construction of these communal houses, which housed extended families.

2.1.3 Inuit and Igloo Architecture The Inuit people of the Arctic areas of North America are responsible for the development of the well-known snow housing in the shape of a dome called an igloo. These constructions, which are constructed from blocks of compacted snow and provide insulation and warmth in chilly situations, are built from snow.

2.2 Traditional Building Styles Found in Oceania

2.2.1 Bure and Tiki homes: Communities such as the Fijians and Maori of New Zealand traditionally built thatched-roof homes in the Pacific Islands. These huts were referred to as "bure" and "tiki huts." The construction of these constructions involves the use of palm leaves, bamboo, and other resources that are readily available in the area.

2.2.2 Gathering Places Traditional indigenous communities in Oceania frequently constructed ornate gathering places, such as the "marae" that the Maori people of New Zealand utilize. These structures acted as focal points for gatherings and rituals that brought the community together.

3. **The Significance to History and the Circumstances of the Culture**

    3.1 The Importance of African Architecture in the World

    3.1.1 Egypt's Pyramids The ancient Egyptians built the pyramids to serve as tombs for their pharaohs. Not only did these renowned monuments demonstrate the cutting-edge architectural and engineering knowledge of their day, but they also possessed an enormous amount of religious and symbolic value.

    3.1.2 Great Zimbabwe The stone buildings of Great Zimbabwe are all that remain of a great monarchy that existed during the middle ages. The social and political order of the region is reflected in the construction of these buildings.

    3.2 The Significance of Native American Architecture

    3.2.1 Navajo Hogans The significance of the circle in Navajo culture is reflected in the circular design of Navajo hogans since the circle is seen as the center of the universe. These buildings are significant components in Navajo rituals as well as Navajo life in general.

    3.2.2 Maori Wharenui Maori meeting buildings, also known as wharenui, are characterized by exquisite carvings and have a great deal of cultural weight. The Maori sense of identity and heritage is strengthened via the telling of stories, the performance of ceremonies, and the meeting of members of the community in these places.

4. **Persistent Impact on the Design of Contemporary Architecture**

ART AND ARCHITECTURE

4.1 Design that is Sustainable and Friendly to the Environment

A lot of indigenous architectural forms put an emphasis on being environmentally friendly and efficient with resources. Contemporary architects who are interested in designing environmentally friendly and energy-efficient buildings are increasingly adopting these ideas in their work. The use of natural materials, passive heating and cooling systems, and interaction with the natural surroundings are some of the elements that have been taken from indigenous architecture.

4.2 The Interaction of Cultures and Syncretism

The varied and singular architectural traditions of Africa and other indigenous civilizations are a significant source of inspiration for contemporary architects. Syncretic architectural expressions are those that represent a fusion of traditional and contemporary aesthetics.

Old expressions are often the result of the incorporation of the fundamentals of old architectural forms into modern design.

4.3 Conservation and Protecting Our Heritage

The number of initiatives that seek to maintain and propagate the architectural traditions of indigenous communities is growing. Native American tribes and groups are actively working to preserve the architectural history and traditional building practices of their people. Modern architects work closely with these communities to ensure that the traditional architectural styles of these communities are honored and preserved.

4.4 Recognition and Appreciation Across the World

Structures such as the Great Mosque of Djenné and the rock-hewn chapels of Lalibela, Ethiopia, have been recognized as UNESCO World Heritage sites, attesting to the widespread acclaim that African architectural traditions have garnered around the world. These architectural treasures continue to motivate today's architects and bring people from all over the world to see them.

The rich and varied cultural legacy of these places is reflected in the African and indigenous architectural forms that may be seen in these areas. They respond to the social and environmental circumstances in which they exist while reflecting the values, beliefs, and practices of the communities to which they belong. Not only have these architectural styles had a significant impact on architecture of the modern era, but they also continue to serve as a source of inspiration for architects and designers all over the world.

The protection of cultural heritage and the promotion of environmentally responsible and sustainable design methods both require the preservation and celebration of these architectural traditions as key components. In a time when people all around the world are looking for ways to live in a more sustainable manner and be better stewards of the environment, the wisdom and principles that are ingrained in African and indigenous architectural forms contain important lessons for the future of architecture and design.

Chapter 10

Preservation and Challenges in the Digital Age

A new era of information has begun with the advent of the digital age, one in which the storage, diffusion, and access to knowledge have all been revolutionized by technological advancements. The protection of our cultural, scientific, and historical heritage has been confronted with a variety of opportunities and problems as a result of this shift. While the advent of digitization has made it possible to access massive archives of knowledge like never before, it has also given rise to a number of difficult problems regarding the legitimacy and long-term preservation of digital assets. The significance of preserving our cultural heritage and the knowledge that we have accumulated for the benefit of future generations is emphasized throughout this paper, along with the difficulties and opportunities presented by the digital age.

1. **The Beginning of the Digital Era: The Beginning of a New Era of Preservation**

    1.1 The Emergence of the Digital Age

    The rise of personal computers, the internet, and other digital technologies has ushered in a new era in terms of how information is generated, disseminated, and stored. This change is known as the digital revolution. It has enabled the spread of large volumes of information around the globe in a matter of seconds, thereby democratizing access to knowledge and opening it up to more people. Even though the ease of sharing digital information has brought about a multitude of positive effects, it has also given birth to a number of urgent concerns regarding the maintenance of digital content over the long term.

    1.2 The Meaning of "Digital Preservation"

    The term "digital preservation" refers to the processes, rules, and procedures that are put into place to guarantee that digital material will continue to be accessible, authentic, and usable throughout the course of time. It is a field that incorporates aspects of technology, information science, as well as archival administration. This makes it a multidisciplinary field. The purpose of digital preservation is to protect digital materials from being lost, corrupted, or rendered obsolete in the future, thereby ensuring that they can continue to be used by future generations.

1.3 The Significance of the Preservation of Digital Information
1.3.1 Cultural Heritage Digital materials provide rich records of our cultural heritage, such as historical documents, artworks, and cultural objects. These types of materials include historical documents, artworks, and cultural artifacts. Taking measures to ensure their preservation keeps alive our link to the past and paves the way for future generations to investigate their own cultural origins.

1.3.2 Scientific Research The collection of digital data, which may include datasets, simulations, and research articles, is essential to the conduct of scientific research. The safekeeping of these data is absolutely necessary for the furthering of scientific understanding as well as the reproducibility of scientific results.

1.3.3 Compliance with Legal Requirements and Regulatory Obligations Many businesses are obliged by law to store particular kinds of digital documents for predetermined amounts of time. In the event that you fail to do so, there may be legal repercussions.

1.3.4 Memory Institutions Libraries, archives, and museums are all important players in the conservation of cultural history. They have entered the digital age, and as a result, they are need to modify their preservation techniques in order to safeguard their digital holdings.

2. **Obstacles to Conservation in the Age of Digitalization**
  2.1 The Rapid Accumulation of Outdated Technology
  The rapidly accelerating rate of technological, software, and file format obsolescence is one of the most critical issues presented by digital preservation. As technology advances, digital content that was originally developed on antiquated systems will become inaccessible. It may be difficult, for instance, to retrieve data that has been stored on floppy disks, CD-ROMs, or older software if the necessary gear and software are not compatible.

  2.2 The Authenticity and Completeness of the Data
  The integrity of digital information can easily be compromised, and unauthorized parties may get access to it. Particularly important, particularly for historical documents and legal records, is the process of ensuring the validity and integrity of data. Protecting digital content from being tampered with or altered in a manner that is not allowed is a difficult and continual task.

  2.3 The Deterioration of Digital Content
  In the course of time, digital resources are vulnerable to a variety of different types of degradation, which are frequently referred to as "bit rot" or digital decay. This might happen as a result of the media degrading (for example, a hard drive failing), the file format becoming obsolete, or the data becoming corrupt.

Valuable digital assets run the risk of being lost if adequate maintenance and migration are not performed.

2.4 The Protection of Intellectual Property and Copyright

It can be difficult to successfully preserve digital content while also adhering to copyright and intellectual property rights. When digitizing and preserving items that are protected by intellectual property rights, institutions such as libraries, archives, and museums must traverse difficult legal and ethical considerations.

2.5 Costs Related to Data Volume and Storage

The sheer number of digital data that is created today is mind-boggling, and the storage of this data and the management of it is expensive. When it comes to storing digital materials, maintaining them, and providing access to them, organizations need to set aside resources.

2.6 Confidentiality and Safety

Concerns regarding users' privacy and data protection need to be taken into account during digital preservation initiatives, in particular when dealing with sensitive personal information. A careful equilibrium needs to be maintained in order to safeguard the privacy of individuals without compromising access to important historical information.

2.7 Materials That Were Born Digital

The preservation of "born-digital" materials is becoming an increasingly important obstacle to overcome as more and more content is produced digitally. This includes preserving content in many digital formats such as emails, websites, social media, and digital art, amongst others.

3. Methods and Solutions for the Preservation of Digital Content

3.1 Migratory Status

Migration is the process of shifting digital content from outmoded file formats or technologies to more modern formats that are more easily accessible. Using this method will ensure that digital content is always compatible with the latest technological developments. Migration, on the other hand, can be resource-intensive and carries the danger of compromising the original authenticity in some ways.

3.2 Modeling after

The process of establishing software or hardware environments that are capable of running older software and file formats, which enables access to legacy digital assets, is known as emulation. Emulation is very helpful when it comes to the preservation of interactive multimedia or works that are dependent on software. However, the implementation of this solution can be difficult and expensive.

3.3 Online Archival Storage Facilities

Digital repositories are safe storage systems that are meant to keep digital resources, as well as the metadata and organizational information that pertains to those digital materials, intact. Digital libraries and archives are two examples of repositories, which provide a controlled environment for the preservation of digital materials as well as access to those assets.

3.4 Verification and Correction of the Data
Data validation and fixity checks guarantee that the digital content will not be altered and will retain its original authenticity. Techniques like as checksums, cryptographic hashing, and audit trails are able to assist in the monitoring of the content's integrity when it is stored digitally.

3.5 The Process of Digital Curation
The administration of digital content along with its arrangement and recording is what's known as "digital curation," and it's done with the goal of ensuring its longevity. This comprises the formulation of policies and processes, as well as the generation of metadata and controls on access.

3.6 Standards at the National and International Level
It is absolutely necessary, for the purposes of effective digital preservation, to adhere to both national and international standards as well as best practices. Guidelines and standards for the digital preservation of information have been produced by many organizations, such as the International Organization for Standardization (ISO) and the Digital Preservation Coalition (DPC).

3.7 Working Together and Making Our Voices Heard
In the realm of digital preservation, collaboration across different types of institutions, academics, and experts is absolutely necessary. It makes possible the sharing of information, resources, and the skills of various individuals. Both increasing awareness of the significance of digital preservation and securing money for preservation activities can be accomplished through advocacy efforts.

4. Examples of Successful Archiving of Digital Content

4.1 The Archive of the Internet
The Internet Archive is a charitable organization that has saved copies of billions of websites and gives users access to historical glimpses of the internet. The success of this enormous project illustrates that it is possible to archive digital content on a broad scale.

4.2 The Digital Collections of the Library of Congress
An extensive variety of cultural and historical artifacts has been digitized and made available thanks to the efforts of the Library of Congress in the United States. Their digital collections provide access to a vast amount of cultural material, including a variety of artifacts such as maps, pictures, manuscripts, and audio recordings.

4.3 The Rosetta Space Mission
The Rosetta Project is an endeavor to save extinct languages by storing linguistic data and dictionaries. This project was started in 2001. This study highlights the significance of digital preservation in preserving linguistic variation and provides an example of its use.

5. The Prospects for Digital Archiving in the Future

5.1 Artificial intelligence and machine learning

Artificial intelligence (AI) and machine learning have recently seen significant advancements, which have made it possible to automate digital preservation operations. The categorization of content, the production of metadata, and even the prediction of preservation concerns are all possible applications for AI.

5.2 The Archiving of Websites

In spite of the ongoing development of the internet, web archiving will continue to be an essential component of digital preservation. The issues associated with preserving digital content are giving rise to the development of new methods, such as decentralized web archiving and archiving that is based on blockchain technology.

5.3 Digital Art and Materials Born in the Digital Age

The preservation of digital art and resources that were born digital, such as interactive media, 3D models, and virtual reality experiences, will become an increasingly pressing issue for cultural organizations and museums.

5.4 The Technology Behind Blockchain

The immutability of blockchain technology and the distributed ledger capabilities it offers make it a promising candidate for improving digital preservation. This would be accomplished by verifying the authenticity and integrity of digital materials.

5.5 The Role of Crowdsourcing and Citizen Archivists

The capacity for digital preservation can be increased by the participation of citizen archivists and the use of crowdsourcing. The transcription, annotation, and curation of digital collections are all areas that can benefit from the participation of online communities and volunteers.

5.6 Free and Open Access to Content and Licensing

The practices of digital preservation will continue to place a large emphasis on open access and licensing policies. Policies that allow for open access to digital content provide for more widespread and equal access to those items, while suitable licensing frameworks help balance the preservation of cultural heritage with issues of copyright.

The advent of the digital age has fundamentally altered the landscape of preservation, ushering in both previously unimaginable potential and difficult obstacles. It is of the utmost importance to undertake the job of ensuring the long-term preservation of digital information, ranging from cultural heritage to scientific data. The establishment of comprehensive preservation plans, the adoption of standards and best practices, and continued collaboration between institutions and people working in the field of digital preservation are the ways in which these problems might be overcome.

It is imperative that preservation efforts be adapted in order to maintain our digital legacy for the generations that will come after us as technology continues to advance. The advent of the digital age has the potential to endow individuals and organizations

ART AND ARCHITECTURE

with the ability to maintain their heritage, knowledge, and creativity, thereby serving as a connecting mechanism between the present and the future. Digital preservation is an undertaking that crosses cultural, geographic, and historical barriers; it is becoming increasingly important in a world that is becoming increasingly defined by its digital legacy.

10.1 Digital Documentation and Restoration

The use of digital documentation and restoration has emerged as a significant tool for the preservation and protection of cultural heritage in our age marked by rapid improvements in technological capability. This forward-thinking method makes it possible to compile exhaustive digital recordings of historical artifacts, monuments, and locations; as a result, both the preservation of these items and their accessibility to subsequent generations are ensured. The fields of heritage preservation and digital recording and restoration have seen a revolution in recent years, which has facilitated the conservation of priceless cultural assets and enabled a greater understanding of our collective history. This essay investigates the significance of digital documentation and restoration in the field of cultural heritage preservation, focusing on the impact that it has on study, conservation, and public interaction with the subject matter.

1. **The Importance of Digital Documentation to the Archiving Process**
   1.1 The Purpose and Boundaries of the Study
   The term "digital documentation" is used to describe the procedure of photographing, recording, and storing cultural artifacts, locations, and monuments in digital formats during the process of heritage preservation. This in-depth documentation features 3D scanning, high-resolution imagery, and detailed data collection, all of which contribute to the creation of digital reproductions of the original physical objects or structures. This procedure makes it possible to accurately preserve minute characteristics and proportions, so assuring that cultural material will be preserved for the foreseeable future.
   1.2 The Safeguarding of Heritage That Is In Danger
   The documenting of cultural artifacts and history in digital format is critically important to the protection of at-risk historical sites. Heritage conservationists can secure the virtual perpetuation of these assets even if the physical items are lost or destroyed by generating correct digital records of artifacts and places that are vulnerable to natural disasters, human intervention, or environmental degradation. This can be accomplished by creating accurate digital records of artifacts and locations that are vulnerable to natural disasters, human intervention, or environmental degradation.
   1.3 Improving the Quality of Research and Study
   Researchers and academics have access to vital resources, such as digital documentation, which they can use to conduct in-depth studies and analyses. Researchers now have the possibility to explore and understand cultural items and

historical locations in greater detail than ever before thanks to high-resolution 3D models and digital archives. This has led to the discovery of new information and new insights into the history and value of various cultural treasures.

2. **The Importance of Analog and Digital Restoration**

    2.1 An Explanation of What Digital Restoration Is

    The process of digital restoration involves the use of advanced digital technology to reproduce and restore cultural items and structures that have been damaged or are in the process of decaying. Digital restoration enables the rebuilding of historical situations, architectural features, and artistic aspects for contemporary audiences by applying computer-generated imagery (CGI), virtual reality (VR), and augmented reality (AR). This helps to revitalize cultural heritage for modern audiences.

    2.2 Restoring Locations of Cultural Heritage

    The preservation of heritage sites and their subsequent regeneration both benefit greatly from the use of digital restoration. Restoration specialists are able to restore historical environments and provide visitors with immersive experiences that evoke the ambiance and beauty of the past because they digitally reconstruct architectural components, ornamental details, and original color schemes. This allows the specialists to offer historical environments that have been reconstructed.

    2.3 Enhancing Presentations in Museums

    The presentation of objects and works of art in museum exhibitions can be improved by the use

    of digital restoration. Museums are able to offer visitors dynamic and interesting displays by incorporating digital visualizations and reconstructions into their exhibits. These displays can offer viewers a comprehensive understanding of the historical background, artistic approaches, and cultural relevance of the exhibits.

3. **The Steps Involved in the Digital Documentation and Restoration Process**

    3.1 Scanning and Imaging in Three Dimensions

    The process of digital documentation and restoration relies heavily on various imaging and scanning technologies, particularly those that can capture three-dimensional data. The thorough digitization of cultural artifacts and heritage locations is ensured by the use of high-resolution 3D scanners, which record detailed geometric data, in conjunction with modern imaging techniques, which record color, texture, and material properties.

    3.2 Processing of Data and Reconstruction of Images

    The processing and reconstruction of data requires the transformation of unprocessed digital data into precise three-dimensional models and virtual worlds. The processing of scanned data, the reconstruction of missing pieces, and the recreation of historical surroundings are all made possible thanks to the use of specialist software and digital platforms by restoration experts. This makes it possible to accurately preserve and restore cultural material.

3.3. The Implementation of Virtual Reality

Users are able to explore and engage with digital copies of cultural artifacts and heritage locations thanks to the incorporation of virtual reality technologies, which makes it possible for immersive digital experiences to be created and distributed. Applications for virtual reality provide a dynamic platform for public participation and educational outreach, which helps to build a greater awareness and comprehension of cultural heritage.

4. The Applications and Repercussions of Digital Documentation and Restoration

4.1 Interactive Online Exhibitions and Virtual Tours

Virtual tours and online exhibitions have been made possible thanks to improvements in digital documentation and restoration techniques. These advancements have made it possible for audiences all over the world to view and interact with cultural material without leaving the comfort of their own homes. These digital platforms offer participatory experiences that are not restricted by physical location, so facilitating cross-cultural communication and elevating global awareness of heritage.

4.2 Educational Community Involvement and Outreach

Teaching outreach initiatives have been completely transformed by digital documenting and restoration, which has enabled students and teachers to gain access to interactive learning resources as well as immersive teaching materials. Heritage preservationists can motivate the next generation to appreciate cultural heritage and advocate for its conservation by integrating digital reproductions and virtual reconstructions into school curriculum. This is one way to preserve cultural heritage.

4.3 Strategies for the Planning and Management of Conservation

The thorough digital records that are produced as a result of the process of documenting and restoring an area are beneficial to the proper planning and administration of conservation efforts. Digital data can be used by conservationists and heritage professionals to evaluate the state of cultural items, monitor changes over time, and establish sustainable preservation policies that assure the long-term protection of cultural heritage as well as its accessibility.

5. Obstacles to Overcome and Plans for the Future

5.1 The Boundaries of Current Technology and Its Availability

The lightning-fast progression of digital technologies creates issues for digital preservation platforms in terms of both their accessibility and their ability to remain operational. The deployment of standardized formats and the development of user-friendly interfaces that are able to suit a variety of audiences are required in order to guarantee the compatibility and accessibility of digital archives and virtual reconstructions for the long term.

5.2 Considerations Regarding Ethical Standards and Authenticity

Concerns about historical veracity and authenticity arise in connection with the application of
digital restoration technology, which raises ethical problems. Experts in restoration and heritage conservation continue to struggle with the difficulty of striking a balance between the use of digital upgrades and the maintenance of the building's historical integrity.

5.3 Sources of Financial Support and Funding

Obtaining the necessary financial resources can be a substantial challenge for initiatives involving full digital documentation and repair. The procurement of cutting-edge scanning equipment, the creation of cutting-edge software, and the hiring of highly skilled experts are all dependent on having sufficient funding.

5.4 Participation of the Public and Advocacy

To successfully promote the value of digital documentation and restoration, it is vital to involve the public in productive dialogue and make advocacy efforts. It is necessary to run advocacy efforts, educational activities, and public outreach programs in order to increase support for heritage preservation and create more understanding about its importance.

5.5 The Protection of Nonmaterial Cultural Heritage

Even while tangible cultural artifacts are the primary focus of digital recording and restoration efforts, intangible cultural artifacts, such as oral traditions, rituals, and performing arts, continue to present a barrier for those interested in their preservation. To successfully incorporate intangible cultural property onto digital platforms, creative ways are required.

In this day and age, the documentation and restoration of cultural artifacts using digital technology is an innovative strategy for the preservation and protection of cultural heritage. Heritage preservationists have unlocked new options for the conservation of cultural items and heritage sites, as well as for the study of those artifacts and for public interaction with those sites. These new opportunities are made possible by advanced 3D scanning, imaging, and virtual reality technology.

Even though there are still obstacles to overcome in terms of accessibility, authenticity, funding, and public participation, it is indisputable that digital documentation and restoration have had a significant impact on the conservation of cultural property. These technologies have the potential to break down geographical barriers, promote an appreciation for other cultures, and encourage future generations to become stewards of our common history. When we talk about preserving cultural heritage in this day and age, we aren't just talking about preserving the past; we're also talking about making sure that its presence in the present and the future is dynamic, engaging, and long-lasting.

10.2 Cultural Heritage Preservation and Politics

The act of protecting, conserving, and promoting the tangible and intangible legacies left behind by a society is an undertaking that is intricate and varied, and it falls under the category of "cultural heritage preservation." Nevertheless, the preservation of cultural legacy is not just a matter of historical or artistic significance; rather, it is intricately entangled with political elements that create the narratives, identities, and power relations within a community. Politics is a significant factor in influencing whether pieces of cultural heritage are highlighted, preserved, or even purposefully eradicated. In this essay, we dig into the complex relationship that exists between the preservation of cultural heritage and politics. In particular, we focus on the ways in which political ideologies, power conflicts, and the development of national identities all have an impact on how cultural heritage is preserved and interpreted.

1. **The Political Aspects of Trying to Preserve Cultural Heritage**
   1.1 Determining What Constitutes Cultural Heritage
   The factors, both physical and intangible, that contribute to the formation of a community's identity and history are included in its cultural legacy. It consists of culturally significant artifacts, monuments, traditions, languages, and practices that have been handed down from generation to generation. Protecting these aspects of cultural heritage for future generations and ensuring that their significance is acknowledged and appreciated are both necessary steps in the preservation of cultural heritage.
   1.2 The Role of Politics in the Protection of Cultural Heritage
   When governments and policymakers develop the narratives and interpretations of history to fulfill specific agendas, the preservation of cultural heritage is frequently subject to political pressures. This is because governments and policymakers affect the narratives and interpretations of history. The selection, interpretation, and presentation of cultural legacy are all susceptible to being greatly influenced by political ideology, nationalism, and power relations.
   1.3 The Relationship Between the National Identity and Cultural Heritage
   The formation of national identity is inextricably intertwined with the preservation of cultural heritage. Cultural legacy is frequently utilized by governments as a tool in an effort to cultivate a sense of national pride and unity. This is accomplished by placing an emphasis on particular historical narratives and symbols that are congruent with the predominate political ideas and ambitions of a nation.
2. **The Importance of Politics in the Protection of Cultural Heritage**
   2.1 The Practice of Selective Archiving and Deletion
   Politics has the potential to result in the selective preservation of cultural legacy or the intentional eradication of that which does not conform to the dominant narrative. Certain historical events, monuments, or cultural practices may be

emphasized or hidden in order to either promote a certain political ideology or obliterate the memory of previous injustices or conflicts. This could be done for either of these reasons.

2.2 Commemoration and the Building of the Nation

Cultural heritage is frequently used by political authorities as a means of commemorating historical events and personalities in order to bolster national narratives and cultivate a sense of collective identity among the populace. The purpose of erecting monuments, museums, and memorials is to memorialize significant events in the history of a nation and to shape the collective memory of the people living in that nation.

2.3 Diplomacy of Culture and the Use of Soft Power

In the context of international relations, cultural diplomacy and soft power are both viable applications of the concept of cultural heritage. The cultural heritage of a nation is often used by governments to create a positive image overseas, with the goals of fostering international collaboration, promoting tourism, and increasing their influence on the global stage.

3. Obstacles Facing the Conservation of Cultural Heritage

3.1 The Plagiarism and Exploitation of Different Cultures

The commodification of customs, artifacts, and indigenous knowledge can be the outcome of political and economic interests driving the exploitation and commercialization of cultural heritage. This can lead to the destruction of that legacy. Appropriation of culture has the potential to diminish the authenticity and relevance of cultural activities and artifacts, which is detrimental to the preservation of those traditions and artifacts as well as the integrity of the culture.

3.2 Memory Politics and Narratives That Contradict One Another

Memory politics is when various groups within a society defend varied views of the past in response to competing narratives about historical events and cultural heritage. This can be a result of conflicting narratives about historical events and cultural heritage. These conflicts frequently reveal long-standing social, cultural, and political divisions, which presents a challenge to the conservation and understanding of cultural assets.

3.3 The Destruction of Heritage Caused by Armed Conflict

The destruction of cultural heritage places, monuments, and artifacts can be an unintended consequence of armed conflicts and acts of warfare. During times of conflict, cultural heritage is often destroyed as unintentional "collateral damage," resulting in the loss of vital historical and cultural legacies that cannot be restored.

4. Methods for the Protection of Cultural Heritage with an Awareness of Political Considerations

4.1 Methods That Are Both Participatory And Inclusive

It is possible to hear a variety of voices and points of view when preservation efforts for cultural assets are conducted using methods that are inclusive and participatory. Participation from local communities, indigenous groups, and populations at the margins of society in the process of preserving cultural heritage contributes to the development of a more holistic understanding of cultural heritage and builds social cohesion.

4.2 Public Awareness and Educational Initiatives

It is essential to encourage public education and knowledge about the relevance of cultural heritage in order to cultivate a greater appreciation and comprehension of the complexity of history and identity. A cultural heritage that is interpreted in a way that is both more nuanced and more inclusive can be encouraged by educational efforts that place an emphasis on critical thinking and historical empathy.

4.3 Openness to the Public and Personal Responsibility

To reduce the degree to which heritage management is influenced by politics, it is vital to incorporate principles of transparency and accountability into preservation methods for cultural resources. It is possible to help avoid the exploitation and misuse of cultural property for the purposes of political gain or commercial gain by establishing explicit norms, ethical frameworks, and oversight procedures.

5. The Prospects for the Politically Conscientious Preservation of Cultural Heritage

5.1 Dismantling the Colonial Heritage

The process of decolonizing heritage requires identifying the past injustices, inequities, and exploitation that are related with cultural heritage and finding ways to solve these issues. It requires the reevaluation of colonial legacies in heritage management, as well as the recognition of indigenous knowledge and the return of looted artifacts to their rightful owners.

5.2 The Archiving and Documentation of Digital Content

Opportunities to protect cultural material from deterioration and destruction have emerged as a result of recent developments in digital documenting and preservation technology. The use of digital repositories, 3D modeling, and applications for virtual reality all give novel approaches to the documentation and sharing of history in a way that is both inclusive and easily accessible.

5.3 The Importance of International Cooperation and Solidarity

The preservation of culturally valuable heritage calls on the cooperation and unity of people from all around the world. The importance of preserving cultural heritage on a worldwide scale is highlighted by the participation of international organizations in initiatives such as UNESCO's World Heritage program, which play a pivotal role in encouraging the preservation of cultural heritage on a global scale.

5.4 The Influence that Grassroots Movements Can Have

In order to effectively advocate for the culturally sensitive protection of heritage, grassroots movements and community initiatives are extremely helpful. These movements have the potential to challenge political narratives and power dynamics, working toward the goal of ensuring that cultural legacy continues to be a representation of a varied range of voices and experiences.

The protection of cultural assets is a nuanced and intricately interconnected field that is deeply shaped by political considerations. The political ideologies, power dynamics, and national narratives that are prevalent in a culture are frequently reflected in the ways in which cultural heritage is interpreted, protected, and presented within that society. Societies may ensure that their legacy continues to be a lively and authentic representation of their diverse and growing identities if they acknowledge the politics of cultural heritage preservation, confront the issues it presents, and embrace a strategy that is more inclusive and participatory. Those who cherish and conserve the history of the past while also appreciating the inherent complexities and nuances that come with it hold the key to the future of culturally conscious heritage preservation.

10.3 The Threat of Climate Change

The threat posed by a changing climate is one of the most significant global problems we face today. It is a threat that is multifaceted and extensive, with the potential to have enormous repercussions for the environment, society, and economy all across the world. The term "climate change" refers to gradual shifts over an extended period of time in the typical weather patterns and temperature found on Earth. These shifts are mostly caused by the actions of humans. In this essay, we will investigate the factors that have led to climate change, as well as its effects, and we will look at the preventative measures that are necessary to lessen the impact of this existential risk to our planet.

1. **Factors Contributing to Climate Change**

    1.1 The Emission of Greenhouse Gases

    The release of greenhouse gases (GHGs) into the atmosphere is the principal factor responsible for the current state of the climate. These gases, which include carbon dioxide (CO_2), methane (CH_4), and nitrous oxide (N_2O), act as a blanket, retaining the heat that is generated by the sun. This results in an increase in the average temperature of the earth. The majority of greenhouse gas emissions come from human activities such as the burning of fossil fuels for energy, the destruction of forests, and various industrial processes.

    1.2 Destruction of Forests

    The capacity of the globe to absorb CO_2 is decreased as a direct result of deforestation, which is one of the main contributors to climate change. Carbon dioxide is taken in by trees and forests, which act as "sinks" for the gas and store it. This carbon that has been stored is then released into the atmosphere when forests are cut down or burned, which makes the greenhouse effect even worse.

    1.3 Methods Employed in Agriculture

Methane and nitrous oxide, two powerful greenhouse gases, are produced in substantial quantities as a byproduct of agricultural practices like animal husbandry and the application of synthetic fertilizers. Methane is produced during the digestive process of livestock, whereas nitrous oxide is produced when fertilizers are broken down in the soil.

1.4 Methods Employed in Industries

GHGs, such as carbon dioxide (CO_2) and synthetic gases like hydrofluorocarbons (HFCs), are produced as a byproduct of a number of manufacturing activities, including the production of cement and chemicals. These emissions are the byproduct of production processes that require a lot of energy as well as chemical reactions.

2. **The Effects That Climate Change Will Have**

2.1 The Increase in Temperature

Temperature increases all around the world are one of the most obvious effects that climate change will have. The global mean temperature has risen by a large amount over the course of the last century, which has resulted in heatwaves that are both more common and intense.

2.2 Ice Caps Dissolving and Rising Water Levels

The glaciers and ice caps at the poles are melting at an accelerated rate as a direct result of the higher temperatures. As a direct consequence of this, sea levels are climbing, which represents a huge risk to the communities and ecosystems that are located along the coast. The effects of rising sea levels include a rise in the frequency and severity of flooding, as well as increased erosion and population displacement.

2.3 Unusually Severe Weather Occurrences

The rise in frequency and severity of extreme weather events, such as hurricanes, droughts, wildfires, and heavy rains, has been related to climate change. These occurrences have the potential to cause severe harm to both human settlements and agricultural and other types of infrastructure.

2.4 The Depletion of Biodiversity

The effects of climate change include the disruption of ecosystems and the threat to biodiversity. A great number of species are having trouble adapting to the shifting environmental conditions, and some of them are in danger of going extinct. Temperature changes and changes in the patterns of precipitation can have an effect on food chains and ecosystems all over the world.

2.5 Acidification of the Ocean

seas around the world are taking in a disproportionate amount of carbon dioxide, which is contributing to the acidity of the seas. This process is harmful to marine life, particularly creatures with calcium carbonate shells or skeletons because it erodes the calcium carbonate. The acidification of the seas poses a risk to global food security and can destabilize entire marine ecosystems.

3. **Strategies for Risk Reduction**
   3.1 Transition to Alternative and Renewable Sources of Energy
   The shift away from fossil fuels and toward renewable energy sources like solar, wind, and hydropower is one of the most important things that can be done to slow or stop climate change. Renewable energy is sustainable, produces fewer greenhouse gas emissions, and lessens our reliance on energy sources that are high in carbon intensity.
   3.2 Effective Use of Energy
   It is possible to drastically cut greenhouse gas emissions by increasing energy efficiency across multiple sectors, including buildings, transportation, and industrial activities. Increased insulation, more fuel-efficient automobiles, and appliances that use less energy are a few examples of the types of steps that can assist conserve energy and reduce emissions.
   3.3 Reforestation and the Creation of New Forests
   Both reforestation, which is the process of restoring formerly wooded areas, and afforestation, which is the process of creating new forests, are necessary steps in the process of removing CO_2 from the atmosphere. These methods increase the capacity of carbon sinks, promote biodiversity, and reduce the rate of deforestation.
   3.4 Agriculture that is Sustainable
   A reduction in greenhouse gas emissions from the food industry is one of the potential benefits of adopting sustainable agriculture techniques. The health of the soil can be improved and emissions from livestock and fertilizers can be reduced by employing agricultural practices such as crop rotation, precision farming, and agroforestry.
   3.5 Capture and Storage of Carbon Dioxide (also Known as CCS)
   The method of carbon capture and storage involves removing emissions of carbon dioxide (CO_2) from sources such as factories or power plants and storing them in underground reservoirs. The carbon capture and storage (CCS) technology can assist cut emissions from industries that are difficult to decarbonize completely.
   3.6 Policy Concerning the Climate and International Agreements
   The United Nations Framework Convention on Climate Change and other international agreements, such as the Paris Agreement, provide a framework for coordinated action to combat climate change. Countries make a public commitment to reduce their emissions and collaborate on climate change mitigation efforts.
   In order to accomplish these objectives, it will be necessary to implement policy measures such as pricing carbon and setting emissions targets.
4. **The Significance of Collaborative Efforts Around the World**

4.1 Reducing Inequalities on a Global Scale

The effects of climate change are not being experienced in the same way by everyone. Communities that are already fragile and countries still struggling to grow typically experience the brunt of its repercussions. The pursuit of equity and assistance for these communities ought to be at the forefront of mitigation efforts.

4.2 Strategies for Climate Change Adaptation

Communities that are already being negatively impacted by the effects of climate change absolutely need to take measures to adapt. Preparedness for natural disasters, improvements to existing infrastructure, and the creation of agricultural systems that are more robust are some of these strategies.

4.3 The Advancement of Technology Via Scientific Research

It is essential to maintain scientific research and innovation in order to grasp the intricacies of climate change and discover solutions to these problems. It is possible for progress in climate change adaptation and mitigation to be driven by funding for climate research and the development of innovative technology.

The Earth and all of its inhabitants face a danger brought on by climate change that has never been seen before. Its origins can be traced back to human actions, and it will have far-reaching repercussions, having an effect not only on ecosystems but also on economies and civilizations. In order to successfully mitigate the effects of climate change, we need to make a coordinated effort to cut emissions of greenhouse gases (GHG), shift to renewable energy sources, and encourage responsible land use and agriculture.

The path toward limiting the effects of climate change is difficult, but it is not impossible to do so. We can mitigate the negative effects of climate change by working together to implement a variety of solutions, such as increasing our use of renewable energy sources and preserving our natural habitats, such as forests and oceans. It is absolutely necessary for nations all over the world to work together, with the backing of climate policies and accords, in order to address this urgent problem, safeguard our planet, and provide a sustainable future for future generations.

Chapter 11

Art and Architecture Tourism

Art and architectural tourism is a subset of cultural tourism that has seen significant growth in popularity in recent years. This is likely due to the fact that tourists are increasingly interested in having experiences that are meaningful to them and that immerse them in the rich cultural legacies of the places they visit. This specialized form of tourism includes the investigation of historical landmarks, iconic architectural marvels, renowned museums, and active art communities. It provides tourists with the opportunity to interact with a wide variety of artistic traditions and architectural styles. This essay dives into the diverse world of art and architectural tourism, focusing on its cultural value, its impact on the economy, and the life-altering experiences it provides to tourists.

1. An Awareness of the Role of Art and Architecture in Tourism

1.1 The Purpose and Boundaries of the Study

The worlds of art and architecture Traveling involves investigating and appreciating the numerous art forms, artistic traditions, and architectural marvels that may be found at different locations around the world. As they do so, tourists immerse themselves in the cultural and historical milieu of the locations they visit by engaging with the artworks, monuments, and constructions of the past and the present, both in terms of their spatial and visual aesthetics.

1.2 Importance in Cultural Aspects

Art and architecture are strong mirrors that reflect a society's norms and values as well as its history and sense of shared identity. Traveling allows individuals to get insights into the cultural fabric and artistic achievements of a particular location or group. This can be accomplished by exploring the art and architecture of the destination. This type of tourism promotes better understanding between other cultures, a greater appreciation for diversity, and the protection of existing cultural traditions.

2. The Allure of Traveling to See Works of Art and Architecture

2.1 Total Submersion in the Aesthetic and Cultural Environment

Travelers who are looking for engaging experiences that go beyond typical sightseeing are drawn to the fields of art and architecture as tourist destinations. Travelers can immerse themselves in the artistic and cultural narratives of a location by visiting historical landmarks, modern art exhibitions, and architectural wonders. This results in a deeper understanding for the destination's heritage and creative manifestations.

2.2 The Potential for Inspiring Learning and Growth

Travelers have the opportunity to learn about the development of artistic forms and architectural trends, as well as the historical settings that have affected them, which makes art and architecture tourism both informative and inspirational. Having exposure to a variety of artistic traditions can stimulate creative thought, critical analysis, and a deeper comprehension of the ways in which art and culture are intertwined.

2.3 Unforgettable Adventures Await You

Travelers can have experiences that are one-of-a-kind and unforgettable by taking part in art and architectural tourism, which can frequently be adapted to cater to the interests and preferences of individual tourists. Travelers have the opportunity to engage with local communities and cultural practitioners when they go to renowned art institutions, take architectural tours, and participate in cultural festivals and art events. This type of interaction helps to develop authentic and life-changing travel experiences.

3. Investigating World-Famous Works of Art and Buildings

3.1 Important Centers of Art and Cultural Diversity

Art and architecture aficionados from all over the world congregate in global cities such as Paris, New York, and Florence because of these cities' well-deserved reputations for having thriving art scenes and rich cultural offerings. These locations are home to some of the world's most illustrious art museums, galleries, and architectural masterpieces, which together weave together a vibrant tapestry of artistic history and modern inventiveness.

3.2 Marvels of Architecture and Important Historical Sites

Travelers are mesmerized by the intricate designs of architectural marvels such as ancient ruins, medieval cathedrals, and modernist skyscrapers due to the fact that these structures have significant historical value.

Iconic buildings and structures from all over the world, such as the Taj Mahal in India, the Colosseum in Rome, and the Sydney Opera House in Australia, are excellent examples of the wide range of architectural styles and engineering accomplishments that characterize various eras throughout history.

3.3 Neighborhoods Devoted to Contemporary Art and Vibrant Creative Scenes

Travelers will have the opportunity to engage with contemporary art movements and rising artistic expressions if they visit places like Berlin, Tokyo, and Cape Town, which all include emerging art districts and creative populations. These dynamic spaces encourage artistic creativity, cultural interchange, and the investigation of cutting-edge artistic techniques, which is a reflection of the ever-changing character of art and culture in today's modern world.

4. **The Contribution of Tourism to the Economy in the Fields of Art and Architecture**

   4.1 The Contribution of Tourism to the Economy Regarding Cultural Expenditures

   The global tourism business would not exist without the huge contributions made by art and architecture tourism. These types of tourism bring in significant revenue for destinations thanks to the money spent by tourists on things like lodging, dining, transportation, and cultural events. Tourism that focuses on art and architecture generates economic benefits that are beneficial to local companies, cultural institutions, and the preservation of heritage buildings and artistic traditions.

   4.2 The Creation of Cultural Facilities and Institutions

   The expansion of art and architecture tourism is facilitated by expenditures made in cultural infrastructure, such as the building of museums, galleries, and art centers. The economic potential of cultural tourism is recognized by both public and private organizations, and as a result, resources are allocated to the development of cultural institutions and the support of creative industries in order to create both sustainable economic development and the creation of jobs.

   4.3 Innovative Business Models and the Art Market

   Tourism centered on art and architecture encourages creative enterprise and the growth of the art market, which in turn fosters the expansion of art studios, galleries, and artisanal workshops that are geared toward meeting the needs of cultural tourists. The vitality of the local economy and cultural environment is enhanced by the cultivation of traditional forms of economic activity such as handicrafting, artistic collaboration, and the purchase of original works of art and mementos.

5. **Obstacles and Long-Term Prospects for the Art and Architecture Tourism Industry**

   5.1 The Impact of Overtourism on the Protection of Heritage

   Overtourism, which places undue stress on historically significant but fragile sites and places a burden on the community's ability to provide necessary services, can result when large numbers of tourists visit popular art and architectural areas. The integrity and authenticity of cultural landmarks and artistic treasures must be preserved by employing sustainable tourism techniques. These activities include visitor control, the implementation of carrying capacity, and community engagement.

5.2 The Misappropriation of Culture and Its Effects on Ethical Tourism

Concerns concerning cultural appropriation and the monetization of indigenous artistic traditions and history might be brought up as a result of the commercialization of art and culture in the tourism industry. For the purpose of ensuring an ethical engagement with art and architectural tourism, responsible tourism practices that promote cultural sensitivity, respect for local customs, and the fair representation and pay of cultural practitioners are essential.

5.3 Methods That Are Friendly to the Environment and Help Save the Environment

The environmental impact of art and architectural tourism, which includes carbon emissions from travel and the use of natural resources for cultural infrastructure, highlights the significance of supporting sustainable and environmentally friendly practices. These impacts include carbon emissions from travel. For the purpose of limiting the negative impact that art and architectural tourism has on the natural environment, it is essential to implement programs that place an emphasis on energy efficiency, waste reduction, and the incorporation of green technologies into cultural institutions and tourism operations.

6. The Role of New Technology and Innovation in the Tourism Industry for Art and Architecture

6.1 Electronic Documentation and Interactive Virtual Environments

Recent developments in digital documentation, virtual reality (VR), and augmented reality (AR) technology offer novel platforms for the conservation of art and architecture as well as the promotion of tourism in these fields. Through the use of digital archives, online exhibitions, and immersive virtual experiences, audiences from all over the world are able to interact with artistic expressions and cultural heritage in a way that is neither constrained by physical distance or the passage of time.

6.2 Innovative Strategies for the Tourism Industry and the Protection of Cultural Heritage

The use of "smart tourism" solutions, such as digital guides, interactive maps, and mobile applications, can improve the experience that tourists have when visiting art and architectural locations. These technologies make navigation more streamlined, give users access to information in real time, and encourage the preservation of cultural heritage through the use of digital storytelling and interactive learning experiences.

6.3 Adaptive Reuse and Environmentally Responsible Design

The concepts of green architecture and historic conservation can be supported by the use of sustainable design techniques and adaptive reuse strategies in the building of cultural infrastructure and architectural spaces. The expansion of art and architectural tourism in a sustainable manner is helped along by projects of transformation such as repurposing ancient buildings, including renewable materials, and placing an emphasis on energy-efficient design.

7. The Prospects for Tourism Involving Art and Architecture

7.1 Intercultural Communication and Affirmation of Difference

It will be important for art and architectural tourism to place an emphasis on cultural interchange and inclusivity. This will help to create collaborations between different artistic communities and encourage tourists to engage with the genuine expressions of local cultures. Tourism practices that are inclusive will cater to a wide variety of interests, so guaranteeing that the opportunity to enjoy art and architecture is available to all visitors.

7.2 Tourism That Is Good for the Environment and Responsible

The expansion of art and architectural tourism will place a strong emphasis on environmentally conscious and ethical travel practices. Travelers will increasingly seek out destinations and experiences that promote environmental conservation, ethical participation, and the preservation of cultural heritage. As a result, the travel industry will be driven to adopt more sustainable practices.

7.3 The Innovation and Accessibility of Digital Technology

Travelers will be able to enjoy cultural riches and architectural wonders through digital platforms thanks to the innovations brought about by the digital revolution, which will make art and architecture tourism more accessible. The technologies of virtual reality and augmented reality will allow interactive and instructional experiences that bring art and architecture to audiences all over the world, regardless of where they are physically located.

7.4 International Cooperation and the Promotion of Cultural Diplomacy

Travel centered around the appreciation of art and architecture will become an increasingly important component of international cooperation and cultural diplomacy. Dialog, mutual comprehension, and the celebration of cultural history as a universal and uniting aspect of the human experience will all be supported through the development of international alliances, cultural exchange programs, and the promotion of creative and architectural diversity.

The worlds of art and architecture Traveling gives tourists the chance to experience life-changing trips that completely submerge them in the world's myriad cultural manifestations and architectural marvels. This specialized form of tourism highlights the inextricable connection between art, architecture, and cultural identity. As a result, it helps to encourage understanding between different cultures, as well as economic growth and environmentally responsible activities.

The impact that art and architectural tourism has on cultural preservation, sustainable development, and global connectedness is only going to become more evident as time goes on and the industry continues to mature. Travelers, cultural practitioners, governments, and industry stakeholders all have a part to play in creating the future of art and architecture tourism. This will ensure that art and architecture tourism continues to be a vehicle for discovery, education, and the celebration of the artistic and architectural history of the world.

11.1 The Role of Tourism in Cultural Heritage

The dynamic interaction between tourism and cultural heritage helps to both maintain and promote the varied and rich legacies left behind by societies all over the world. This relationship is intertwined with both tourism and cultural heritage. The term "cultural heritage" refers to both the tangible and intangible parts of a community's identity. Some examples of tangible aspects of cultural heritage include historical places, traditions, art, and architecture. On the other hand, tourism refers to the movement of individuals who are looking for one-of-a-kind experiences, with cultural heritage frequently serving as the primary lure for tourists. This essay investigates the role that tourism plays in the preservation and promotion of cultural heritage by analyzing its relevance, benefits, and the problems it poses to these important endeavors.

1. **The Value of a Country's Cultural Heritage to the Tourism Industry**
   1.1 The Role of Cultural Heritage as an Attraction for Tourists
   The preservation of cultural traditions is essential to the success of tourism efforts. Travelers who are looking for genuine and enlightening experiences are attracted to different aspects of a country's cultural legacy, such as historical landmarks, archaeological sites, museums, traditional festivals, and architectural marvels.
   1.2 Enhancing the Vacation Experiences of Visitors
   The presence of cultural heritage can enrich visitor experiences by providing a more profound connection to the locations that are explored. The travel experience can be enhanced by cultivating an appreciation for the destination's cultural fabric through activities such as learning about local customs, artwork, historical events, and architectural landmarks.
   1.3 Promoting Understanding Across Different Cultures
   Understanding and tolerance between different cultures can be fostered through tourism that places an emphasis on cultural heritage. Travelers who immerse themselves in the practices and customs of a variety of societies and communities come away with a deeper appreciation for the importance of intercultural conversation.
2. **The Advantages of Visiting Cultural Heritage Attractions**
   2.1 The Effect on the Economy
   Destinations reap significant economic benefits from the tourism associated with their cultural heritage. It generates revenue thanks to the money spent by tourists on things like lodging, dining, getting around, and participating in cultural activities. Visiting historic sites can be beneficial to the local economy, as it helps local businesses thrive while also producing new jobs.

2.2 The Practice of Preserving and Conserving

Cultural heritage can benefit from tourism's ability to support its preservation and conservation. It is possible to reinvest funds gained by tourism activities, such as entrance fees to heritage sites or donations to museums, in initiatives to maintain and restore cultural assets, so assuring their long-term preservation.

2.3 Intercultural Communication

The practice of cultural heritage tourism makes it easier for tourists to engage in cultural activities with local people. Travelers have the opportunity to interact with local residents, cultural practitioners, and craftspeople, so helping to the continuation of cultural traditions and fostering the free flow of information and ideas.

2.4 Promotion and Educational Activities

Both outsiders and residents can learn from each other through the practice of heritage tourism. It stimulates cultural promotion and revival, creates knowledge about the significance of heritage preservation, and develops cultural awareness and appreciation.

3. The Difficulties Presented by Tourism to Cultural Heritage

3.1. Excessive Tourism

Over Tourism is one of the most significant challenges that come with cultural heritage tourism. It is possible for popular heritage sites to become overcrowded, which can have a variety of unfavorable effects, including the desecration of the sites, the exhaustion of local resources, and the disruption of local populations.

3.2 The Degradation of the Heritage

The flood of tourists can cause cultural heritage places and artifacts to get worn out and damaged over time. It is possible for visitors to do long-term damage to heritage sites by engaging in activities such as climbing on ancient structures, touching fragile artwork, and releasing pollution into the environment.

3.3 Cultural Appropriation

When tourists participate in local traditions and customs without properly appreciating or respecting the value of those traditions and customs, this behavior can be considered cultural appropriation. The result of this might be the commercialization of culture, which can threaten both the genuineness and the integrity of many cultural activities.

3.4 The Widening Gaps in Economic Status

Cultural heritage tourism has the potential to increase revenue, but it also has the potential to worsen existing economic imbalances. It is possible that local communities would not receive the full economic benefits of tourism, and that a small number of stakeholders will receive the majority of the cash generated by tourism.

4. Tourism That Does Not Harm the Cultural Heritage

4.1 Activities That Contribute to Responsible Tourism

It is imperative that responsible tourism practices be implemented in order to reduce the detrimental effects of tourism on cultural heritage. These practices include visitor management, the determination of carrying capacity, and cultural sensitivity training for tourists.

4.2 Participation in the Community
It is imperative that local communities be involved in the design and administration of cultural heritage tourism.
The cultural heritage of local communities should be presented to tourists in a way that is compatible with local values, and the local economy should be a primary focus of tourism development efforts.

4.3 An Awareness of Other Cultures
Tourists are expected to have a fundamental level of cultural awareness and sensitivity. The local customs, traditions, and practices should be respected by tourists, and they should be informed about the cultural significance of heritage sites and items before they visit those locations.

4.4 The Promotion of Long-Term Sustainability
The tourism industry that relies on cultural assets should put an emphasis on protecting the environment and making positive contributions to the community as a whole. It is possible for methods of sustainable development to ensure that the economic, social, and environmental components of tourism are in harmony with the preservation and promotion of cultural heritage by bringing these facets together.

5. **The Role of Technology and Innovation in the Tourism of Cultural Heritage**

5.1 Documentation and Experiences Conducted Digitally and Virutally
The manner in which tourists interact with cultural material has been fundamentally changed as a result of developments in digital documentation, virtual reality (VR), and augmented reality (AR) technologies. Through the use of digital archives, online exhibitions, and immersive virtual experiences, audiences all over the world are given the opportunity to investigate cultural heritage, removing geographical and temporal barriers in the process.

5.2 Innovative Answers for the Tourism Industry
At cultural heritage sites, the use of "smart tourism" technologies, such as mobile applications, interactive maps, and digital guides, improves the experience for tourists visiting these locations. These technologies deliver information in real time, assistance with navigation, and immersive learning experiences that bring the past to life.

5.3 The Conservation and Repair of Cultural Property
The protection and maintenance of cultural assets can benefit from the application of cutting-edge technology. Conservationists and restorers are able to evaluate, document, and restore heritage places and artifacts with increased

precision and efficiency because to 3D scanning, GIS (Geographic Information System) mapping, and digital modeling.

6. **The Prospects for Tourism in Cultural Heritage Areas**

6.1 Permanence and Resistance to Disruption

Destinations will progressively embrace eco-friendly methods and prepare for potential disruptions caused by climate change and other problems in order to meet the growing demand for cultural heritage tourism. This will place a greater emphasis on sustainability and resilience.

6.2 International Cooperation and the Role of Cultural Diplomacy

The field of cultural heritage tourism will be an essential component of both cultural diplomacy and international cooperation. Dialogue, mutual comprehension, and the enjoyment of cultural history as a common human experience will continue to be supported by international collaborations, cultural exchange programs, and the promotion of varied cultural manifestations.

6.3 Accessibility in the Digital Age

The accessibility of heritage sites, artworks, and cultural practices through digital platforms will become an essential component of cultural heritage tourism. This will enable people from all over the world to interact with heritage sites, artworks, and cultural practices, overcoming limits imposed by their physical locations.

6.4 The Principles of Inclusivity and Equity

The tourism industry that focuses on cultural heritage will work toward the goals of inclusivity and equity. This will ensure that the advantages of tourism are distributed among the local people and that the experiences may be enjoyed by a diverse group of tourists.

Cultural heritage tourism provides a platform for the preservation of varied cultural expressions and historical legacies around the world, as well as for their promotion and meaningful engagement with those expressions and legacies. While it does bring issues relating to overtourism, historical protection, and cultural appropriation, the future of cultural heritage tourism will be shaped by practices that are ethical and sustainable in the tourism industry, as well as by community involvement and the incorporation of emerging technologies.

Participants in cultural heritage tourism, cultural practitioners, policymakers, and industry stakeholders all have a part to play in the development of cultural heritage tourism in a responsible and sustainable manner. In this way, cultural heritage tourism can continue to act as a bridge between different cultures, so contributing to the promotion of intercultural understanding, economic expansion, and the protection of our common human heritage.

11.2 Iconic Landmarks and World Heritage Sites

The rich cultural legacies and significant historical contributions of civilizations from all over the world are attested to by iconic sites and World Heritage Sites all

ART AND ARCHITECTURE

across the planet. These locations, which are frequently recognized by the grandeur of their architecture, the significance of their historical significance, or the natural beauty of their surroundings, serve as global emblems of human achievement and of the vast cultural fabric that humans have created. This essay investigates the relevance of iconic landmarks as well as World Heritage Sites, focusing on their significance from a cultural and historical standpoint, as well as the obstacles they confront and the efforts that are dedicated to the promotion and protection of these sites.

1. **The Importance of Famous Sights and Attractions**
   1.1 Its Importance to Our Cultural and Historical Past
   Iconic landmarks are significant not only historically but also culturally since they reflect the accomplishments, values, and identities of the societies that were responsible for building them. They provide insights into the cultural history and creative expressions of past populations, embodying the architectural, artistic, and engineering skill of ancient civilizations. In addition, they were built by ancient civilizations.
   1.2 Symbolism and the Construction of Identity
   Iconic monuments frequently serve as emblems of national or regional identity, representing the distinct narratives, goals, and values of a particular town or nation. These landmarks may be found all over the world. They instill a sense of pride, solidarity, and cultural continuity in people of all ages and from a variety of ethnic backgrounds, resonating with all of these values.
   1.3 The Role That Tourist Attractions Play in the Economy
   Numerous historically significant locations have been transformed into important tourist attractions, which in turn have attracted tourists from all over the world and contributed to the economic growth of the areas in which they are located. The cash brought in by tourism thanks to these landmarks helps support local companies as well as the development of infrastructure and the conservation of cultural property.
2. **The Importance of the Sites That Make Up the World Heritage List**
   2.1 Designation as a World Heritage Site by UNESCO
   The United Nations Educational, Scientific, and Cultural Organization (UNESCO) bestows the title of "World Heritage Site" to locations that are acknowledged for their cultural, historical, or natural significance and that are considered to be of exceptional worth to all people.
   These locations are important for fostering global cooperation and intercultural communication since they symbolize the common heritage of all people.
   2.2 The Diversity of Cultures and Their Intangible Heritage
   The term "World Heritage Site" refers to a variety of cultural expressions, such as architectural marvels, archaeological sites, cultural landscapes, and intangible cultural traditions. They develop an understanding for the interconnection of

world heritage by providing insights into the depth and variety of human culture, which is a result of their contribution.

2.3 Environmentalism and the Promotion of Sustainable Development

The recognition of a location as a World Heritage Site highlights how critical it is to preserve it

and maintain it in an environmentally responsible manner. Efforts made toward the preservation of these sites frequently include the engagement of the local community, the practice of sustainable tourism, and the protection of natural ecosystems. This helps to promote the harmonious coexistence of humans and the natural world.

3. Obstacles Facing World Heritage Sites and Other Iconic Landmarks

3.1 The Negative Effects of Overtourism on the Environment

Overtourism is a problem that has arisen as a consequence of the growing popularity of iconic monuments and World Heritage Sites. This problem has resulted in overcrowding, the damage of the environment, and the deterioration of infrastructure. An excessive amount of tourism can put a strain on the available local resources and cause disruptions to the natural ecosystems in the area.

3.2 Dangers Caused Both by Nature and by Humans

There is a risk that natural disasters, pollution, and the effects of climate change will have an adverse effect on iconic landmarks and World Heritage Sites. These locations are subject to considerable dangers from factors such as rising sea levels, earthquakes, and harsh weather, which makes it imperative that appropriate conservation and disaster management policies be put into place.

3.3 Urbanization and Development That Is Not Under Control

The degradation of the surrounding environment can be caused by unregulated urban development and the extension of infrastructure around renowned landmarks and World Heritage monuments. This has the potential to have a negative impact on the historical context of these monuments as well as their overall visual integrity.

Finding a happy medium between the needs of contemporary development and the protection of cultural assets will continue to be a difficult task.

4. Efforts Made in the Areas of Preservation and Promotion

4.1 Management of Tourism That Is Sustainable

It is absolutely necessary to put sustainable tourism management techniques into action in order to reduce the detrimental effects that tourism can have on important sites and World Heritage Sites. Overcrowding and the destruction of the natural environment can be mitigated by the implementation of strategies such as tourist quotas, approved tour routes, and the promotion of appropriate travel practices.

4.2 Preservation of the Cultural and Natural Environment

It is absolutely necessary for the preservation of iconic sites and World Heritage

Sites to have conservation efforts that put an emphasis on the preservation of cultural heritage in addition to the natural environment. These efforts encompass the implementation of heritage preservation plans, the completion of restoration projects, and the promotion of environmentally friendly behaviors in order to reduce the negative impact that tourism has on the environment.

4.3 Participation in and Empowerment of the Community

Residents are more likely to feel a feeling of ownership and responsibility if their communities are involved in the process of preserving famous sites and World Heritage Sites and promoting awareness of these places. The long-term preservation of these locations can be helped along by the implementation of educational programs, community-based initiatives, and the participation of local stakeholders.

5. **The Role of Digital Technology in the Conservation of Heritage**

5.1 The Integration of Virtual Reality and Digital Documentation

The protection and promotion of historically significant landmarks and sites on the list of World Heritage Sites has been profoundly impacted by recent developments in digital recording and virtual reality technologies. The creation of digital archives, 3D models, and immersive virtual experiences has made it possible for audiences all over the world to study these places remotely, which has led to increased educational participation and accessibility.

5.2 Geotourism and the Protection of Geoheritage

Geotourism, which encourages the preservation of natural heritage and geological marvels, was developed as a result of the realization that geological features and landscapes are important components of heritage. This realization led to the creation of geotourism. Initiatives that are part of the geoheritage program enhance awareness of the geological significance of locations, which in turn fosters a broader understanding of the natural history of the Earth.

5.3 Virtual and Augmented Reality Experiences in Interactive Exhibitions

The use of augmented reality and interactive exhibitions in heritage sites and museums enriches the experiences of visitors by giving possibilities for individuals to connect with the historical and cultural narratives of these locations in a way that is both immersive and educative. Visitors are given the opportunity to engage with historical items and contexts through the use of interactive technologies, which results in a heightened understanding for cultural heritage.

6. **The Prospects for Historic Preservation and Cultural Promotion**

6.1 The Sustainable Development Goals and the Conservation of Cultural Heritage

It is possible to promote the integration of heritage conservation with larger initiatives for environmental sustainability, social inclusion, and economic growth by aligning preservation efforts with the Sustainable Development Goals (SDGs) of the

United Nations. This will ensure that the preservation of cultural heritage contributes to the well-being of communities and the planet as a whole.

6.2 International Partnerships and the Role of Cultural Diplomacy

When it comes to encouraging international collaboration for the preservation and promotion of renowned landmarks and World Heritage Sites, cultural diplomacy and global collaborations are two of the most important factors. Support for the preservation of global history and the celebration of cultural diversity can come from a variety of sources, including multilateral and bilateral agreements, cultural exchange programs, and the sharing of best practices.

6.3 Learning and Being Aware of Other Cultures

Education and cultural awareness efforts will continue to play a critical role in engaging the public and developing a sense of responsibility toward iconic landmarks and World Heritage Sites. This will be the case in the foreseeable future. A deeper understanding for the historical and cultural significance of these locations can be fostered through the implementation of educational programs, community outreach initiatives, and cultural exchange activities.

Landmarks that are instantly recognizable and places that have been designated as World Heritage Sites are significant examples of human ingenuity, cultural distinctiveness, and historical accomplishment. Their preservation and promotion call for an all-encompassing strategy that strikes a balance between the needs of the tourism industry and the requirement to safeguard cultural and natural assets. The world will continue to evolve, and as it does, innovative technology, sustainable practices, community participation, and global collaboration will play a crucial role in shaping the future of famous landmarks and World Heritage Sites. This will ensure that these sites continue to serve as unchanging icons of human culture and heritage.

11.3 Responsible Tourism and Preservation

Tourism has grown to become one of the most important industries in the world. Every year, millions of tourists travel to a variety of locations throughout the globe. Tourism presents enormous obstacles to the conservation of natural and cultural heritage, despite the fact that it has the potential to generate economic advantages and open up chances for cultural exchange. Responsible tourism, sometimes referred to as sustainable tourism, is an approach that seeks to find solutions to these problems by striking a healthy balance between the positive features of tourism and the preservation of the natural environment and cultural traditions. The idea of responsible tourism, as well as its principles, benefits, and obstacles, are investigated in this essay, with a particular emphasis placed on the role that responsible tourism plays in the preservation of cultural and natural heritage.

1. Comprehending the Concept of Responsible Tourism
   1.1 The Meaning of the Term "Responsible Tourism"

The term "responsible tourism" refers to a strategy to the travel industry that places a priority on the health and happiness of the communities that tourists visit, as well as the local environment. Its goal is to have as few negative effects as possible while having as many favorable effects as possible. This strategy encourages travelers to engage in responsible tourism and promotes ethical business practices across the board in the tourism industry.

1.2 Core Values and Guidelines for Responsible Tourism

Responsible tourism attempts to lessen the environmental footprint of travel by preserving resources, reducing waste, and supporting environmentally friendly behaviors. One way to do this is to minimize the impact that tourism has on the environment.

Travelers are strongly encouraged to respect the traditions, customs, and way of life of the places they visit and should do so out of courtesy to the local residents. This includes having an awareness of and respect for prevailing social norms and cultural mores in the area.

Promote economic growth by ensuring that tourism is beneficial to local communities by way of the creation of jobs, the promotion of sustainable business possibilities, and the payment of fair wages. Responsible tourism is a driver of economic growth.

Involve and interact with the local community One of the guiding principles of the tourism industry is to involve local communities in decision-making and to share the advantages of tourism with them. This helps to ensure that the local people benefit from tourism in a way that gives them more power.

Travelers should be encouraged to pick environmentally friendly modes of transportation, reduce the amount of energy they use, and reduce the amount of garbage they produce while yet maintaining a respectful attitude toward the natural world.

2. The Advantages of Engaging in Responsible Tourism

2.1 The Protection of the Nation's Cultural Heritage

By showing respect for and actively encouraging the continuation of local customs and rituals, responsible tourism is an essential component in the protection of cultural assets. Travelers help to preserve local customs and historical landmarks when they participate in the cultural activities of their host communities and financially support those cultures.

2.2 The Protection of the Country's Natural Heritage

The necessity of safeguarding natural heritage is emphasized when responsible tourism is practiced. Travelers and the tourism sector can lessen their negative influence on fragile ecosystems and natural habitats by engaging in activities such as responsible wildlife viewing, hiking in an environmentally responsible manner, and other ecotourism activities.

2.3 The Positive Economic Effects on the Surrounding Communities

The local economies of several popular tourist locations are entirely dependent on revenue from the industry. The practice of responsible tourism ensures that a fair share of the revenue generated by tourists is distributed directly to the local companies and communities, hence fostering economic growth.

2.4 The Promotion of Lasting Growth

By attempting to strike a healthy balance between the industry's social, environmental, and

financial impacts, responsible tourism serves as a vehicle for advancing the tenets of sustainable development. Through the preservation of resources and the upholding of the destinations' original character, this strategy guarantees that tourism will be beneficial to both current and future generations.

3. Obstacles Facing a Responsible Tourism Industry

3.1 Striking a Balance Between Economic Expansion and Conservation

Finding a happy medium between expanding the economy and protecting the local culture is one of the most significant issues that responsible tourism must face. Tourism may be essential to the economic health of individual towns, but an increase in visitor numbers may place a strain on the area's natural resources and cultural traditions.

3.2 Excessive Vacationing

An area is said to be experiencing overtourism when it receives an excessively high number of tourists, which can result in overcrowding, the destruction of natural habitats, and the disruption of local residents. Responsible tourism needs to find solutions to these problems, such as limiting the amount of tourists and minimizing the damage they cause.

3.3 The Taking of Ideas From Other Cultures

Travelers who adopt aspects of the culture they are visiting without fully comprehending or respecting the cultural value of those characteristics are guilty of cultural appropriation. Responsible tourism fosters cultural awareness as well as respect for the norms and practices of the destinations visited.

3.4 The Function of the Travel and Tourism Sector

Within the realm of ethical tourism, the tourism sector plays an essential part. Even while many companies have made a commitment to sustainable operations, it's possible that some of them put profits ahead of preservation. The difficulty that needs to be tackled by responsible tourism is getting the industry to embrace responsible practices and policies.

4. Conservation attained by the Practice of Responsible Tourism

4.1 Tourism Based on Local Communities

A kind of responsible tourism known as community-based tourism gives members of the surrounding community the ability to take an active role in tourism activities and reap the economic benefits of tourism. It grants communities the ability to exercise control over their cultural and natural heritage, allowing for the establishment of tourism activities that are congruent with the communities' core beliefs and customs.

4.2 Initiatives Towards a Sustainable Tourism

The term "sustainable tourism" refers to a wide variety of approaches that are implemented with the intention of mitigating the unfavorable effects of tourism. These include the utilization of renewable sources of energy, the reduction of waste, the preservation of natural environments, and the conservation of species. The general preservation of places is aided by efforts such as these many kinds of initiatives.

4.3 The Interpretation of Heritage

The interpretation of cultural heritage is an essential component of sustainable tourism. It entails teaching tourists about the cultural and ecological legacy of a particular location before they visit. The provision of context and the promotion of understanding are two benefits that might result from interpretation, which in turn helps to cultivate respect and appreciation for the local heritage.

4.4 Interacting With Passengers

It is crucial for the protection of history to engage travelers in engaging in responsible tourism practices. Travelers may reduce their negative influence on the environment, show respect for the cultures they visit, and patronize businesses that uphold ethical standards. They can also promote ethical travel within their social networks by sharing their experiences and encouraging others to do the same.

5. **The Role of New Technologies and Creative Thinking in Responsible Tourism**

    ## 5.1 Alternatives that Are Better for the Environment and Digital Platforms

    Travelers now have easier access to information regarding environmentally friendly options, responsible travel alternatives, and sustainable enterprises thanks to the proliferation of digital platforms and mobile apps. These technologies assist passengers in making decisions based on accurate information, which are consistent with the ideals of responsible tourism.

    ## 5.2 Virtual Tourist Attractions and Activities

    The technologies of virtual reality (VR) and augmented reality (AR) give novel ways to experience heritage sites and travel destinations. Virtual tourism experiences enable people to discover locations without actually traveling to such locations, hence lessening the negative effects of travel on the environment.

    ## 5.3 Innovative Answers for the Tourism Industry

    Responsible tourism practices can be encouraged through the use of innovative tourist solutions such as interactive maps and digital guides. They offer real-time information about sustainable transit, eco-friendly hotels, and ethical enterprises, which enables visitors to make more responsible decisions while they are on their trips.

6. **The Prospects for Conservation and Responsible Tourism in the Future**

6.1 Cooperation on a Global Scale

The difficulties of responsible tourism and the protection of heritage can only be effectively addressed through international cooperation. The management of overtourism, the protection of sensitive ecosystems, and the promotion of cultural awareness will all be assisted by international accords, partnerships, and cooperative efforts.

6.2 Instruction and Becoming Aware

Initiatives aimed at raising awareness and educating the public will continue to be an essential component of responsible tourism. Travelers have a responsibility to be informed about the fundamentals of safe travel as well as the significance of preserving cultural traditions. These efforts will not be complete without including the promotion of cultural sensitivity and environmental responsibility.

6.3 Policies for a Sustainable Tourism Industry

At the municipal, national, and international levels, tourism regulations that are sustainable are going to be very necessary for responsible travel. It is imperative that groups and governments collaborate in order to draft and enact regulations that encourage cultural preservation and environmentally responsible tourism practices.

6.4 Significant Developments in Technology

The future of environmentally conscious tourism will continue to be influenced by developments in technology. The growth of responsible tourism will be greatly aided by the development of innovative solutions that lessen the negative effects of travel on the environment, improve the experience of tourists, and advance cross-cultural understanding.

The practice of responsible tourism is essential to striking a healthy balance between the economic advantages of travel and the protection of natural and cultural resources. Responsible tourism makes a contribution to the long-term preservation of the world's heritage by putting an emphasis on activities that are environmentally friendly, participation in local communities, and ethical conduct. As the tourism industry continues to expand, the movement toward responsible tourism will play an increasingly important part in preserving and honoring the singular cultural and natural resources that contribute to the extraordinary wealth and variety of our planet.

Chapter 12

Future Trends in Art and Architecture

The realms of art and architecture have always been dynamic and continually evolving, reflecting the transitions in society, technological advancement, and human ingenuity. This has been the case since the beginning of time. As we progress farther into the 21st century, the fields of art and architecture are getting ready to see revolutionary shifts in their respective fields. This essay goes into the probable future developments in these domains, showing how rising technology, environmental concerns, social dynamics, and cultural transformations will impact the way we produce, experience, and engage with art and the built environment in the future.

1. **Developments in Art and Architecture Caused by Advances in Technology**
   1.1 The Relationship Between Virtual Reality (VR) and Digital Art
   Integration of digital technologies is having a tremendous impact on the landscape of art and architecture, both of which are being transformed as a result. The popularity of digital art, which includes a wide variety of subgenres such as computer-generated art, algorithmic art, and interactive installations, is only expected to grow. Virtual reality (VR) and augmented reality (AR) technologies are transforming the way we experience art by delivering immersive and interactive encounters with both traditional and digital works of art. These technologies are also changing the way we engage with one another.
   The use of virtual reality (VR) and augmented reality (AR) in architecture is radically altering the design and visualization processes. Virtual reality (VR) can be used by interior designers, architects, and other design professionals to produce virtual walkthroughs of buildings and spaces for clients to experience the design of the place before construction begins. By superimposing digital information on top of the real world, augmented reality (AR) helps us better comprehend architectural components and the context in which they are used.
   1.2 Applications of 3D Printing in Architectural Design

The use of 3D printing is quickly becoming a game-changer in the field of architecture. Large-scale 3D printers have made it possible for architects to produce detailed facades, complex architectural components, and even complete buildings using these machines. This technology has the ability to completely change the way that building is done, making it both more effective and more environmentally friendly while also opening the door to more creative and individualized design options.

1.3 Art and Design Produced by Artificial Intelligence

The use of artificial intelligence (AI) to create works of art and design is becoming increasingly common. The use of machine learning algorithms enables the creation of novel artistic styles, the generation of architectural designs, and even the optimization of building structures with the purpose of achieving the highest possible levels of efficiency and sustainability.

1.4 Design Based on Generations

Generative design, which is powered by algorithms and artificial intelligence, enables architects to input certain criteria, such as structural requirements and sustainability goals, and then allows the software to create various design possibilities that match these criteria. Generative design is becoming increasingly popular in the architectural industry. This method may result in architectural solutions that are more environmentally friendly, cutting-edge, and efficient.

2. Environmental Responsibility and Eco-Friendly Buildings

2.1 Materials That Are Eco-Friendly

The usage of eco-friendly and renewable resources will likely become increasingly prevalent in architectural design in the near future. It is expected that recycled and upcycled materials, in addition to novel materials such as engineered wood and sustainable alternatives to concrete, will become increasingly widespread. Using these materials to create buildings helps to minimize the overall carbon footprint of construction.

2.2 Components of Passive Design

It is expected that passive design concepts, which put an emphasis on making the most of natural ventilation, daylighting, and insulation, will continue to acquire more significance. To improve energy efficiency and the level of comfort experienced by building occupants, architects will increasingly employ passive design principles into construction projects.

2.3 Rooftop Gardens and Other Vertical Plantings

Green roofs and vertical gardens will become more widespread in urban areas, giving several benefits such as increased air quality, temperature regulation, and enhanced aesthetics. Green roofs and vertical gardens will become more common in urban areas. These urban parks and other green spaces contribute to mitigating the urban heat island effect and fostering biodiversity inside urban areas.

ART AND ARCHITECTURE

2.4 Buildings That Generate Positive Energy or Use None At All

The construction of positive-energy buildings (PEBs) and net-zero energy buildings (NZEBs) is expected to increase as the concept of sustainability becomes increasingly important. These structures generate as much or even more energy than they need, primarily through the use of renewable energy sources such as solar panels and wind turbines.

3. Creative Repurposing and the Preservation of Heritage

3.1 Creative Repurposing of Existing Structures

It will be increasingly vital to repurpose and repurpose existing buildings in innovative ways. The historical and architectural significance of older buildings will be preserved as architects and designers find new uses for them, transforming them into lively and practical spaces in the process. This technique not only lessens the amount of waste produced, but it also shows respect for the historical and cultural traditions of cities.

3.2 Heritage Conservation and Contemporary Development

Finding a happy medium between preserving cultural traditions and embracing modernization will be a continuous issue. The incorporation of modern architecture and technology into historic buildings while still paying homage to those structures' unique significance will become increasingly popular in the coming years.

3.3 The Role of Social Inclusion and Cultural Patrimony

The protection of cultural assets and the promotion of social inclusion will receive increased focus from architects and urban planners. A future increasing trend will be the design of spaces that respect and promote the cultural variety of the community while also generating a sense of belonging for all members of the community.

4. Intelligent Urban Design and Adaptive Structures

4.1 The Concept of the Smart City

The idea of "smart cities" will develop further as a result of the combination of technological advancements, data, and environmentally conscious practices. In the design of smart cities, the emphasis is placed on strengthening urban infrastructure, transit systems, and services in order to raise the standard of living, lessen the negative impact on the environment, and increase accessibility.

4.2 A Architecture That Is Responsive

Architecture that is responsive can adjust itself to the shifting requirements of its users and the surrounding environment. In the future, buildings and urban areas will contain responsive characteristics such as adjustable layouts, intelligent systems, and dynamic facades in order to maximize the efficiency of energy usage and improve the comfort of users.

4.3 The Integration of the Internet of Things (IoT)

The Internet of Things is going to become an essential component of urban planning and architecture. IoT sensors and gadgets will collect data on numerous elements of city life, such as traffic flow, energy usage, and air quality. This data will enable city planners and architects to make decisions based on the collected information.

5. **Considerations Regarding Society and Culture**

   5.1 An Inclusive Approach to Design

   The ideas of inclusive design will become more prominent, making it more likely that locations, goods, and services will be accessible to people of varying ages, abilities, and socioeconomic backgrounds. The principles of universal design will be prioritized by architects and designers so that the spaces they build may satisfy the requirements of a wide variety of users.

   5.2 Environments That Promote Wellness

   The concept of wellness will play an increasingly important role in the design of buildings and interiors. There will be a significant demand for environments that foster both physical and mental well-being, such as those with a biophilic design that integrates elements of nature. To improve the health and comfort of building occupants, architects will take into account elements such as air quality, acoustics, and lighting.

   5.3 Housing That Is Both Affordable and Sustainable

   The demand for housing solutions that are both inexpensive and environmentally friendly will be a driver of architectural innovation. Modular building, prefabricated homes, and community-driven design strategies will be investigated by architects as potential solutions to the problems of housing affordability and environmental impact.

6. **The Importance of Art in the Process of Urban Planning**

   6.1 The Role of Urban Interventions and Public Art

   Cities will continue to see improvements in both their aesthetic appeal and their cultural vitality as a result of public art and other urban initiatives. Communities will have access to focal points in the form of installations, sculptures, murals, and interactive artworks, all of which will promote creative and cultural expression in public areas.

   6.2 The Art of Placemaking

   The idea of "placemaking," which entails the construction of areas that encourage a sense of identity and belonging, will impact both the practice of urban planning and the design of buildings. The growth of cities will center on the production of spaces that are singular, welcoming, and have a cultural resonance of their own.

   6.3 Art and Environmental Responsibility

   Expressions of creativity will be important in bringing attention to issues of environmental preservation and sustainability. Communities will be engaged in a debate about climate change and ecological responsibility through the use of

art installations and architectural designs that use recycled materials, renewable energy sources, and ecological themes.
7. **Obstacles to Overcome and Ethical Considerations**

7.1 Protection of Personal Information and Data
Privacy and data security are two issues that have been brought to the forefront as a result of the growing incorporation of technology into the design of buildings and cities. It will be a huge problem to find a balance between the activities of smart cities and the security of the personal information of individuals.

7.2 The Relationship Between Gentrification and Social Equity
A increasing source of concern is the possibility of gentrification, which occurs when low-income neighborhoods are displaced as a result of urban development. In order to forestall the unfavorable effects of gentrification, urban planners and architects have a responsibility to give thought to issues of social fairness and affordable housing.

7.3 Ethical Design and the Appropriation of Cultural Values
Ethical considerations will be of increasing importance in the design process. In order to avoid engaging in cultural appropriation, architects and designers need to be aware of the practice and make sure that their work respects the historical and cultural context of the people they work with.

The terrain of the future of art and architecture is one that is both intriguing and dynamically shifting. The way in which we design and experience the built environment will continue to be shaped by developing technology, growing pressures to reduce environmental impact, and shifting patterns of social interaction. Art and architecture will play an important role in resolving the issues of the 21st century, which range from the preservation of the natural environment to the broadening of social participation. We can create spaces that are not only aesthetically inspirational but also functional, inclusive, and sustainable by embracing these future trends, which will enrich the lives of individuals as well as communities.

12.1 Technological Advancements in Design and Construction
The design and construction industries are undergoing a tremendous transformation as a result of technological developments. These advancements offer new tools, materials, and processes that improve productivity, sustainability, and creative capacity. These technologies are moving the construction industry into a future in which buildings are smarter, more sustainable, and easier to construct. Some of these technologies include the use of advanced software and automation, while others include the creation of revolutionary construction materials. This essay investigates the major technological advances in design and construction, focusing on the possible influence these developments could have on the built environment.

1. **Building Information Modeling, or BIM for short.**
   1.1 The Meaning and Importance of the Term
   The acronym BIM stands for "building information modeling," which refers to the digital depiction of the structural and operational aspects of a building. It is a tool for group collaboration that makes effective design, construction, and project administration more possible. BIM makes it possible for contractors, engineers, and architects to collaborate in an environment that is well-coordinated and full of data, which ultimately leads to improved decision-making and enhanced project outcomes.
   1.2 The Most Important Benefits
   BIM encourages collaboration between design and construction teams, which helps reduce errors, discrepancies, and disputes in the project plans. Improved communication also results from this increased level of collaboration.
   Better visualization: Building information modeling (BIM) offers a three-dimensional visual
   representation of a structure, which makes it simpler for stakeholders to comprehend the design and engage with it.
   Changes to the design can be made efficiently using BIM, which enables fast, undetectable alterations that save both time and resources during the design process.
   Clash detection: architectural information modeling (BIM) software has the capability to automatically detect clashes and conflicts between various architectural parts, hence lowering the possibility of errors occurring during construction.
   Decisions that are based on data: Building information modeling (BIM) gives users access to specific information about the building's components, which enables them to make improved choices regarding the building's materials, energy efficiency, and upkeep.
2. **Construction Through Prefabrication and Modularization**
   2.1 Fabrication in Advance
   In prefabrication, the individual components of a building are put together in a factory setting rather than on the construction site. After being transported to the construction site, these modules, wall panels, and floor systems, as well as full building modules, are ready for speedy assembly. Prefabrication offers a number of benefits, including a reduction in the amount of time needed for construction, an improvement in quality control, and a reduction in the amount of trash generated on-site.
   2.2 Construction Using Modular Components
   Prefabrication is taken to the next level with modular construction, in which entire parts or rooms of a building are made away from the construction site before being assembled into the finished structure on the construction site. This

strategy is especially useful for undertakings that require swiftness and effectiveness, such as the construction of low-cost homes and emergency shelters.

2.3 The Many Benefits That Come With Prefabrication and Modular Building

Off-site production can considerably cut down on the amount of time needed to complete a project, which results in accelerated construction schedules.

These strategies have the potential to lead to cost savings by lowering the amount of on-site labor as well as waste.

Improved quality control: Factory settings that are carefully monitored and managed ensure that building components always have a high level of quality.

Reduced waste, increased energy efficiency, and the opportunity to recycle materials all contribute to a construction process that is more environmentally friendly.

3. Robotics and Computerized Automation

3.1 Applications of Robots in Construction

Bricklaying, pouring concrete, and even site inspection are just some of the duties that are increasingly being done by robots in the construction industry. These robots are capable of completing operations that are repetitive and physically demanding with accuracy and efficiency, which ultimately improves both worker productivity and worker safety.

3.2 Drones and Other Unmanned Aerial Vehicles

Unmanned aerial vehicles (UAVs), sometimes known as drones, are extremely helpful instruments for evaluating construction sites, monitoring progress, and conducting safety inspections. They have the ability to gather data and photos with a high resolution, which assists project managers in making informed decisions and reducing risks.

3.3 Fully Self-Propelled Construction Machinery

It is anticipated that the development of autonomous construction equipment, such as self-driving trucks and bulldozers, will usher in a period of profound change throughout the industry. These machines are able to function with precision and consistency and are available around the clock, which eventually increases construction productivity.

4. The Use of 3D Printing in the Construction Industry

The additive manufacturing technique known as 3D printing is making its mark in the construction industry by enabling the creation of intricate architectural pieces and even entire buildings. Large-scale 3D printers have the ability to use a wide variety of building materials, such as concrete and recycled materials, to construct buildings in a short amount of time with a low amount of waste.

Printing in three dimensions (also known as 3D printing) enables the creation of intricate geometries at a far faster and more efficient rate than more conventional manufacturing techniques.

The use of recycled materials and the generation of very little waste are two ways in which 3D printing can contribute to more environmentally responsible building practices.

Architectural and industrial designers now have the opportunity to experiment with novel forms and shapes that would have been difficult to produce in the past.

5. **Technologically Advanced Materials and Eco-Friendly Building**

   5.1 Environmentally Friendly Materials

   To lessen its effect on the surrounding ecosystem, the construction sector is progressively shifting its focus toward environmentally friendly materials, such as recycled and renewable resources. Materials that fall within this category include, among others, engineered wood, recycled plastic composites, and sustainable alternatives to concrete. These materials retain the structural integrity of the building while also providing increased environmental performance.

   5.2 Materials Capable of Repairing Themselves

   The use of materials that can repair themselves is a game-changing innovation in the building industry. These materials have the potential to mend minor cracks and damage, which in turn extends the lifespan of structures and reduces the expenses associated with their upkeep. Self-healing concrete is one example. This type of concrete can fix cracks and heal itself when it comes into contact with water.

   5.3 Wood that is See-Through

   An intriguing new material, transparent wood combines the inherent structural strength of wood with the ability to see through the substance. It has the potential to be used in windows and walls, where it would provide insulation while also allowing natural light to enter the locations it was installed in.

6. **Environmental Monitoring and the Efficient Use of Energy**

   6.1 BEMS, which stands for Building Energy Management Systems

   Building Energy Management Systems, often known as BEMS, are rapidly becoming an essential component in the management of energy usage in buildings as well as the improvement of their sustainability. These systems gather data on energy use and assist in optimizing heating, cooling, lighting, and other systems in order to reduce the amount of energy that is wasted.

   6.2 Standards for Eco-Friendly Buildings and Passive Designs

   Architectural projects are increasingly incorporating passive design concepts, which aim to maximize the effects of natural elements like as ventilation, daylighting, and insulation. In addition, the adoption of sustainable and energy-efficient construction methods is being driven by green building standards such as LEED (Leadership in Energy and Environmental Design) and BREEAM (construction Research Establishment Environmental Assessment Method).

7. **The Prospects for Architecture and Building Construction**

ART AND ARCHITECTURE

7.1 Buildings That Are Smarter And More Connected
The incorporation of Internet of Things (IoT) technology into the architecture of buildings is going to radically alter the ways in which people interact with the places in which they live and work. The use of energy, the level of user comfort, and the level of security will all be able to be monitored and optimized in smart buildings.

7.2 Cities That Are Sustainable
There will be a significant increase in the focus placed on urban development that is environmentally responsible as the rate of urbanization continues to rise. The development of sustainable cities will rely heavily on the installation of renewable energy sources, green infrastructure, and resilient urban planning.

7.3 A Focus on the User Experience
The creation of spaces that improve human health and productivity will receive a growing amount of attention from the design and construction industries. The use of biophilic design, which brings elements of nature into man-made environments, is expected to become more widespread.

7.4 Considerations of an Ethical Nature
There will be ongoing development in the ethical issues that go into design and construction. To guarantee that their projects make a constructive contribution to society, architects and builders will need to address challenges relating to cultural sensitivity, inclusivity, and the appropriate use of technology.

The design and construction industries are being propelled into a future that places a greater emphasis on creativity, efficiency, and sustainability as a result of technological breakthroughs. These technologies are transforming the way we conceive of and create the built environment. Some examples of these technologies are building information modeling (BIM), prefabrication, 3D printing, and the use of sustainable materials. The future contains the possibility of buildings and cities that are more intelligent, more sustainable, and more human-centered in order to fulfill the demands of a world that is changing swiftly. These technologies, as they continue to progress, will be extremely helpful in meeting the issues posed by urbanization, sustainability, and the shifting requirements of society.

12.2 Cultural Exchange and Fusion
People, ideas, and influences cross national borders in a globalized world, which creates a rich tapestry of diversity and connection. Cultural interchange and fusion are fundamental components of a globalized society, which enables these things to occur. The migration of humans, the exchange of cultural materials, and the blending of traditions are the factors that shape these processes. This essay investigates the significance of cultural exchange and fusion, looking into the ways in which they effect societies, inspire innovation, and contribute to the ever-evolving identities of individuals, communities, and the world at large.

1. The Workings of Intercultural Communication
   1.1 The Meaning of It
   An individual, a group, or an entire society can participate in a cultural exchange when they interact with one another and share cultural components, ideas, practices, and traditions. It can happen as a result of many different activities, such as traveling, migrating, trading, communicating, or expressing oneself creatively.
   1.2 A Look Back at Some Historical Perspectives
   The practice of exchanging one culture for another is not a recent development but rather one that has ancient historical roots. Throughout the course of history, trade routes such as the Silk Road made it easier for people from the East and the West to exchange commodities, ideas, and cultures with one another. Between the 15th and the 20th centuries, European, African, Asian, and Indigenous American cultures came into touch with one another as a result of exploration and colonialism. This resulted in the mixing of linguistic styles, cultural practices, and culinary techniques.
   1.3 The Part That Technology Plays
   The contemporary period has seen a significant increase in the amount of cultural exchange due to the developments in technology, notably in the fields of communication and transportation. People from all over the world are now connected thanks to the proliferation of the internet, social media, and travel, which has made it possible for them to instantaneously share information and experiences with one another.
2. Syncretism and the Fusing of Different Cultures
   2.1 The Meaning of It
   Syncretism is another name for the process that cultural fusion refers to. Cultural fusion is the process wherein components of multiple cultures mix, melting together to generate new cultural forms, practices, or traditions. This occurrence takes place whenever two or more cultural groups contact, which results in a blending of the traditions, languages, and artistic expressions of both of the participating groups.
   2.2 Some Instances of the Merging of Cultures
   Cuisine: The coming together of different culinary traditions has resulted in the creation of dishes such as currywurst, which is a blend of Indian curry and German sausages. Sushi burritos, on the other hand, are a fusion of Japanese and Mexican cuisines.
   Jazz, for example, is a kind of musical expression that originated as a result of the collision of African, European, and American musical influences.
   Creole languages, such as Haitian Creole, are the outcome of a linguistic fusion that brought together elements of African, European, and Indigenous languages.

Art: Contemporary art frequently combines a wide range of artistic forms, approaches to material construction, and cultural references and inspirations.

3. **The Importance of Intercultural Communication and Merging of Cultures**

   3.1 Strengthening the Existence of Diverse Cultures

   Through the introduction of novel concepts, behaviors, and points of view, cultural interaction and fusion contribute to the richness of the fabric that is cultural diversity. The interactions between people of other cultures allow individuals to accept and appreciate one another's unique qualities, which ultimately leads to more tolerance and comprehension.

   3.2 Promoting Creative Thinking

   The interaction of different cultures is frequently a source of inventiveness and creativity. Individuals might be motivated to generate fresh artistic expressions, culinary creations, technological advances, and social behaviors when they are exposed to new ideas and viewpoints.

   3.3 Encouraging Citizenship in the World Community

   Individuals are encouraged to identify with humankind as a whole rather than merely with their own local or national identity through the cultivation of a feeling of global citizenship through the practice of cultural exchange. This way of thinking encourages cooperation on a global scale, as well as empathy and solidarity.

4. **Problems and Debates**

   4.1 The Taking of Ideas From Other Cultures

   A complicated problem known as cultural appropriation emerges when components of one culture are taken from or imitated by members of another culture without the former group having an understanding, authorization, or respect for the cultural significance of the items in question. It typically leads to the perpetuation of prejudices and can result in the misrepresentation and commercialization of certain cultural practices.

   4.2 The Maintenance of a Cultural Sense of Self

   Cultural interaction and fusion have the potential to be beneficial experiences, but they also have the potential to provide obstacles to the maintenance of cultural identities.

   For instance, the rapid globalization of popular culture can contribute to the degradation of traditional traditions and languages, particularly among indigenous and underprivileged populations. This is especially true in the case of indigenous communities.

   4.3 Uneven Distribution of Power

   The process of cultural exchange does not necessarily occur in a balanced manner. It is sometimes influenced by power inequalities, in which dominant cultures push their customs and values on less powerful ones. This can have a significant impact. This can lead to the suppression of alternative voices and ideas as well as the establishment of cultural hegemony.

5. **Some Modern Illustrations of Cultural Mixing and Exchange**

    5.1 The Culture of Food

    In the realm of substantial cultural interaction and fusion, the realm of food is one of the most prominent examples. The proliferation of food trucks and restaurants that serve dishes that combine elements from a variety of different cuisines exemplifies the phenomena that is fusion cuisine's rise to prominence on a worldwide scale.

    5.2 Language and the Appropriation of Other Languages

    Language is a living, evolving thing that frequently adopts words, phrases, and idioms from other countries and cultures. The English language, for instance, is full of words borrowed from other languages; this is a reflection of centuries' worth of cultural contact and trade.

    5.3 Creative Expressions: Art and Music

    Frequently serving as examples of cultural fusion is contemporary art and music. Artists usually take their inspiration from a variety of different civilizations, fusing together a wide variety of artistic styles and mediums. Composers and musicians are renowned for their ability to create music that defies categorization according to standard genres.

6. **The Prospects for Intercultural Communication and Merging of Cultures**

    6.1 Technologies and Methods of Connection

    The ease of communication and travel will further accelerate the mixing of different cultures as technological advancements continue to be made. Immersive experiences will be created via revolutionary technologies such as virtual reality, augmented reality, and others. These experiences will allow individuals to interact with people from other cultures in ways that have never been possible before.

    6.2 Respect for Cultural Traditions and Preserving Traditions

    It is very possible that in the future, there will be an increasing focus placed on honoring and preserving cultural customs and traditions, particularly within populations that are excluded. The efforts that are made to resist cultural appropriation and to enhance understanding of the cultural value of behaviors and symbols are going to become more prominent.

    6.3 Education and Conscientization of the World

    The development of a global awareness and the promotion of cultural interaction will largely be the responsibility of educational institutions. The curriculum will place an emphasis on cross-cultural communication, the development of empathy, and the promotion of a feeling of global citizenship among the student body.

    The interconnected world we live in is defined in large part by the transformational forces of cultural exchange and fusion. Our lives are enriched as a result of their presentation of novel concepts, practices, and points of view. However, this does not mean that there aren't any difficulties associated with these processes; for example, cultural appropriation and the loss of cultural identities. Respect, comprehension, and empathy are the three most important qualities to cultivate in order to successfully develop healthy cultural interaction and fusion. As we move forward, we should enjoy the diversity that these processes provide while also protecting the authenticity of the distinctive customs and rituals that are associated with each culture. By doing so, we can establish a global society that is more welcoming, harmonious, and that recognizes and respects the richness that comes from the diversity of cultural traditions.

12.3 The Role of Art and Architecture in Shaping the Future

Art and architecture have always played an important part in the process of building the environment we live in by reflecting the ideals, aspirations, and technological capabilities of the times in which they were created. The roles that art and architecture play in defining our future are more important than they have ever been before, given the fast shifting global context we find ourselves in today. This essay investigates the complex link that exists between art, architecture, and the future. It focuses on the ways in which these three fields impact one another and contribute to the development of both our built environment and cultural landscape.

1. **The Point of Confluence Between Art and Architecture**
   1.1 An Explanation of What Art and Architecture Are
   Although many people consider art and architecture to be two separate fields, there are many underlying connections between the two. Both of these ways of expressing oneself creatively require the manipulation of space, form, and materials, as well as the use of cultural symbols, in order to convey thoughts, feelings, and principles.
   The border that separates art and architecture is an arbitrary one because both fields constantly inspire and are influenced by one another.
   1.2 The Relationship Throughout History
   Art and architecture have constantly influenced one another and co-evolved throughout the course of history. Ancient civilizations such as the Greeks and Romans incorporated artistic aspects into their architectural designs. During the Middle Ages, Gothic cathedrals were famous for successfully fusing structural and artistic features into a single building. Art and architecture began to converge during the Renaissance period, which was characterized by its emphasis on humanism and proportion. This convergence can be seen in the works of artists such as Leonardo da Vinci and Filippo Brunelleschi.
2. **Art and Architecture as Forms of Identity Expression**
   2.1 Sense of Belonging to a Culture
   Expressions of cultural identity can be powerfully conveyed via the mediums of art and architecture. They reflect a society's historical narratives and worldviews

while also transmitting its values, beliefs, and collective memory to subsequent generations. A culture's artistic expressions and architectural styles provide a visual depiction of the culture's individuality through their aesthetic qualities.

2.2 Movements and Styles in Architectural Design

A number of architectural styles and movements, including Gothic, Neo-classicism, and Modernism, have left indelible impressions on both the built environment and the cultural history of our society. They frequently manifested themselves as a reaction to societal shifts and advances, and they reflected the zeitgeist of the era in which they were created. For instance, the modernist movement echoed the profound upheavals that occurred at the beginning of the 20th century by placing an emphasis on functionality, simplicity, and a break from tradition.

3. **Influencing the Future Through Eco-Friendly Product Design**

   3.1 Environmental Awareness and Concern for the Future of the Planet

   Art and architecture have been thrust to the forefront of conversations about the future in the 21st century as a direct result of the critical need for environmentally responsible design. The goal of sustainable architecture is to reduce the amount of environmental damage caused by the built environment by lowering energy consumption, increasing the use of renewable energy sources, and increasing the use of materials that are less harmful to the environment.

   Art installations, such as those found at the Eden Project in the United Kingdom, help bring attention to environmental problems and emphasize the significance of living in a more sustainable manner.

   3.2 Eco-Friendly Construction and Biophilic Architecture

   Building methods that are considered green place an emphasis on energy efficiency, the minimization of waste, and the use of materials that are sustainable. The practice of incorporating natural elements into man-made places, also known as biophilic design, aims to foster a greater sense of wellbeing and connection to the natural world. These fundamentals of design are essential to the process of fashioning a future that is ecologically responsible and in harmony with the surrounding environment.

4. **Innovation as well as progress made in technological areas**

   4.1 Technology in the Building Industry

   The architectural design process has been revolutionized as a result of developments in technology such as Building Information Modeling (BIM), three-dimensional printing, and parametric design. For example, Building Information Modeling (BIM) helps architects to develop precise, data-rich models that improve cooperation and cut down on error rates. The use of 3D printing has the potential to completely change the building industry by facilitating the speedy production of sophisticated architectural components.

   4.2 Works of Digital Art and Experiences in Virtual Reality

The bounds of creative expression and architectural visualization are being pushed further and further by the rise of virtual reality and digital art. The use of virtual reality by architects to create immersive experiences that allow customers and users to examine concepts before construction begins is possible thanks to this technology. Digital art, such as the works of Olafur Eliasson, presents a challenge to our understanding of space, light, and form, and this has an impact on the aesthetics of architectural design.

5. **Social Interactions and Community Gathering Places**
   5.1 The Importance of Art in Public Places
   The appearance of urban environments in the future will be greatly influenced by works of public art. It encourages community participation, helps people develop a feeling of identity, and highlights various cultural manifestations. Murals, sculptures, and installations placed in public locations have the ability to communicate social messages, encourage contemplation, and stimulate solidarity.
   5.2 Inclusive Architecture and Community Participation
   The overarching goal of inclusive design is to produce environments that are accessible to people of varying abilities, experiences, and requirements. Making environments accessible to everyone and promoting social inclusion will become increasingly important in the field of architecture in the years to come. The practice of inclusive design encourages a constructed environment that is more equitable and diverse.

6. **Preservation and Adaptive Reuse of Existing Materials**
   6.1 Protecting Our Cultural Heritage
   For the purpose of preserving historical and culturally significant buildings, preservation efforts and adaptive reuse are absolutely necessary. The preservation of architectural legacy establishes a link between the past and the present, so contributing to a feeling of cultural continuity and identity. The Colosseum in Rome and the Great Wall of China are two examples of iconic structures that serve as reminders of the achievements and progress made by humans.
   6.2 Revisions Made in the Present Day and Age
   Reimagining classic buildings in light of modern sensibilities is one path that may be taken by the architectural profession in the years to come. Existing buildings are given a new lease on life through adaptive reuse projects such as converting ancient warehouses into residential lofts or transforming historic factories into cultural institutions. This is accomplished while the structures' historical qualities are maintained.

7. **Art and Architecture as Agents of Social Transformation**
   7.1 Expression of Social and Political Ideologies
   Both works of art and buildings can serve as a catalyst for social and political transformation. Artists and architects who take a stand for social justice and

equality may use their work to confront societal issues, question prevalent standards, and advocate for these causes. For instance, the AIDS Memorial Quilt is an impactful piece of art that celebrates those who have lost their lives to the AIDS pandemic and raises awareness of the disease.

7.2 Reconceptualizing Existing Urban Settings

The rethinking of urban landscapes for the future relies heavily on the contributions of art and architecture.

Issues like housing affordability, transportation, the availability of green areas, and the overall health of communities can all be improved by innovative urban planning and architecture. Architectural initiatives such as the High Line in New York City illustrate the possibilities for change by repurposing outdated industrial infrastructure into a lively public park.

8. Challenges and Ethical Considerations in the Eighth Section

8.1 The Taking of Ideas From Other Cultures

The appropriation of other cultures is a barrier that must be overcome in the fields of art and architecture. It is imperative that the cultural relevance of creative aspects and architectural traditions be recognized and respected. It is essential to avoid spreading stereotypes and inaccurate depictions by engaging in cultural activities and symbols in an ethical manner.

8.2 Evictions and the Process of Gentrification

Gentrification presents obstacles for the continued development of art and architecture in a number of different metropolitan locations. It is possible that long-established communities would be displaced, which would have a negative impact on the cultural richness of the area, as districts undergo gentrification and become more appealing to wealthy inhabitants. The ethical challenge here is to find a balance between renewal and the protection of the community's distinctive identity.

The significance of art and architecture in determining the course of future events is immense, and the ways in which they do so are varied. Art and architecture are dynamic forces that continue to affect the world we live in. They continue to do so in a variety of ways, including having an effect on cultural identity and aesthetics, pushing sustainability, and driving technical innovation. They have the ability to inspire a more sustainable and fair future while they are tackling the issues of the 21st century, which they also have the potential to promote social change, inclusivity, and social justice. The enduring relationship that exists between art, architecture, and society holds the promise of a world that is not only more appealing to the senses aesthetically, but also one that is more empathetic, just, and in tune with nature.